THE ENGLISH CONSTITUTION

WALTER BAGEHOT was born in Langport, Somerset, in 1826, the son of a banker. After taking BA and MA degrees from University College London he studied for the bar, and was called in 1852. However, he decided to return home and join his father's bank, devoting his leisure to contributing literary, historical and political reviews to the leading periodicals of the 1850s. In 1861 he returned to London, succeeding his father-in-law as editor and director of the *Economist*. Three books ensured Bagehot's reputation as one of the most distinguished and influential Victorian men-of-letters: *The English Constitution* (1867), published at the height of the debate over parliamentary reform; *Physics and Politics* (1872), his application of Darwinian ideas to political science; and *Lombard Street* (1873), a study of the City of London. Walter Bagehot died in 1877.

MILES TAYLOR is a Lecturer in Modern History at King's College, London. He is the author of *The Decline of British Radicalism, 1847–60* (Clarendon Press, 1995) and is currently completing a biography of the last Chartist leader, Ernest Jones.

OXFORD WORLD'S CLASSICS

For almost 100 years Oxford World's Classics have brought readers closer to the world's great literature. Now with over 700 titles—from the 4,000-year-old myths of Mesopotamia to the twentieth century's greatest novels—the series makes available lesser-known as well as celebrated writing.

The pocket-sized hardbacks of the early years contained introductions by Virginia Woolf, T. S. Eliot, Graham Greene, and other literary figures which enriched the experience of reading. Today the series is recognized for its fine scholarship and reliability in texts that span world literature, drama and poetry, religion, philosophy and politics. Each edition includes perceptive commentary and essential background information to meet the changing needs of readers.

OXFORD WORLD'S CLASSICS

WALTER BAGEHOT

The English Constitution

Edited with an Introduction and Notes by
MILES TAYLOR

OXFORD
UNIVERSITY PRESS

OXFORD
UNIVERSITY PRESS

Great Clarendon Street, Oxford OX2 6DP

Oxford University Press is a department of the University of Oxford.
It furthers the University's objective of excellence in research, scholarship,
and education by publishing worldwide in

Oxford New York

Athens Auckland Bangkok Bogotá Buenos Aires Calcutta
Cape Town Chennai Dar es Salaam Delhi Florence Hong Kong Istanbul
Karachi Kuala Lumpur Madrid Melbourne Mexico City Mumbai
Nairobi Paris São Paulo Shanghai Singapore Taipei Tokyo Toronto Warsaw

with associated companies in Berlin Ibadan

Published in the United States
by Oxford University Press Inc., New York

First published as an Oxford World's Classics paperback 2001

British Library Cataloguing in Publication Data

Data available

Library of Congress Cataloging in Publication Data

Data available

ISBN 0-19-283975-6

1 3 5 7 9 10 8 6 4 2

Typeset in Ehrhardt
by RefineCatch Limited, Bungay, Suffolk
Printed in Great Britain by
Cox & Wyman Ltd.
Reading, Berkshire

CONTENTS

INTRODUCTION

WALTER BAGEHOT'S *The English Constitution* (1867) was not the first word on the subject written in the 1860s. Nor has it proved the last, or even the most enduring. But it remains the best. First published as a series of articles in the *Fortnightly Review* between May 1865 and January 1867, *The English Constitution* is a stylish analysis of the workings of the cabinet system, the monarchy, and the Houses of Parliament, especially at times of political crisis and difficulty It is not a conventional text-book. Neither constitutional case-law nor historical narrative are allowed to get in the way of a good read. Bagehot's wit and irreverence, his endless supply of anecdotes and stories, and his pragmatic approach to the problems of government make *The English Constitution* a lively and unpredictable book. In many ways it belongs to the tradition of the political essay as polemic—the style and tone is of Edward Bulwer Lytton, or Thomas Carlyle or Hilaire Belloc—rather than to that classic canon of constitutional authorities represented by Henry Hallam, A. V. Dicey, and A. L. Lowell. But Bagehot's work is authoritative in a way that other polemics are not. It is informed by a lightly-worn evolutionary sociology and psychology, which, though somewhat arcane, remain persuasive. It is not doctrinaire: Bagehot describes a fluid and not a static system, some of which he admires, of some of which he disapproves. Above all, *The English Constitution*, for all its levity, is a deft and penetrating account of an age-old set of institutions beset by modernity. It has influenced countless later constitutional commentators, including Dicey and James Bryce, acted as a primer for future monarchs such as Edward VII, and furnished sketch-writers and essayists alike with memorable one-liners. *The English Constitution* remains such a classic because, as one reviewer noted at the time, it is 'wise chat'.[1]

Bagehot's Reputation

'Wise chat' sums up the achievement but also the problem of Bagehot's great work. *The English Constitution* is enjoyable, but also

---

[1] *Spectator*, 24 March 1866.

vulnerable in the face of posterity. Few have doubted its readability. Many have questioned its accuracy and utility with the passage of time. Even in his own generation Bagehot was better known for his later Darwinian work, *Physics and Politics*, than for *The English Constitution*. *Physics and Politics* went through eight editions in fifteen years; *The English Constitution* took twenty-four years to reach a sixth edition, an by then Bagehot's constitutional writing was perhaps better known overseas than at home. A German translation of *The English Constitution* had been produced in 1868, an American edition (which included amongst its admirers the future President Woodrow Wilson) in 1873. It was in America too that the first edition of Bagehot's collected writings was released in 1889, a quarter of a century before the first definitive English edition. Only after the First World War did Bagehot's domestic audience really swell, as nostalgia for the Victorian age increased and concerns for the constitution flared up with the extension of the suffrage. In 1928 *The English Constitution* appeared for the first time in the World's Classics series, with an appreciative introduction by a former Prime Minister, Earl Balfour. Since then, however, wider readership has not ensured venerability. Bagehot nowadays is more noted for what he got wrong than what he got right. 'There can be very few studies of our party system that were so rapidly overtaken by events as Walter Bagehot's *English Constitution*', declared Richard Crossman in 1963, and, although more brazen than most, this verdict has been widely shared. Twentieth-century supporters of the Commons, such as Leo Amery, have suggested that Bagehot misunderstood the separation of powers; supporters of the monarchy and the Lords, such as Norman St John Stevas, have argued that Bagehot underestimated the continuing importance of those institutions; apologists for the cabinet, such as Richard Crossman, have pointed out that Bagehot overlooked the importance of party and the Prime Minister.[2] Some historians simply think Bagehot got it all wrong, whilst others have implied that it does not really matter anyway, since few Victorians were interested in the thoughts on an

[2] Leo Amery, *Thoughts upon the Constitution* (London, 1947); Norman St John Stevas, *Walter Bagehot: A Study of his Life and Thought together with a Selection from his Political Writings* (London, 1959), 63–86; Richard Crossman, 'Introduction' to Bagehot, *The English Constitution* (London, 1963), 1.

esoteric subject of a financial journalist with an unpronounceable name.[3]

Bagehot, who often seemed not to be treating his own subject very seriously, has thus not been taken seriously—either by modern historians who have aspired to be politicians, or by politicians who think of themselves as historians. This is partly a matter of tone. 'Wise chat' endears but does not endure. But it is also the result of how Bagehot's *English Constitution* is read. If the book continues to be read simply as an accurate portrayal of the fundamental operations of the British political system, then not surprisingly its veracity will diminish over the course of time. Bagehot himself suggested as much in his introduction to the second edition of *The English Constitution* published in 1872, five years into the working of the new electoral system ushered in by the second Reform Act. He drew back from many of the conclusions he had reached in the 1860s, rearranged the sequence of chapters so that his discussion of monarchy was more prominent, and dropped entirely his gloomy conclusions about the extension of the suffrage. By revising his own work so quickly, Bagehot implied that it was a descriptive work requiring updating as the circumstances it described changed. Ironically, this was also to admit its fallibility. So Bagehot himself invited in the corrective and reproving criticism that has been the hallmark of scholarship on *The English Constitution* ever since. The 1872 edition of the book, with its *mea culpa* prologue, continues to be the standard modern edition. Yet it is not the real thing. It is the errata and not the original. Bagehot's introduction to the 1872 edition and the changes therein make descriptive accuracy appear to be his main concern. However, in the original articles of 1865–7, and in the first edition, Bagehot's purpose was more prescriptive and polemical. Taken out of context, Bagehot's meaning has been rendered obscure.

The full force of *The English Constitution* can only be captured if it is relocated within the deep debate about parliamentary reform which enveloped British political life from the late 1850s onwards. *The English Constitution* is above all a contribution to that debate, reflecting on what had been achieved since the 1830s under the

---

[3] Brian Harrison, 'Bagehot's System', in Harrison, *The Transformation of British Politics, 1860–1995* (Oxford, 1995); Ruth Dudley Edwards, *The Pursuit of Reason: The 'Economist', 1843–1993* (London, 1993). Bagehot is pronounced 'Badge-ot' and not 'Baggy-ho' or 'Baggot' or 'Beige-hot'.

reformed political system, what required alteration, and what demanded retention. Bagehot's lifetime (he was born in 1826) encompassed the first decades of the reformed Parliament at work. In 1832 around half a million voters were added to the franchise, largely through extending the vote in the boroughs to householders occupying property worth at least £10 rental per annum, and some 150 seats were transferred from old small constituencies to newer counties and boroughs. Invigorated by reform, the House of Commons became the lynchpin of the constitution in the 1830s, taking on more legislation and subjecting governments of the day to greater scrutiny. By the time Bagehot wrote in the 1860s the new system was at its apotheosis. The memoirs, collected essays, and speeches of the leading protagonists of that system were beginning to be published. Modern practical accounts of parliamentary procedure, the drafting of legislation, and the operation of election laws poured from the presses in the 1840s and the 1850s. Newspapers of the day devoted huge column space to parliamentary debates, and to parliamentary elections which occurred with unprecedented regularity between 1830 and 1865. Having survived Chartism, the revolutions of 1848 and a battering of confidence during the Crimean war, the reformed Parliament was basking in its own glory. In the summer of 1859, the House of Commons approved the presentation of George Hayter's famous collective portrait of the reformed Commons to the National Portrait Gallery.

But at the same time, by the 1860s, the reformed system was bursting at the seams. Demographic change and economic prosperity meant that in many constituencies the £10 rental franchise set in 1832 now bore little relation to the wealth and distribution of the population. The economic prosperity of the mid-Victorian boom also brought new challenges. The needs of local government, the plans of private investors (especially in the railways), and the interests of both employers and workers in the heavy industries required a more representative and efficient legislative chamber. Few politicians or contemporaries argued against such logic. But equally few were impressed by the options for parliamentary reform. Whereas in 1832 Britain (and especially England) shone as a beacon of democracy to the rest of the world, with one-fifth of its adult male population enfranchised, by the 1850s the rest of the world had begun to catch up and overtake. Effective full adult suffrage was a feature of the constitution in France, much of the USA and indeed in the new constitutions of the British white settlement colonies. Yet the results were worrying. Bonapartist military imperialism had re-emerged in France, the United States were on the verge of civil war, and stories of corruption and mob-rule in colonial government were rife. Something was amiss in the evolution of civilization when the most advanced democracies were proving to be the most unstable.

This is the context in which the articles that comprised *The English Constitution* were originally written in the mid-1860s. Bagehot wrote from the left-centre of British politics, supportive of reform, but anxious at its likely consequences. He also wrote using the tools of a social anthropologist, seeking to understand the barbarism at the heart of the modern condition. In order to understand Bagehot's *The English Constitution* we therefore need to know a little more about his own distinctive intellectual evolution and about his reaction to political developments worldwide in the 1850s and 1860s. By setting out the background and context in this way the polemical purpose of his work will become clear. We can do this by turning our attention first to Bagehot's own intellectual odyssey, and then to the two major constitutional phenomena of his times: the French Empire and the American Civil War.

Bagehot's Life and Times

Bagehot was born into a West Country banking family and, after university in London, trained as a barrister. In his mid-twenties he opted to return to banking, a career he continued until taking over the direction of the *Economist* full-time on the death of James Wilson, its founding editor (and Bagehot's father-in-law) in 1860. On the face of it, Bagehot's background is not that of a mid-Victorian intellectual. His father was not only a country banker, but also a Unitarian (a small but very influential branch of non-conformity), which meant that the universities of Oxford and Cambridge were not an option for Bagehot, although he himself, like his mother, was Anglican. Bagehot spent most of the 1850s viewing events from afar down in Somerset, and when he did eventually become part of the London scene in the 1860s it was as editor of a trade paper with a small circulation (it sold 3,690 copies per week in 1873), replete with details of money markets, stocks and shares, but short on intellectual speculation. Bagehot's background seems to confirm his status as a political outsider, rough-hewn and more used to the practical world of commerce than to the deliberative science of politics. But appearances are deceptive. Bagehot was as much of an intellectual as any of his contemporaries. Indeed, his education, both formal and practical, had exposed him to some of the principal new ideas of the mid-nineteenth century.

Bagehot completed his schooling at Bristol College where his masters included the ethnologist, James Cowles Prichard (1786–1848), whose *Researches into the Physical History of Man* (1813) remained the standard reference point for most accounts of evolution until the publication of Charles Darwin's *Origin of the Species* in 1859. Bagehot was also taught by William Carpenter (1813–85), one of the leading natural scientists of his generation, whose work on mental physiology proved very influential. And in Bristol Bagehot also came to know John Addington Symonds (1807–71) a leading physician and writer on the mind and the unconscious. Although scientists, none of these men was slow in coming forward to apply the fruits of their researches to history and to contemporary events. From Bristol Bagehot went up to study at University College London, then a haven not only for dissenting families who objected to the religious tests required by the older universities, but also for leading Unitarians and other heterodox scholars. By the late 1840s the college could boast an impressive roll-call of thinkers and writers, including Francis Newman, the religious sceptic, Augustus de Morgan, the mathemetician, and Robert Grant, the unorthodox anatomist. At University College, Bagehot's best friends were Unitarians, namely Richard Holt Hutton and William Roscoe, and although Bagehot's religious views remained secure, they were not unchallenged. Interestingly, the ideas of John Henry Newman, Francis's elder brother and the leading Anglo-Catholic, tested the faith of the young Bagehot to the limit. As well as exposure to intellectual radicalism, Bagehot received a large dose of radical politics, observing the great London meetings of the Anti-Corn Law League, the free trade pressure group led by Cobden and Bright, at first hand. From an early age, therefore, Bagehot was mixing with controversial figures instrumental in opening up natural science to rational inquiry, established religion to critical thought, and aristocratic government to liberal agitation.

Bagehot was also of a generation that came of intellectual age in 1848, the year of revolutions across Europe. On 10 April 1848, whilst studying for the bar, he was sworn in as a special constable, deputed to protect Lincoln's Inn from the expected Chartist mobs. Bagehot was no friend of revolution. As a banker's son he knew only too well that flourishing commerce required political stability. But the breakdown of political order in Europe in the late 1840s and early 1850s served to undermine any lingering faith Bagehot had in political or moral certainty. Here he was influenced by Arthur Hugh Clough, the poet and the principal of University Hall, the college residence where Bagehot lived whilst studying for his MA and then later at the bar. Clough, who had witnessed the contagion of revolutionary events in Paris in the early summer of 1848, produced perhaps the most famous political poem of that year, *The Bothie of Tober-na-Vuolich*, a narrative verse which articulated the dilemma of the educated liberal—incensed by poverty and misrule, but unconvinced by working-class social and political experiment. Bagehot's appreciation of Clough's sceptical resolve 'to go on living quietly and obviously, and see what truth would come to him'[4] is an insight into Bagehot's own frame of mind at mid-century as well.

Completing his legal studies in 1851, Bagehot left London to spend a few months in Paris. He caught the tail-end of the republican government, and witnessed Louis Napoleon's *coup d'état* in December and his re-establishment of imperial power the following year. In the new year of 1852 Bagehot contributed a pseudonymous series of seven articles to a Unitarian journal back in England, *The Inquirer*, then edited by his friend Hutton. Going against the grain of much English opinion, Bagehot welcomed Louis Napoleon's seizure of power, arguing that he had restored peace and security, and returned the French to a system of autocratic rule which although offensive to liberal tastes, was more suited to their headstrong national character. Returning from Paris in the spring of 1852, Bagehot laid down his political pen and returned to his father's bank. Over the next seven years his journalism was never in abeyance, but it was confined mainly to literary and historical essays.

Bagehot's schooling inside and beyond the academy suggests that he was not quite the country cousin of constitutional writing that he

[4] Quoted in Alastair Buchan, *The Spare Chancellor: The Life of Walter Bagehot* (London, 1959), 52.

may sometimes appear. In political terms by the 1850s he occupied the ground of a sceptical Whig, a space he shared with men such as Robert Lowe, George Cornewall Lewis, and the 3rd Earl Grey, all three particular heroes of Bagehot, and all three eventually his good friends as well. These men had all found their theoretical commitment to liberal institutions tempered by the practical needs of different people in different places in changing times. Lowe and Grey had practical experience of colonial democracy in the years after 1848— Lowe as a member of the legislative assembly of New South Wales, Grey as the colonial secretary responsible for devising new colonial constitutions for the Australian states, New Zealand, the Cape and the crown colonies of the West Indies. Lewis was editor of the leading Whig intellectual quarterly, the *Edinburgh Review*, but was also a member of the crisis-ridden cabinet of Lord Palmerston during the latter half of the Crimean war. Like them, Bagehot in his writings on France, and later on England as well, displayed a worldly disdain for democracy at work, and a low expectation of politicians in power. Compared to these rather gloomy Whigs, Bagehot's tone erred on the side of hilarity, but there is no mistaking his sceptical premise.

But Bagehot was also a modern Whig, in the sense that his understanding of political institutions was increasingly informed by the new turn in the natural sciences. The most obvious expression of this intellectual debt is his *Physics and Politics*, published in book form in 1872, in which he attempted to apply the ideas of Darwin, Thomas Huxley, Henry Maine, and others to politics. Such influences also surface in *The English Constitution* as well, where his emphasis on the need to observe internal function rather than outward appearance, reflected the advances that had been made in human biology since the 1840s. Indeed, in choosing to launch *The English Constitution* in the first number of the *Fortnightly Review* in 1865, Bagehot was self-consciously aligning himself with the new liberal social science. The first editor of the *Fortnightly* was George Henry Lewes, partner of Mary Ann Evans (George Eliot), biographer of Goethe, author of popular accounts of psychology and physiology, and the leading English disciple of Auguste Comte, the French positivist. When Lewes's editorship of the *Fortnightly* came to an end in 1867, he was succeeded by John Morley, admirer of Huxley and friend to the English positivists.

Bagehot, then, wrote not from the margins of political and intellectual life in mid-Victorian Britain, but from a point quite near to the centre. Whilst it true that his style is closer to the great literary essayists whom he admired, and that his analysis is peppered with homely truths derived from the world of the counting-house and the boardroom, his basic concerns were the same as those of many other Whig and liberal commentators in the 1850s and 1860s, namely, which political institutions were best adapted for a rapidly changing world. One answer to that question lay, for Bagehot, in the fate of governments outside Britain.

France, America, and the British Empire

The English Constitution is not just about England, or even Britain. Bagehot discusses the peculiar virtues of the English system in the light of his country's closest neighbour and then greatest rival, France; and also in comparison to, as Bagehot saw it, the only other free government in the world, the United States of America. He also at different points in the book alludes to the constitutional experiences of the Australian states. Bagehot's purpose in deploying this comparative method is simple but effective. He wished to disabuse his readers of the quaint notion that English-style parliamentary institutions could be exported to other countries, irrespective of national differences, differences of character, and differences of historical development. Much of his venom over conventional 'literary' theories of the constitution is in fact reserved for people who believe that the separation of powers model of government had been copied from England by the founding fathers of the American Constitution in the mid-eighteenth century, and was capable of transplantation to the new Australian states in the mid-nineteenth.

Louis Napoleon's France was the first constitution to occupy Bagehot's attention. He was there at its inception—quite literally: he delighted in telling friends back in England that he had helped to build barricades in the streets of Paris in December 1851. And he recorded its demise at the hands of the Prussian army and the Communards in 1870–1. For Bagehot the second empire was the '*best finished* democracy',[5] for under the Emperor Napoleon an efficient bureaucracy—a sort of Benthamite despotism—dispensed welfare

---

[5] Bagehot, 'Caesarism as it now Exists', *Economist*, 4 March 1865, in Norman St John Stevas, *The Collected Works of Walter Bagehot* (1965–86), iv. 112.

to the masses. According to Bagehot this was preferable to the republican socialism which had dominated the National Assembly between 1848 and 1851. Socialism had alarmed the commercial classes, and brought government to a state not far off anarchy. The French had a 'want of stupidity';[6] they liked to teach rather than learn, to innovate rather than adapt, and so their national character ill-equipped them for deliberative parliamentary government on the English model. This is not to say that Bagehot completely endorsed Napoleon's rule. Although welcoming the strong executive, he insisted that there should be a consultative council, an intermediary between the omnipotent Emperor and the powerless Assembly, otherwise there would be no channel at all for public opinion. When Napoleon fell Bagehot argued that it was precisely because of this 'absence of all intermediate links of moral reponsibility and co-operation'.[7] The government of the second Empire passed Bagehot's test of efficiency, but it failed his standards of public consultation.

America exercised Bagehot's interest and intrigue to a much greater degree than France, and perhaps unusually so, since he never visited the country nor had much practical acquaintance of Americans themselves. He wrote thirty-one articles on America for the *Economist*, most of them during the Civil War of 1861–5, as well as a long piece for the *National Review*. He considered all aspects of the war: slavery, the cotton 'famine' in Lancashire, the economic blockade, the rights and wrongs of British neutrality, and Abraham Lincoln, to whom he eventually warmed. But Bagehot returned again and again to one particular theme in his analysis of the American Civil War, namely, how the inherent flaws of the federal constitution had worsened the conflict between the states. '[I]t is impossible for Englishmen', wrote Bagehot in April 1861, 'not to observe that the whole mischief has been, not caused but painfully exacerbated by the unfortunate mixture of flexibility and inflexibility in the United States Constitution.' The southern, slave-holding states dominated the federal congress and the senate, but they had no control over the new President Lincoln. Indeed, once in office for a fixed term of years, the President was accountable to no one, and shared responsi-

---

[6] Bagehot, 'Letter IV: On the Aptitude of the French Character for Self-Government', *Inquirer*, 31 Jan. 1851, in *Collected Works*, iv. 55.

[7] Bagehot, 'The Collapse of Caesarism', *Economist*, 20 Aug. 1870, in *Collected Works*, iv. 156.

bility for his policies with no other branch of the constitution—unlike the English system, Bagehot pointedly remarked, where '[t]he mutual influence of the Cabinet on the House, and the House on the Cabinet, keeps the country in a vital connection with the ministry'.[8] Not only was the President beyond accountability, but the manner of his election ensured that he seldom enjoyed public respect. The system of double election or selection of the President by an electoral college meant that the least-known candidate usually won. Moreover, once he was elected there was then an interregnum, whilst the whole of his government—political and administrative staff alike—left office and made way for the new regime. On coming into power the new President was preoccupied with handing out the spoils of office, rather than the pressing political issues of the day. Into this power vacuum had leapt the southern states in 1861, declaring their secession, and, in Bagehot's view establishing a new constitution which was a great improvement on the old one. The American constitution was not only flawed in operation, argued Bagehot, but in its very origins. The federal union established in the eighteenth century was a compromise between different peoples who 'had hated one another at home', and had created their own little commonwealths in their separate states. Federal union was 'essentially a collection of *imperia in imperio*' and presidential elections always acted as a focus for inter-state tension.[9] The founding fathers may have believed they were putting into place an English system based on the separation of powers, but Bagehot argued that this was wrong. The England of George III was no more a mixed constitution than the England of Victoria.

Following Alexis de Tocqueville, the French liberal and author of *Democracy in America* (1835), Bagehot also feared the consequences of the rapid populating of America by the émigrés of Europe. In the days of the founding fathers a transplanted landed gentry had ensured a steady supply of statesmen, but ante-bellum America had seen the constitution turn into 'an almost umitigated ochlocracy',[10] in which mob law and manners had come to dominate presidential

---

[8] Bagehot, 'The American News and its Lessons', *Economist*, 20 April 1861, in *Collected Works*, iv. 238–40.

[9] Bagehot, 'The American Constitution at the Present Crisis', *National Review*, 13 (Oct. 1861), in *Collected Works*, iv. 284–5, 290–1.

[10] Bagehot, 'What May Be in America', *Economist*, 17 Aug. 1861, in *Collected Works*, iv. 272–3.

elections. Similar developments characterized colonial society in Australia, where, as Earl Grey had found, it was almost impossible to introduce a bi-cameral legislature without the resident authority of the Crown, for settler society was too socially egalitarian to produce the classes of rank and status who normally gave stability and leadership to politics. Like America, Australia was a reminder of the difficulty and not the ease with which parliamentary government could be exported from Westminster. Political institutions worked in Britain, not because of the inherent logic of a paper constitution, but because they matched the civilization of which they were a part. Bagehot's reasoning was Burkean, and like Edmund Burke in the 1790s, it was a reasoning he hoped to communicate to English liberals as they confronted the prospect of parliamentary reform.

Bagehot and Parliamentary Reform

Bagehot burst back into political journalism in 1859, when a pamphlet version of his two *National Review* articles on parliamentary reform was published by Chapman and Hall. The winter and spring of 1858–9 saw a proliferation of similar books, articles, and ephemera on the subject from all shades of political opinion, as Lord Derby's Conservative government reluctantly prepared a moderate reform bill and the radical John Bright stormed the public platforms of England and Scotland demanding an extensive one—an 'Americanization' of English institutions, so his critics chided. In his pamphlet Bagehot came down somewhere in the middle, arguing that on the whole Parliament had done well enough since 1832, although its expressive function was no longer working properly, as artisans in the towns were not adequately represented. At the same time there was a danger that a uniform lowering of the franchise would swamp the voices of the higher orders, and also increase corruption in the small borough constituencies where the manners and progress of urban society had made less inroad. The ability or 'fitness' of an individual to elect a 'ruling assembly' was not, concluded Bagehot, an attribute shared by everyone: '[E]very person has a right to *so much political power as he can exercise without impeding any other person who would more fitly exercise such power.*'[11] Bagehot's solution

---

[11] Bagehot, *Parliamentary Reform: An Essay* (London, 1859), 18.

was to propose the introduction, or reintroduction, of a variety of suffrages. There might be a simple low ratepaying franchise, as Bright was calling for, in the larger towns (with a population of more than 75,000), but nowhere else; and in order to prevent corruption the smaller boroughs might be combined into groups. It was an idea to which Bagehot was to return in 1860, in *The English Constitution* itself, and in later essays.[12] It was, as he acknowledged, an idea drawn from the Whig luminaries, Sir James Mackintosh and Lord John Russell. In true Whig style it rewarded civilization and progress where it had developed, and attempted to neutralize barbarism where it still lingered.

Bagehot's 1859 pamphlet was widely acclaimed, and in subsequent years, now established in London at the helm of the *Economist*, he followed it up with many articles on British and American politics. He began to develop a theme that was to dominate *The English Constitution*. This was the idea that the functions of the House of Commons were not merely expressive and legislative, but also elective. The House of Commons, in Bagehot's view, effectively chose the Prime Minister and his cabinet. In that way the English parliamentary system was superior to the American, for in America there existed no such mechanism, and as a result, the President treated Congress as inferiors.[13] British voters therefore had a special responsibility: they were required not just to choose fit representatives, but also to select men who would be able to elect wise ministers. Of course, Bagehot cannot have meant that MPs *directly* elected the Prime Minister and his cabinet, for they did not then and have never done since. But anyone familiar with the party politics of the 1850s, when successive administrations rarely survived without the confidence and support of the House of Commons, would have recognized Bagehot's argument.

The Conservative reform bill of 1859, which proposed a series of new 'fancy' franchises but little else, was defeated, and Lord

---

[12] Bagehot, 'Plurality of Votes. The True Principle of a Reform Bill', *Economist*, 24 March, 1860, in *Collected Works*, vi. 323–7; 'The New Reform Bill', *Economist*, 2 March 1867, in *Collected Works*, vi. 366–70; 'Lord Althorp and the Reform Act of 1832', *Fortnightly Review*, 20 (Nov. 1876), in *Collected Works*, iii. 201–31.

[13] Bagehot, 'The Unseen Work of Parliament', *Economist*, 9 Feb. 1861, in *Collected Works*, vi. 45–8; 'The Defect of America', *Economist*, 6 Dec. 1862, in *Collected Works*, vi. 161–4; 'Presidential and Ministerial Governments Compared', *Economist*, 13 Dec. 1862, in *Collected Works*, vi. 165–7.

Palmerston again came into office. Palmerston was no great supporter of parliamentary reform and the issue disappeared below
the surface once more, only re-emerging in 1864 as the Liberal
party confronted the probability of a general election or the death of
Palmerston, or, as it turned out, both. Following Palmerston's death
in October 1865, Russell formed a new government, led in the
House of Commons by William Gladstone. As Bagehot's series of
articles in the *Fortnightly Review* reached the halfway mark in March
1866, Gladstone announced his government's proposals for reform:
a £7 rental franchise in the boroughs, a £14 occupational franchise
in the counties, with the question of the redistribution of constituencies put off for a future parliament. What Bagehot had dreaded all
along—a new urban franchise based on a uniform qualification—
was the principal feature of not only Gladstone's measure, which
was defeated, but also of the eventual successful Conservative
reform bill, introduced by Disraeli in May 1867 and based on household suffrage in the boroughs, that is, no rental qualification, just
simple occupation. Several leading Liberals, including Robert Lowe,
voiced their opposition to the indiscriminate lowering of the franchise, believing, like Bagehot, that it would make cabinet government more difficult. But although Lowe and his followers, dubbed
'Adullamites' after Bright's likening of them to the followers of
Daniel, who, according to the Bible took refuge in the cave of
Adullam, helped defeat Gladstone's bill, they were left with a more
extensive one instead. They were left with Disraeli's 'leap in the
dark'.

   The English Constitution was thus written against the backdrop of
civil war in America, Caesarist-style imperialism in France, and the
reopening of the parliamentary question at home. These events set
the agenda of inquiry in Bagehot's book. Why did parliamentary
government work in some countries and not in others? To what
extent was its success or failure the result of national character, or
the intrinsic operation of the institutions themselves? Why was a
constitutional monarchy more effective than a President or an
Emperor? And was parliamentary government compatible with mass
democracy? We shall examine the responses that Bagehot gave to
these questions in *The English Constitution*, but first we need to
review and place on one side some of the existing contexts into
which the work has been forced.

Bagehot and the Study of the Constitution

To appreciate Bagehot's contribution to mid-Victorian political debate it is important to recognize what he was *not* writing about in *The English Constitution*. The book is often celebrated for two main reasons. First, Bagehot is credited with seeing off what he called the 'literary theory' of the constitution, that is the idea that the English constitution rests on a harmonious balance between sovereign, Lords, and Commons, and that there is a separation of powers between the executive, legislature, and the judiciary. Bagehot argued that the modern cabinet, accountable to parliament, in fact combined all these separate functions, and therefore the 'literary theory' was erroneous. Montesquieu, Blackstone, De Lolme, Hallam, J. S. Mill, and a whole host of legal and historical writers, subsequent commentators suggest, were left standing still by Bagehot's discovery of the cabinet. The second achievement usually claimed for Bagehot is his articulation of a new role for the monarchy, not as the working head of state, but as the bearer of ceremonial in politics, a 'dignified' symbol of authority which ordinary people are more likely to obey and revere than the professional politicians who actually run the 'efficient' institutions of government. Bagehot's depiction of the value of monarchy as a totem has often been taken as one of the most effective arguments against the introduction of a republic in Britain.

These sorts of claims for Bagehot's novelty are rather misleading. Neither on the cabinet nor on monarchy was Bagehot particularly original, although both issues are absolutely essential to his wider concerns. For Bagehot the system of cabinet government was not so much new and unnoticed, as simply preferable to the imperial and presidential system of governments existing in France and the USA. Similarly, Bagehot was not trying to save monarchy from a republican challenge—a challenge which was intense at the time of the publication of the second edition of *The English Constitution* in 1872, but barely perceptible in 1865—rather he was trying to explain how a monarchy which combined prerogative and symbolic power could actually make quasi-republican institutions work more effectively. Let us examine these points in more detail.

It is not at all clear in *The English Constitution* to whom Bagehot's invective over the 'literary theory' of the constitution is directed. Montesquieu and De Lolme are possible candidates, inasmuch as

they were widely read in eighteenth- and nineteenth-century Britain, especially the latter whose *Constitution of England* (1771) went
through eleven English editions between 1807 and 1839. But neither
are mentioned at all by Bagehot. Nor is Blackstone mentioned,
although his *Commentaries on the Laws of England* (1765–9) was the
standard work both on common law and the workings of Parliament.
Two literary talents who had famously turned their attention to
constitutional history were Hallam (in 1827) and Macaulay (in 1848),
but both men earn Bagehot's praise rather than his censure. Finally,
John Stuart Mill is often put forward as an exponent of the 'literary
theory'. His *Considerations on Representative Government* had been
published to widespread interest in 1861. Bagehot had reviewed it
twice, and, of course, the opening lines of his own book cite Mill in
an apparently tongue-in-cheek manner. But Mill's work treats of
representative government in general and does not have a great deal
to say in a descriptive sense on the English case. In *The English
Constitution* Bagehot does criticize at length Mill's support for proportional representation, but he welcomed his election to Parliament
in 1865 and lamented his death in 1873.[14] The constitutional writer
to whom Bagehot took most exception was Lord Brougham, the
former Whig Lord Chancellor, whose political philosophy he found
pompous and whose political achievements he wrote off as those of a
soap-box orator.[15] In inveighing against the 'literary theory' of the
constitution Bagehot may have had in mind the loose and rather
coarse simplicity of Brougham. But for the most part his attack on
orthodoxy is an exaggerated sense of special pleading, a device to
highlight his argument.

For constitutional writing had moved on considerably by the
1860s. True enough, it was still dominated by historians and by
lawyers. But, influenced by French romanticism and by Carlyle, the
historians now had attitude, and the lawyers, anxious for work, now
knew a great deal more about the practical workings of Parliament,

[14] Bagehot, 'Considerations on Representative Government', *Economist*, 11 May
1861, in *Collected Works*, vi. 336–41; 'Considerations on Representative Government',
Economist, 18 May 1861, in *Collected Works*, vi. 342–6; 'Mr Mill's Address to the
Electors of Westminster', *Economist*, 29 April 1865, in *Collected Works*, iii. 541–6; 'The
Late Mr Mill', *Economist*, 17 May 1873, in *Collected Works*, iii. 555–9.

[15] Bagehot, 'Lord Brougham', *National Review*, 5 (July 1857), in *Collected Works*, iii.
159–93. The *Spectator* thought that Bagehot would be read long after Brougham's
'windy dissertations': 9 March 1867.

particularly parliamentary draughtsmanship and electoral law. Narrower legalistic discussions of the separation of powers were replaced from the 1830s onwards with strident Whiggish accounts of the unfolding of political liberty in Britain through the growth of parliamentary control over the monarchy, a development as rooted in the emergence of 'public opinion' as it was in the rise of an aristocracy independent of the Crown. Macaulay's *History of England* (1848) was the best example of this genre, and in the years that followed it spawned a series of paler imitations, many of which were concerned to see off the extreme versions of republicanism which had surfaced across Europe at mid-century. The idea of England as an aristocratic republic thus became something of a commonplace in the mid-Victorian period, noted by foreign commentators such as Ledru Rollin, Louis Blanc, and Hippolyte Taine. In this sense Bagehot's depiction of a 'republic in kid-gloves' (as a German reviewer called it)[16] built on rather than departed from recent historical writing. Similarly more was known about the inner workings of government by the time Bagehot took up his pen. The sheer volume of legislative activity in the 1830s and 1840s accelerated the demand for manuals and advice-books on many different aspects of parliamentary business. The doyen of such procedural writers was Thomas Erskine May, clerk of the House of Commons, whose *Treatise on the Law, Privileges, Proceedings, and Usage of Parliament* was first published in 1844. The operations of other branches of the constitution were also being revealed more or less reliably by the middle of the century: for example, John Campbell's *Lives of the Lord Chancellors* began to be published in 1845, and in 1858 there appeared the 3rd Earl Grey's *Parliamentary Government, considered with Reference to Reform*, which offered a survey and a distinctive argument about the whole operation of the constitution since 1832. To see Bagehot as writing within a vacuum of constitutional commentary, on a subject untouched since the mid-eighteenth century, is rather to overlook just how much had been written about the English constitution in the three decades after 1832.

The pace did not let up in the 1860s. It intensified. Erskine May's *Constitutional History* was published in 1861, as was Lord Brougham's *The British Constitution*; Grey's *Parliamentary Government*

---

[16] Mrs Russell Barrington, *The Life of Walter Bagehot* (London, 1914), 430.

appeared in a new edition in 1864; the work written in 1821 by his erstwhile Whig colleague, Lord John Russell, *Essay on the History of the English Government*, was reissued in 1865; and alongside Bagehot's book in 1867 were published two minor classics on the constitution: William Hearn's *The Government of England* and Alpheus Todd's *On Parliamentary Government in England*. With the possible exception of Brougham, Bagehot's particular animus, not one of these books sought to revive the 'literary theory' of the constitution. May described the development of ministerial responsibility ('the king reigned, but his ministers governed'). Grey described parliamentary government as executive and legislative power 'virtually united in the same hands'. Hearn devoted a whole chapter to the cabinet. Todd repeated May's description of the authority of the Crown having passed to ministers who were in turn responsible to Parliament. In other words, the idea of cabinet government had already become well-known by the time Bagehot produced his work. In 1861 he admitted as much himself: '[i]t is upon the cabinet, as we all know, that everything which is important in our public business rests and must rest.'[17] Bagehot's peculiar achievement lay in explaining why cabinet government was the best form of government amongst its rivals in Europe and America, and he did all that in one volume, where his competitors had taken two or three.

Bagehot can mislead on the monarchy as well. The monarchy was at its most unpopular for over fifty years when the second edition of *The English Constitution* went to press. The continued absence from public life of the Queen, still in mourning over the death of Prince Albert a whole decade earlier, political anger over the extent of the civil list fanned by MPs such as Sir Charles Dilke, and the efflorescence of republican clubs and newspapers in the wake of the fall of Napoleon III in France and his replacement by the short-lived Paris Commune—all served to make monarchy controversial in a way it had not been since the trial of Queen Caroline in 1820. Over the next two decades this position was reversed. Incorporated into the pomp and ceremony of empire, Queen Victoria became an essential part of Benjamin Disraeli's Tory democracy, providing the theatrical circus element to the new artisan democracy, while Parliament dealt out the bread of social reform. But of course Bagehot was not preoccupied

---

[17] Bagehot, 'The Unseen Work of Parliament', *Economist*, 9 Feb. 1861, in *Collected Works*, vi. 46.

with any of these developments when he first wrote down his ideas on the role of monarchy in 1865. The republican mood had yet to erupt, and the new populism characteristic of party politics in the era of mass democracy had not yet taken hold. In the mid-1860s Bagehot's concerns were rather different. What he sought to do was to describe how a constitutional monarch, particularly of the experience of the recently deceased Prince Albert, could save a parliamentary system from itself, that is from its two extremes: the excitability of the electorate, and the all too human flaws of ministerial politicians. Only by reconsidering Bagehot's concerns in the 1860s is it possible to appreciate the true value of what he had to say about monarchy.

Bagehot needs then to be understood against the backdrop of his times, engaging with and reacting to constitutional developments and constitutional writing at home and abroad. His style may have been that of a salon wit, or a political pundit, but beneath the gloss lay the abiding concerns of a comparative political analyst. In many respects he was not so much the first modern commentator on the constitution, as many like to see him, but rather, as John Burrow has perceptively observed, the last Whig, determined to root his discussion of political institutions within a sociological perspective and within a sense of historical change.

The English Constitution *then and now*

Cabinet government in England, argued Bagehot, was the best form of constitution because it was neither a bureaucratic despotism, as in Napoleon III's France or Bismarck's Prussia, nor a system based on divided or diffused sovereignty, as in America. The cabinet—'the efficient secret'—was all-powerful, but it was always accountable to the House of Commons. The cabinet was a 'hyphen' or a 'buckle' combining the authority of the Crown (the members of the cabinet were, after all, the Crown's ministers) with the legislative functions of Parliament. It was neither exclusively executive nor exclusively legislative: Bagehot welcomed the fact that ministers who were by and large MPs headed government departments, rather than faceless permanent senior civil servants, and collective responsibility meant it had to show a united and authoritative face to the Commons. With a foot in both camps—executive and legislative—the cabinet avoided

the log-jam to which the American President and the Congress were
often exposed. But the cabinet was removable, it had no fixed term,
and it depended on the confidence of the House of Commons. The
English House of Commons was therefore a real, and not a sham
electoral body, as the American electorate tended to be. It could
make and unmake administrations. Equally, the cabinet had the
power of dissolving the Commons, if the Commons was wilful or
misused its nominal responsibility to check the government of the
day.

Cabinet government was also good government because it was so
deliberative and discursive. The House of Commons could not be
the main source of legislation because it was too subject to the fickle
demands of the constituencies and too liable to act capriciously or
factiously. Although Bagehot enumerated five functions for the
Commons (the elective, the expressive, teaching, informing, and
legislative), it was clear that the most important was its elective
role—the Commons was the 'assembly which chooses our president'.[18] Therefore it was important that the choosing assembly was
composed of MPs who were capable of choosing wisely and
independently of their constituents. Further extension of the suffrage threatened to make such a task more difficult. Manhood suffrage, Bagehot suggested, would create a Commons comprised of
demagogues. Proportional representation, as advocated by Thomas
Hare and supported by John Stuart Mill, would turn election con-
tests over to the control of the caucus, that is a small group of
professional politicians who would manipulate candidate lists in the
interests of the main parties. Whilst there was a case for exending the
franchise, so that Parliament might better fulfil its 'expressive' function and represent working men in the towns, this legitimate aspir-
ation could never be allowed to undermine Parliament's principal
function of 'electing' a cabinet.

Cabinet government worked efficiently, in Bagehot's view, because
the English constitution also contained 'dignified' elements which
siphoned off many of the social and psychological pressures to which
the French and American systems of government were habitually
subjected. The formal powers of a modern English monarch were
few and in some cases rather eccentric, but the 'theatrical' activities

---

[18] *The English Constitution*, 170.

of the court, especially the royal family, deflected ordinary people's minds away from the workings of government. The fiction of monarchical power was a useful fiction, for it enabled poor people to associate the political system with a remote though intelligible figure to whom they could never have access, rather than a parliament to which they might. Similarly, the House of Lords acted as a focus for social ambition and status, although the formal powers and patronage that it exercised were few. Far better, suggested Bagehot, for people to idolize the peers and their wives who held levées and parties in St James's Square and Piccadilly, than a French-style Senate or a bureaucracy who exercised real power. But Bagehot also appreciated the importance of the remaining powers of both the monarchy and the House of Lords. The monarchy could be a crucial figure at moments of crisis, for through advising ministers, appointing ministers, or even creating new peers, it might avert a power vacuum into which systems such as that which operated in America were often pitched because they had no such 'safety-valve'. Few monarchs were wise enough to be able to know when or how to use these powers, although Bagehot implied that Prince Albert, had he lived, might have been effective in this way. But the knowledge that such power existed was an important check on the cabinet and both houses of parliament. In the same way, it was very important for Bagehot that the House of Lords continued to act as a revising chamber, for the House of Commons was usually too busy and sometimes too self-important to give legislation the attention it demanded. A reformed Lords—in other words an active Lords composed of life peers as well as hereditaries—Bagehot deemed to be a crucial part of the English constitution.

The English constitution represented the best of all worlds for Bagehot. It combined the stability and habitual familiarity of monarchy with the legislative efficiency of a bureaucracy, and with the liberal aspirations of a prosperous republic. It was France, America, and England all rolled into one. It was the *juste milieu*. Bagehot sounds almost Aristotelian when he suggests that in England the 'appendages of a monarchy have been converted into the essence of a republic'.[19] But like the great ~~Athenian~~ philosopher Bagehot was preoccupied with how political life could adapt to changing

[19] Ibid. 291.

circumstances without losing its essential function. The English constitution in the 1860s lay in the balance, in an 'equilibrium', to use an analogy of which Bagehot was fond. To tip too far in the direction of democracy would expose it to corruption and the rise of the caucus, of which Bagehot had seen plenty of examples when he attempted unsuccessfully to stand for Parliament on three occasions in the 1860s. To move it too much towards the executive would fuel English distrust of strong government, and precipitate all the problems of federal and imperial rule which had beset America and France.

How does *The English Constitution* look from a distance of nearly a century and a half? Modern readers must judge for themselves, but it is worth speculating on how much Bagehot got right, rather than got wrong. Cabinet government is of course the essence of modern British government, but cabinet government depending on the confidence and support of the whole of the House of Commons no longer exists, indeed it is questionable whether it ever existed in quite the way Bagehot describes. Political parties both in Parliament and in the constituencies now dominate the legislative and electoral processes, and it is political parties who now whip in the votes and majorities which in turn furnish support for cabinet government. Bagehot, to his credit, assumed this might happen. His vision of American democracy, whilst not particularly original or even fair, is a vision of a constitution taken over by professional party politicians, with elections run like a bespoke tailoring service, and parliamentary divisions organized like the herding of cattle. Some might say he was not far off the mark. Cabinet government in the modern age has also come to mean 'big' government, in the sense that there are so many more departments of state now in existence and so many responsibilities now undertaken by central government compared to the mid-Victorian years. Bagehot's world, by contrast, is one in which a minimal state operates. He is prescient on the dangers of Parliament undertaking too much—the problem of government 'overload'—and approved of decentralization where possible, although he was often scornful of the parish–pump qualities of local government politicians. Bagehot would have been a lukewarm supporter of the current measures of regional devolution, perhaps welcoming the release of pressure on business at Westminster, but apprehensive at the prospect of partisan infighting and political inexperience amongst new provincial assemblies.

Conversely, Bagehot can seem quite dated on the more 'dignified' elements of his English constitution. Much of the 'magic of monarchy' has worn off in the last generation or so for fairly obvious reasons, although the role of royalty in giving a measure of pomp, if not quite dignity or even circumstance, to foreign policy, the armed forces, and charitable activity remains immense. And most Britons continue to oppose the idea of replacing the monarchy with a President, on the Bagehot-type grounds that this would involve an inappropriate mixing of unimportant ceremonial duties with important political powers. At the same time Bagehot remains apposite on the House of Lords, which more than ever remains a symbol of social status, the apogee of arrivism in modern Britain. The honours system continues to confer symbolic gravitas, but the Lords itself is an institution without real power. Bagehot's more serious point about the need for an active revising second chamber partially comprised of nominated life peers remains as true now as it did when House of Lords reform was first discussed in the 1850s and 1860s. Debates about the House of Lords still often become embroiled in discussions simply about its composition. But as Bagehot always recognized, the chief consideration to be made with the second chamber was how it could undertake its role most effectively.

In the end, however, it is unfair to subject Bagehot to too much interrogation across the span of time. He was a Victorian Englishman who wrote a clever book—'wise chat'—about the most pressing political issues of his day. In recent years the pace of constitutional change has quickened once more, and the turn of the century begins to resemble the times in which Bagehot was writing. Constitutional commentary is back in vogue. Lacking a modern Bagehot, we would do well to go back and read the original.

NOTE ON THE TEXT

The English Constitution first appeared as a series of nine articles in the *Fortnightly Review*, beginning in May 1865 and ending in January 1867. The nine articles together with an 'Appendix on Reform' (which reproduced an 1864 article by Bagehot) were published as *The English Constitution* by Chapman and Hall in March 1867. In revising the articles for book form Bagehot made many minor excisions and amendments. Readers can compare the text of the original articles with the book version in Norman St John Stevas (ed.), *The Collected Works of Walter Bagehot* (1974), vol. v. A second edition of *The English Constitution* was published in 1872 by Henry S. King. Bagehot wrote a long new introduction for this edition, bringing readers up to date with political developments at home and abroad in the intervening years. But he also distanced himself from some of the conclusions he had reached in the first edition, pointing out that not only had the system he described begun to be transformed by the second Reform Act, but also a whole political generation reared on aristocratic leadership and social deference had passed away. He rearranged the order of the chapters, deleted from the final chapter several pages of negative speculations about the effects of lowering the franchise, and replaced the original appendix with a new appendix discussing Thomas Hare's scheme of proportional representation.

Following convention most subsequent editions of *The English Constitution*—for example, the versions in the two editions of Bagehot's collected works (1915 and 1974), the 1928 World's Classics version, and Richard Crossman's edition of 1963—have been of the 1872 edition, the last published during Bagehot's lifetime. The present edition, however, is of the original 1867 edition, since it remains closer to Bagehot's original purpose and frame of mind in the mid-1860s.

Footnotes to the text, cued by number, are Bagehot's own; editorial notes are cued by asterisk and appear at the end of the text.

SELECT BIBLIOGRAPHY

Editions

Earl Balfour, 'Introduction' to Balfour (ed.), Walter Bagehot, *The English Constitution* (Oxford, 1928).

Richard Crossman, 'Introduction' to Crossman (ed.), Walter Bagehot, *The English Constitution* (London, 1963).

Norman St John Stevas (ed.), *The Collected Works of Walter Bagehot*, 15 vols. (London, 1965–86).

Biography

Mrs Russell Barrington, *Life of Walter Bagehot* (London, 1914).

Alastair Buchan, *The Spare Chancellor: The Life of Walter Bagehot* (London, 1959).

Norman St John Stevas, *Walter Bagehot: A Study of his Life and Thought Together with a Selection from his Political Writings* (London, 1959).

Critical Studies

Asa Briggs, 'Trollope, Bagehot and the English Constitution', in Briggs, *Victorian People: Some Reassessments of Peoples, Institutions, Ideas and Events* (London, 1954), 87–115.

Crane Brinton, 'Bagehot', in Brinton, *English Political Thought in the Nineteenth Century* (London, 1933), 180–98.

John Burrow, 'Sense and Circumstance: Bagehot and the Nature of Political Understanding', in Stefan Collini, Donald Winch, and John Burrow, *That Noble Science of Politics: A Study in Nineteenth-Century Intellectual History* (Cambridge, 1983), 161–81.

R. W. Chapman, 'The Text of Bagehot's Constitution', *Philological Quarterly*, 31 (1952), 446–7.

Michael Churchman, 'Walter Bagehot and the American Civil War', *Dublin Review*, 240 (1966), 377–93.

C. H. Driver, 'Walter Bagehot and the Social Psychologists', in J. F. C. Hearnshaw (ed.), *The Social and Political Ideas of Some Representative Thinkers of the Victorian Age* (London, 1933), 194–221.

Mark Francis and John Morrow, *A History of English Political Thought in the Nineteenth Century* (London, 1994), 213–18.

R. A. Greenberg, 'Mill on Bagehot and reform', *Notes and Queries*, 203 (1958), 83–4.

Mohammed Abdul-Muizz Nasr, *Walter Bagehot: A Study in Victorian Ideas* (Alexandria, 1959).

David Spring, 'Bagehot and Deference', *American Historical Review*, 81 (1976), 524–31.

K. C. Wheare, 'Walter Bagehot', *Proceedings of the British Academy*, 40 (1974), 173–97.

Constitutional Background

David Cannadine, 'The Last Hanoverian Monarchy? The Victorian Monarchy in Historical Perspective', in A. L. Beier, David Cannadine, and James M. Rosenheim (eds.), *The First Modern Society: Essays in Honour of Lawrence Stone* (Cambridge, 1989), 127–65.

Ruth Dudley Edwards, *The Pursuit of Reason: 'The Economist', 1843–1993* (London, 1993).

John D. Fair, 'Walter Bagehot, Royal Mediation and the Modern British Constitution, 1869–1931', *Historian*, 43 (1980), 36–54.

Frank M. Hardie, *The Political Influence of Queen Victoria, 1861–1901* (1935).

Brian Harrison, 'Bagehot's System', in Harrison, *The Transformation of British Politics, 1860–1995* (Oxford, 1996), 13–53.

Angus B. Hawkins, ' "Parliamentary Government" and Victorian Political Parties, c.1830–1860', *English Historical Review*, 104 (1989), 638–69.

William Kuhn, *Democratic Royalism: The Transformation of the British Monarchy, 1861–1914* (1996).

Jon Roper, *Democracy and its Critics: Anglo-American Democratic Thought in the Nineteenth Century* (1989).

F. B. Smith, *The Making of the Second Reform Bill* (Cambridge, 1966).

Further Reading in Oxford World's Classics

Henry Adams, *The Education of Henry Adams*, ed. Ira B. Nadel.

Thomas Carlyle, *Reminiscences*, ed. K. J. Fielding and Ian Campbell.

John Stuart Mill, *On Liberty and Other Essays*, ed. John Gray.

—— *Principles of Political Economy*, ed. Jonathan Riley.

Anthony Trollope, *Phineas Finn*, ed. Jacques Berthoud.

A CHRONOLOGY OF WALTER BAGEHOT

1826   Born 3 February at Langport, Somerset, the son of Thomas Bagehot, partner and manager of Stuckey's Bank.

1832   Passing of the 'great' Reform Act.

1837   Accession of Queen Victoria.

1839–42   Studies at Bristol College.

1842–6   A student at University College London. Takes a BA Honours in Classics in 1846.

1843   The *Economist* commences publication.

1847–8   Contributes reviews of recent works on the currency question (by Thomas Tooke, Robert Torrens, and James Wilson) and John Stuart Mill's *Principles of Political Economy* to the *Prospective Review*.

1848   Gains his MA from University College, and is awarded the college's gold medal for Moral and Intellectual Philosophy and Political Economy.
Enters Lincoln's Inn to begin studying for the bar.
Revolutions break out across Europe.

1851   Moves to Paris in August. Witnesses Louis Napoleon's *coup d'état* in December.
The 'Exhibition of All Nations' is held in London.

1852   As 'Amicus' contributes a series of seven weekly letters on events in France to *The Inquirer*, a Unitarian journal. Returns to London in the spring. Gives up the bar in the summer, and returns to Langport to work in Stuckey's bank with his father. Contributes further articles to the *Prospective Review*.

1854   Britain enters the Crimean War.

1855   Establishment of the *National Review*, which he edits with his college friend Richard Holt Hutton.
Fall of the Aberdeen coalition over mismanagement of the war effort.

1856   Begins contributing to the *Saturday Review*.

1857   Writes for the *Economist* for the first time, contributing articles under the alias of 'A Banker'.
Indian 'mutiny'.

1858   Marries Eliza Wilson, daughter of James Wilson, the proprietor of the *Economist*. They settle into 'The Arches' in
        Clevedon, Somerset.
        Publication of *Estimates of Some Englishmen and Scotchmen*.

1859   His pamphlet *Parliamentary Reform: An Essay* is published and
        receives widespread notice as Lord Derby's government prepares its reform bill. Takes over temporary direction of the
        Economist, in the absence of James Wilson, who had been
        appointed Financial Member of the Council of India.
        Publication of Charles Darwin's *Origin of the Species*.

1861   Moves to London, becoming director and editor of the *Economist*, following the death of James Wilson in India the previous
        summer.
        Death of Prince Albert. Start of the American Civil War.

1865   The first of nine articles on 'The English Constitution' is published in the opening number of the *Fortnightly Review*, edited
        by George Henry Lewes. Withdraws before the poll from the
        general election contest at Manchester in the summer.
        Death of Lord Palmerston in October.

1866   Again unsuccessful in his attempt to enter Parliament. Comes
        second in a by-election at Bridgwater in July.
        Liberal government of Lord John Russell introduces an unsuccessful reform bill.

1867   Publication of *The English Constitution*.
        Passing of the Second Reform Act.

1872   Publication of *Physics and Politics; or Thoughts on the Application of the Principles of 'Natural Selection', and 'Inheritance' to
        Political Society* and a second revised edition of *The English
        Constitution*.
        Voting by secret ballot introduced.

1873   Publication of *Lombard Street: A Description of the Money
        Market*.

1877   At Bagehot's suggestion the Conservative Chancellor, Stafford
        Northcote, brings in Treasury bills as a new means of raising
        finance. On 24 March Bagehot dies at his home at Herd's Hill
        in Langport.

1879   *Economic Studies: The Postulates of English Political Economy*
        published posthumously.

THE
ENGLISH CONSTITUTION

ADVERTISEMENT

THESE Essays appeared in the *Fortnightly Review* at various times between the spring of 1865 and the first month of this year. I much wish that I were able to recast them, for such a series must have many defects when presented as a continuous book; but many occupations forbid me to hope that I could accomplish this within any moderate limits of time, and as the opinions here set forth (whatever may be their value) have at least cost me much time and thought, I venture to publish them in the only form I can.

The arguments of the first Essay, if it had been rewritten, might have been exceedingly illustrated by the present contest between the President and the Congress of the United States: but I leave it to stand as it was published just a few days after Lincoln's death*— when Mr Johnson was said to be a violent Anti-Southerner, and no such quarrel was thought of. There is a just suspicion in the public mind of principles got up to account for events just occurring; and I prefer to leave what I wrote as it stood, when no such events were looked for.

1

THE CABINET

'On all great subjects,' says Mr Mill,* 'much remains to be said,' and of none is this more true, than of the English Constitution. The literature which has accumulated upon it is huge. But an observer who looks at the living reality will wonder at the contrast to the paper description. He will see in the life much which is not in the books; and he will not find in the rough practice many refinements of the literary theory.

It was natural—perhaps inevitable—that such an undergrowth of irrelevant ideas should gather round the British Constitution. Language is the tradition of nations; each generation describes what it sees, but it uses words transmitted from the past. When a great entity like the British Constitution has continued in connected outward sameness, but hidden inner change, for many ages, every generation inherits a series of inapt words—of maxims once true, but of which the truth is ceasing or has ceased. As a man's family go on muttering in his maturity incorrect phrases derived from a just observation of his early youth, so, in the full activity of an historical constitution, its subjects repeat phrases true in the time of their fathers, and inculcated by those fathers, but now true no longer. Or, if I may say so, an ancient and ever-altering constitution is like an old man who still wears with attached fondness clothes in the fashion of his youth: what you see of him is the same; what you do not see is wholly altered.

There are two descriptions of the English Constitution which have exercised immense influence, but which are erroneous. First, it is laid down as a principle of the English polity, that in it the legislative, the executive, and the judicial powers, are quite divided,—that each is entrusted to a separate person or set of persons—that no one of these can at all interfere with the work of the other. There has been much eloquence expended in explaining how the rough genius of the English people, even in the middle ages, when it was especially rude, carried into life and practice that elaborate division of functions which philosophers had suggested on paper, but which they had hardly hoped to see except on paper.

Secondly, it is insisted, that the peculiar excellence of the British Constitution lies in a balanced union of three powers. It is said that the monarchical element, the aristocratic element, and the democratic element, have each a share in the supreme sovereignty, and that the assent of all three is necessary to the action of that sovereignty. Kings, lords, and commons, by this theory, are alleged to be not only the outward form, but the inner moving essence, the vitality of the constitution. A great theory, called the theory of 'Checks and Balances,' pervades an immense part of political literature, and much of it is collected from or supported by English experience. Monarchy, it is said, has some faults, some bad tendencies, aristocracy others, democracy, again, others; but England has shown that a government can be constructed in which these evil tendencies exactly check, balance, and destroy one another—in which a good whole is constructed not simply in spite of, but by means of, the counteracting defects of the constituent parts.

Accordingly it is believed, that the principal characteristics of the English Constitution are inapplicable in countries where the materials for a monarchy or an aristocracy do not exist. That constitution is conceived to be the best imaginable use of the political elements which the great majority of States in modern Europe inherited from the medieval period. It is believed that out of these materials nothing better can be made than the English Constitution; but it is also believed that the essential parts of the English Constitution cannot be made except from these materials. Now these elements are the accidents of a period and a region; they belong only to one or two centuries in human history, and to a few countries. The United States could not have become monarchical, even if the constituent convention had decreed it—even if the component States had ratified it. The mystic reverence, the religious allegiance, which are essential to a true monarchy, are imaginative sentiments that no legislature can manufacture in any people. These semi-filial feelings in government are inherited just as the true filial feelings in common life. You might as well adopt a father as make a monarchy; the special sentiment belonging to the one is as incapable of voluntary creation as the peculiar affection belonging to the other. If the practical part of the English Constitution could only be made out of a curious accumulation of mediaeval materials, its interest would be half historical, and its imitability very confined.

No one can approach to an understanding of the English institutions, or of others which being the growth of many centuries exercise a wide sway over mixed populations, unless he divide them into two classes. In such constitutions there are two parts (not indeed separable with microscopic accuracy, for the genius of great affairs abhors nicety of division): first, those which excite and preserve the reverence of the population—the *dignified* parts, if I may so call them; and next, the *efficient* parts,—those by which it, in fact, works and rules. There are two great objects which every constitution must attain to be successful, which every old and celebrated one must have wonderfully achieved: every constitution must first *gain* authority, and then *use* authority; it must first win the loyalty and confidence of mankind, and then employ that homage in the work of government.

There are indeed practical men who reject the dignified parts of government. They say, we want only to attain results, to do business; a constitution is a collection of political means for political ends; and if you admit that any part of a constitution does no business, or that a simpler machine would do equally well what it does, you admit that this part of the constitution, however dignified or awful it may be, is nevertheless in truth useless. And other reasoners, who distrust this bare philosophy, have propounded subtle arguments to prove that these dignified parts of old governments are cardinal components of the essential apparatus, great pivots of substantial utility; and so manufactured fallacies which the plainer school have well exposed. But both schools are in error. The dignified parts of government are those which bring it force,—which attract its motive power. The efficient parts only employ that power. The comely parts of a government *have* need, for they are those upon which its vital strength depends. They may not do anything definite that a simpler polity would not do better; but they are the preliminaries, the needful pre-requisites of *all* work. They raise the army, though they do not win the battle.

Doubtless, if all subjects of the same government only thought of what was useful to them, and if they all thought the same thing useful, and all thought that same thing could be attained in the same way, the efficient members of a constitution would suffice, and no impressive adjuncts would be needed. But the world in which we live is organised far otherwise.

The most strange fact, though the most certain in nature, is the unequal development of the human race. If we look back to the early ages of mankind, such as we seem in the faint distance to see them— if we call up the image of those dismal tribes in lake villages, or on wretched beaches;—scarcely equal to the commonest material needs, cutting down trees slowly and painfully with stone tools, hardly resisting the attacks of huge, fierce animals, —without culture, without leisure, without poetry, almost without thought,—destitute of morality, with only a sort of magic for religion; and if we compare that imagined life with the actual life of Europe now, we are overwhelmed at the wide contrast—we can scarcely conceive ourselves to be of the same race as those in the far distance. There used to be a notion—not so much widely asserted as deeply implanted, rather pervadingly latent than commonly apparent in political philosophy— that in a little while, perhaps ten years or so, all human beings might without extraordinary appliances be brought to the same level. But now when we see by the painful history of mankind at what point we began, by what slow toil, what favourable circumstances, what accumulated achievements, civilised man has become at all worthy in any degree so to call himself—when we realise the tedium of history and the painfulness of results, our perceptions are sharpened as to the relative steps of our long and gradual progress. We have in a great community like England crowds of people scarcely more civilised than the majority of two thousand years ago; we have others even more numerous such, as the best people were a thousand years since. The lower orders, the middle orders, are still, when tried by what is the standard of the educated 'ten thousand,' narrowminded, unintelligent, incurious. It is useless to pile up abstract words. Those who doubt should go out into their kitchens: let an accomplished man try what seems to him most obvious, most certain, most palpable in intellectual matters, upon the housemaid and the footman, and he will find that what he says seems unintelligible, confused, and erroneous—that his audience think him mad and wild when he is speaking what is in his own sphere of thought the dullest platitude of cautious soberness. Great communities are like great mountains—they have in them the primary, secondary, and tertiary strata of human progress; the characteristics of the lower regions resemble the life of old times rather than the present life of the higher regions. And a philosophy which does not ceaselessly remember, which does not continually obtrude the palpable differences of the various parts, will be a theory radically false, because it has omitted a capital reality—will be a theory essentially misleading, because it will lead men to expect what does not exist, and not to anticipate that which they will find.

Every one knows these plain facts, but by no means every one has traced their political importance. When a state is constituted thus, it is not true the lower classes will be absorbed in the useful; they do not like anything so poor. No orator ever made an impression by appealing to men as to their plainest physical wants, except when he could allege or prove that those wants were caused by the tyranny of some other class. But thousands have made the greatest impression by appealing to some vague dream of glory, or empire, or nationality. The ruder sort of men—that is, men at *one* stage of rudeness—will sacrifice all they hope for, all they have, *themselves*, for what is called an idea,—for some attraction which seems to transcend reality, which aspires to elevate men by an interest higher, deeper, wider than that of ordinary life. But this order of men are uninterested in the plain, palpable ends of government; they do not prize them; they do not in the least comprehend how they should be attained. It is very natural, therefore, that the most useful parts of the structure of government should by no means be those which excite the most reverence. The elements which excite the most easy reverence will be the *theatrical* elements; those which appeal to the senses, which claim to be embodiments of the greatest human ideas—which boast in some cases of far more than human origin. That which is mystic in its claims;—that which is occult in mode of action; that which is brilliant to the eye; that which is seen vividly for a moment, and then is seen no more; that which is hidden and unhidden; that which is specious, and yet interesting—palpable in its seeming, and yet professing to be more than palpable in its results;—this, howsoever its form may change, or however we may define it or describe it, is the sort of thing—the only sort which yet comes home to the mass of men. So far from the dignified parts of a constitution being necessarily the most useful, they are likely, according to outside presumption, to be the least so; for they are likely to be adjusted to the lowest orders—those likely to care least and judge worst about what *is* useful.

There is another reason which, in an old constitution like that of England, is hardly less important. The most intellectual of men are moved quite as much by what they are used to as by what they choose. The active voluntary part of man is very small, and if it were not economised by a sleepy kind of habit, its results would be null. We could not do every day out of our own heads all we have to do. We should accomplish nothing; for all our energies would be frittered away in minor attempts at petty improvement. One man, too, would go off from the known track in one direction, and one in another; so that when a crisis comes requiring massed combination, no two men will be near enough to act together. It is the dull traditional habit of mankind that guides most men's actions, and is the steady frame in which each new artist must set the picture that he paints. And all this traditional part of human nature is, *ex vi termini*,* most easily impressed and acted on by that which is handed down. Other things being equal, yesterday's institutions are by far the best for to-day; they are the most ready, the most influential, the most easy to get obeyed, the most likely to retain the reverence which they alone inherit, and which every other must win. The most imposing institutions of mankind are the oldest; and yet so changing is the world,—so fluctuating are its needs,—so apt to lose inward force, though retaining outward strength, are its best instruments, that we must not expect the oldest institutions to be now the most efficient. We must expect what is venerable to acquire influence because of its inherent dignity; but we must not expect it to use that influence so well as new creations apt for the modern world, instinct with its spirit, and fitting closely to its life.

The brief description of the characteristic merit of the English Constitution is, that its dignified parts are very complicated and somewhat imposing, very old and rather venerable; while its efficient part, at least when in great and critical action, is decidedly simple and rather modern. We have made, or, rather, stumbled on, a constitution which,—though full of every species of incidental defect— though of the worst *workmanship* in all out-of-the-way matters of any constitution in the world, yet has two capital merits:—it contains a simple efficient part which, on occasion, and when wanted, *can* work more simply, and easily, and better than any instrument of government that has yet been tried; and it contains likewise historical, complex, august, theatrical parts, which it has inherited from a long past,—which *take* the multitude,—which guide by an insensible but an omnipotent influence the associations of its subjects. Its essence is strong with the strength of modern simplicity; its exterior is august with the Gothic grandeur of a more imposing age. Its simple essence may, *mutatis mutandis*, be transplanted to many very various countries, but its august outside—what most men think it is—is narrowly confined to nations with an analogous history and similar political relics.

The efficient secret of the English Constitution may be described as the close union, the nearly complete fusion of the executive and legislative powers. According to the traditional theory, as it exists in all the books, the goodness of our constitution consists in the entire separation of the legislative and executive authorities, but in truth its merit consists in their singular approximation. The connecting link is *the cabinet*. By that new word we mean a committee of the legislative body selected to be the executive body. The legislature has many committees, but this is its greatest. It chooses for this, its main committee, the men in whom it has most confidence. It does not, it is true, choose them directly; but it is nearly omnipotent in choosing them indirectly. A century ago the Crown had a real choice of ministers, though it had no longer a choice in policy. During the long reign of Sir R. Walpole* he was obliged not only to manage parliament but to manage the palace. He was obliged to take care that some court intrigue did not expel him from his place. The nation then selected the English policy, but the Crown chose the English ministers. They were not only in name, as now, but in fact, the Queen's servants. Remnants, important remnants of this great prerogative still remain. The discriminating favour of William IV made Lord Melbourne head of the Whig party, when he was only one of several rivals.* At the death of Lord Palmerston* it is very likely that the Queen may have the opportunity of freely choosing between two, if not three statesmen. But, as a rule, the nominal prime minister is chosen by the legislature—and the real prime minister for most purposes—the leader of the House of Commons almost without exception is so. There is nearly always some one man plainly selected by the voice of the predominant party in the predominant house of the legislature, to head that party, and consequently to rule the nation. We have in England an elective first magistrate as truly as the Americans have an elective first magistrate. The Queen is only at the head of the dignified part of the constitution. The prime minister is at the head of the efficient part. The Crown is, according to the saying, the 'fountain of honour;' but the Treasury is the spring of business. However, our first magistrate differs from the American. He is not elected directly by the people; he is elected by the representatives of the people. He is an example of 'double election.' The legislature chosen, in name, to make laws, in fact finds its principal business in making and in keeping an executive.

The leading minister so selected has to choose his associates, but he only chooses among a charmed circle. The position of most men in parliament forbids their being invited to the cabinet; the position of a few men ensures their being invited. Between the compulsory list whom he must take, and the impossible list whom he cannot take, a prime minister's independent choice in the formation of a cabinet is not very large; it extends rather to the division of the cabinet offices than to the choice of cabinet ministers. Parliament and the nation have pretty well settled who shall have the first places; but they have not discriminated with the same accuracy which man shall have which place. The highest patronage of a prime minister is, of course, a considerable power, though it is exercised under close and imperative restrictions; though it is far less than it seems to be when stated in theory, or looked at from a distance.

The cabinet, in a word, is a board of control chosen by the legislature, out of persons whom it trusts and knows, to rule the nation. The particular mode in which the English ministers are selected; the fiction that they are, in any political sense, the Queen's servants; the rule which limits the choice of the cabinet to the members of the legislature,—are accidents unessential to its definition—historical incidents separable from its nature. Its characteristic is that it should be chosen by the legislature out of persons agreeable to and trusted by the legislature. Naturally these are principally its own members—but they need not be exclusively so. A cabinet which included persons not members of the legislative assembly might still perform useful duties. Indeed the Peers, who constitute a large element in modern cabinets, are members, now-a-days, only of a subordinate assembly. The House of Lords still exercises several useful functions; but the ruling influence—the deciding faculty—has passed to what, using the language of old times, we still call the lower house—to an assembly which, though inferior as a dignified institution, is superior as an efficient institution. A principal advantage of the House of Lords in the present age indeed consists in its thus acting as a *reservoir* of cabinet ministers. Unless the composition of the House of Commons were improved, or unless the rules requiring cabinet ministers to be members of the legislature were relaxed, it would undoubtedly be difficult to find, without the Lords, a sufficient supply of chief ministers. But the detail of the composition of a cabinet, and the precise method of its choice, are not to the purpose now. The first and cardinal consideration is the definition of a cabinet. We must not bewilder ourselves with the separable accidents until we know the necessary essence. A cabinet is a combining committee,—a *hyphen* which joins, a *buckle* which fastens, the legislative part of the state to the executive part of the state. In its origin it belongs to the one, in its functions it belongs to the other.

The most curious point about the cabinet is that so very little is known about it. The meetings are not only secret in theory, but secret in reality. By the present practice, no official minute is kept of them. Even a private note is discouraged and disliked. The House of Commons, even in its most inquisitive and turbulent moments, would not permit a note of a cabinet meeting to be read. No minister who respected the fundamental usages of political practice would attempt to read such a note. The committee which unites the law-making power to the law-executing power—which, by virtue of that combination, is, while it lasts and holds together, the most powerful body in the state—is a committee wholly secret. No description of it, at once graphic and authentic, has ever been given. It is said to be sometimes like a rather disorderly board of directors, where many speak and few listen—but no one knows.[1]

But a cabinet, though it is a committee of the legislative assembly, is a committee with a power which no assembly would—unless for historical accidents, and after happy experience—have been persuaded to entrust to any committee. It is a committee which can dissolve the assembly which appointed it; it is a committee with a suspensive veto—a committee with a power of appeal. Though appointed by one parliament, it can appeal if it chooses to the next. Theoretically, indeed, the power to dissolve parliament is entrusted,

---

[1] It is *said*, at the end of the cabinet which agreed to propose a fixed duty on corn, Lord Melbourne put his back to the door and said,* 'Now is it to lower the price of corn or isn't it? It is not much matter which we say, but mind, we must all say *the same*.' This is the most graphic story of a cabinet I ever heard, but I cannot vouch for its truth. Lord Melbourne's is a character about which men make stories.

to the sovereign only; and there are vestiges of doubt whether in *all* cases a sovereign is bound to dissolve parliament when the cabinet ask him to do so. But neglecting such small and dubious exceptions, the cabinet which was chosen by one House of Commons has an appeal to the next House of Commons. The chief committee of the legislature has the power of dissolving the predominant part of that legislature,—in fact, on critical occasions, the legislature itself. The English system, therefore, is not an absorption of the executive power by the legislative power; it is a fusion of the two. Either the cabinet legislate and act, or, if not, it can dissolve. It is a creature, but it has the power of destroying its creators. It is an executive which can annihilate the legislature as well as an executive which is the nominee of the legislature. It *was* made, but it *can* unmake; it was derivative in its origin, but it is destructive in its action.

This fusion of the legislative and executive functions may, to those who have not much considered it, seem but a dry and small matter to be the latent essence and effectual secret of the English Constitution; but we can only judge of its real importance by looking at a few of its principal effects, and contrasting it very shortly with its great competitor, which seems likely, unless care be taken, to outstrip it in the progress of the world. That competitor is the Presidential system. The characteristic of it is that the President is elected from the people by one process, and the House of Representatives by another. The independence of the legislative and executive powers is the specific quality of Presidential Government, just as their fusion and combination is the precise principle of Cabinet Government.

First, compare the two in quiet times. The essence of a civilised age is, that administration requires the continued aid of legislation. One principal and necessary kind of legislation is *taxation*. The expense of civilised government is continually varying. It must vary if the government does its duty. The miscellaneous estimates of the English Government contain an inevitable medley of changing items. Education, prison discipline, art, science, civil contingencies of a hundred kinds, require more money one year and less another. The expense of defence—the naval and military estimates—vary still more as the danger of attack seems more or less imminent, as the means of retarding such danger become more or less costly. If the persons who have to do the work are not the same as those who have to make the laws, there will be a controversy between two sets of persons. The tax-imposers are sure to quarrel with the tax-requirers. The executive is crippled by not getting the laws it needs, and the legislature is spoiled by having to act without responsibility; the executive becomes unfit for its name since it cannot execute what it decides on: the legislature is demoralised by liberty, by taking decisions of which others (and not itself) will suffer the effects.

In America so much has this difficulty been felt that a semi-connection has grown up between the legislature and the executive. When the Secretary of the Treasury of the Federal Government wants a tax he consults upon it with the Chairman of the Financial Committee of Congress. He cannot go down to Congress himself and propose what he wants; he can only write a letter and send it. But he tries to get a chairman of the Finance Committee who likes his tax;—through that chairman he tries to persuade the committee to recommend such tax; by that committee he tries to induce the house to adopt that tax. But such a chain of communications is liable to continual interruptions; it may suffice for a single tax on a fortunate occasion, but will scarcely pass a complicated budget—we do not say in a war or a rebellion—we are now comparing the cabinet system and the presidential system in quiet times—but in times of financial difficulty. Two clever men never exactly agreed about a budget. We have by present practice an Indian Chancellor of the Exchequer talking English finance at Calcutta, and an English one talking Indian finance in England.* But the figures are never the same, and the views of policy are rarely the same. One most angry controversy has amused the world, and probably others scarcely less interesting are hidden in the copious stores of our Anglo-Indian correspondence.

But relations something like these must subsist between the head of a finance committee in the legislature, and a finance minister in the executive.[1] They are sure to quarrel, and the result is sure to satisfy neither. And when the taxes do not yield as they were expected to yield, who is responsible? Very likely the secretary of the treasury could not persuade the chairman—very likely the chairman could not persuade his committee—very likely the committee could

---

[1] It is worth observing that even during the short existence of the Confederate Government these evils distinctly showed themselves. Almost the last incident at the Richmond Congress was an angry financial correspondence with Jefferson Davis.*

not persuade the assembly. Whom, then, can you punish—whom can you abolish when your taxes run short? There is nobody save the legislature, a vast miscellaneous body difficult to punish, and the very persons to inflict the punishment.

Nor is the financial part of administration the only one which requires in a civilised age the constant support and accompaniment of facilitating legislation. All administration does so. In England, on a vital occasion, the cabinet can compel legislation by the threat of resignation, and the threat of dissolution; but neither of these can be used in a presidential state. There the legislature cannot be dissolved by the executive government; and it does not heed a resignation, for it has not to find the successor. Accordingly, when a difference of opinion arises, the legislature is forced to fight the executive, and the executive is forced to fight the legislative; and so very likely they contend to the conclusion of their respective terms.[1] There, is, indeed, one condition of things in which this description, though still approximately true, is, nevertheless, not exactly true; and that is, when there is nothing to fight about. Before the rebellion in America, owing to the vast distance of other states, and the favourable economical condition of the country, there were very few considerable subjects of contention; but if that government had been tried by the English legislation of the last thirty years, the discordant action of the two powers, whose constant co-operation is essential to the best government, would have shown itself much more distinctly.

Nor is this the worst. Cabinet governments educate the nation; the presidential does not educate it, and may corrupt it. It has been said that England invented the phrase, 'Her Majesty's Opposition;' that it was the first government which made a criticism of administration as much a part of the polity as administration itself. This critical opposition is the consequence of cabinet government. The great scene of debate, the great engine of popular instruction and political controversy, is the legislative assembly. A speech there by an eminent statesman, a party movement by a great political combination, are the best means yet known for arousing, enlivening, and teaching a people. The cabinet system ensures such debates, for it makes them the means by which statesmen advertise themselves for

---

[1] I leave this passage to stand* as it was written just after the assassination of Mr Lincoln, and when every one said Mr Johnson would be very hostile to the South.

future and confirm themselves in present governments. It brings forward men eager to speak, and gives them occasions to speak. The deciding catastrophes of cabinet governments are critical divisions preceded by fine discussions. Everything which is worth saying, everything which ought to be said, most certainly *will* be said. Conscientious men think they ought to persuade others; selfish men think they would like to obtrude themselves. The nation is forced to hear two sides—all the sides, perhaps, of that which most concerns it. And it likes to hear—it is eager to know. Human nature despises long arguments which come to nothing,—heavy speeches which precede no motion—abstract disquisitions which leave visible things where they were. But all men heed great results, and a change of government is a great result. It has a hundred ramifications; it runs through society; it gives hope to many, and it takes away hope from many. It is one of those marked events which, by its magnitude and its melodrama, impresses men even too much. And debates, which have this catastrophe at the end of them—or may so have it—are sure to be listened to and sure to sink deep into the national mind.

Travellers even in the Northern States of America, the greatest and best of presidential countries, have noticed that the nation was 'not specially addicted to politics;' that they have not a public opinion finished and chastened as that of the English has been finished and chastened. A great many hasty writers have charged this defect on the 'Yankee race,' on the Anglo-American character; but English people, if they had no motive to attend to politics, certainly would not attend to politics. At present there is *business* in their attention. They assist at the determining crisis; they retard or help it. Whether the government will go out or remain is determined by the debate, and by the division in parliament. And the opinion out of doors, the secret pervading decision of society has a great influence on that division. The nation feels that its judgment is important, and it strives to judge. It succeeds in deciding because the debates and the discussions give it the facts and the arguments. But under a presidential government a nation has, except at the electing moment, no influence; it has not the ballot-box before it; its virtue is gone, and it must wait till its instant of despotism again returns. It is not incited to form an opinion like a nation under a cabinet government; nor is it instructed like such a nation. There are doubtless debates in the legislature, but they are prologues without a play. There is nothing of catastrophe about them; you cannot turn out the government: the prize of power is not in the gift of the legislature, and no one cares for the legislature. The executive, the great centre of power and place, sticks irremovable; you cannot change it in any event. The teaching apparatus which has educated our public mind, which prepares our resolutions, which shapes our opinions, does not exist. No presidential country needs to form daily, delicate opinions, or is helped in forming them.

It might be thought that the discussions in the press would supply the deficiencies of the constitution; that by a reading people especially, the conduct of their government would be as carefully watched, that their opinions about it would be as consistent, as accurate, as well-considered, under a presidential as under a cabinet polity. But the same difficulty oppresses the press which oppresses the legislature. It can *do nothing*. It cannot change the administration; the executive was elected for such and such years, and for such and such years it must last. People wonder that so literary a people as the Americans—a people who read more than any people who ever lived, who read so many newspapers—should have such bad newspapers. The papers are not as good as the English papers, because they have not the same motive to be good as the English papers. At a political 'crisis,' as we say—that is, when the fate of the administration is unfixed, when it depends on a few votes, yet unsettled, upon a wavering and veering opinion—effective articles in great journals become of essential moment. The *Times* has made many ministries. When, as of late, there has been a long continuance of divided parliaments, of governments which were without 'brute voting power,' and which depended on intellectual strength, the support of the most influential organ of English opinion has been of critical moment. If a Washington newspaper could have turned out Mr Lincoln, there would have been good writing and fine argument in the Washington newspapers. But the Washington newspapers can no more remove a president during his term of place than the *Times* can remove a lord mayor during his year of office. Nobody cares for a debate in Congress which 'comes to nothing,' and no one reads long articles which have no influence on events. The Americans glance at the heads of news, and through the paper. They do not enter upon a discussion. They do not *think* of entering on a discussion which would be useless.

After saying that the division of the legislative and executive in presidential governments weakens the legislative power, it may seem a contradiction to say that it also weakens the executive power. But it is not a contradiction. The division weakens the whole aggregate force of government—the entire imperial power; and therefore it weakens both its halves. The executive is weakened in a very plain way. In England a strong cabinet can obtain the concurrence of the legislature in all acts which facilitate its administration; it is itself, so to say, the legislature. But a president may be hampered by the parliament, and is likely to be hampered. The natural tendency of the members of every legislature is to make themselves conspicuous. They wish to gratify an ambition laudable or blameable; they wish to promote the measures they think best for the public welfare; they wish to make their *will* felt in great affairs. All these mixed motives urge them to oppose the executive. They are embodying the purposes of others if they aid; they are advancing their own opinions if they defeat: they are first if they vanquish; they are auxiliaries if they support. The weakness of the American executive used to be the great theme of all critics before the Confederate rebellion.* Congress and committees of Congress of course impeded the executive when there was no coercive public sentiment to check and rule them.

But the presidential system not only gives the executive power an antagonist in the legislative power, and so makes it weaker; but it also enfeebles it by impairing its intrinsic quality. A cabinet is elected by a legislature; and when that legislature is composed of fit persons, that mode of electing the executive is the very best. It is a case of secondary election, under the only conditions in which secondary election is preferable to primary. Generally speaking, in an electioneering country (I mean in a country full of political life, and used to the manipulation of popular institutions), the election of candidates to elect candidates is a farce. The Electoral College of America is so. It was intended that the deputies when assembled should exercise a real discretion, and by independent choice select the president. But the primary electors take too much interest. They only elect a deputy to vote for Mr Lincoln or Mr Breckenridge,* and the deputy only takes a ticket, and drops that ticket in an urn. He never chooses or thinks of choosing. He is but a messenger—a transmitter: the real decision is in those who chose him; who chose him because they knew what he would do.

It is true that the British House of Commons is subject to the same influences. Members are mostly, perhaps, elected because they will vote for a particular ministry, rather than for purely legislative reasons. But—and here is the capital distinction—the functions of the House of Commons are important and *continuous*. It does not, like the Electoral College in the United States, separate when it has elected its ruler; it watches, legislates, seats, and unseats ministries, from day to day. Accordingly it is a *real* electoral body. The parliament of 1857, which, more than any other parliament of late years, was a parliament elected to support a particular premier—which was chosen, as Americans might say, upon the 'Palmerston ticket'—before it had been in existence two years, dethroned Lord Palmerston. Though selected in the interest of a particular ministry, it in fact destroyed that ministry.

A *good* parliament, too, is a capital choosing body. If it is fit to make laws for a country, its majority ought to represent the general average intelligence of that country; its various members ought to represent the various special interests, special opinions, special prejudices, to be found in that community. There ought to be an advocate for every particular sect, and a vast neutral body of no sect—homogeneous and judicial, like the nation itself. Such a body, when possible, is the best selecter of executives that can be imagined. It is full of political activity; it is close to political life; it feels the responsibility of affairs which are brought as it were to its threshold; it has as much intelligence as the society in question chances to contain. It is, what Washington and Hamilton* strove to create, an electoral college of the picked men of the nation.

The best mode of appreciating its advantages is to look at the alternative. The competing constituency is the nation itself, and this is, according to theory and experience, in all but the rarest cases, a bad constituency. Mr Lincoln, at his second election, being elected when all the Federal states had set their united hearts on one single object, was voluntarily re-elected by an actually choosing nation. He embodied the object in which was every one was absorbed. But this is almost the only presidential election of which so much can be said. In almost all cases the President is chosen by a machinery of caucuses and combinations too complicated to be perfectly known, and too familiar to require description. He is not the choice of the nation, he is the choice of the wire-pullers. A very large constituency in

quiet times is the necessary, almost the legitimate, subject of electioneering management: a man cannot know that he does not throw
his vote away except he votes as part of some great organisation; and
if he votes as a part, he abdicates his electoral function in favour of
the managers of that association. The nation, even if it chose for ✓
itself, would, in some degree, be an unskilled body; but when it does
not choose for itself, but only as latent agitators wish, it is like a large,
lazy man, with a small, vicious mind,—it moves slowly and heavily,
but it moves at the bidding of a bad intention; it 'means *little*, but it
means that little *ill*.'

And, as the nation is less able to choose than a parliament, so it has
worse people to choose out of. The American legislators of the last
century have been much blamed for not permitting the ministers of
the President to be members of the Assembly; but, with reference to
the specific end which they had in view, they saw clearly and decided
wisely. They wished to keep 'the legislative branch absolutely distinct from the executive branch;' they believed such a separation to
be essential to a good constitution; they believed such a separation
to exist in the English, which the wisest of them thought the best
constitution. And, to the effectual maintenance of such a separation,
the exclusion of the President's ministers from the legislature is
essential. If they are not excluded they become the executive, they
eclipse the President himself. A legislative chamber is greedy and
covetous; it acquires as much, it concedes as little as possible. The
passions of its members are its rulers; the law-making faculty, the
most comprehensive of the imperial faculties, is its instrument;
it will *take* the administration if it can take it. Tried by their own
aims, the founders of the United States were wise in excluding the ₹
ministers from Congress.

But though this exclusion is essential to the presidential system of
government, it is not for that reason a small evil. It causes the
degradation of public life. Unless a member of the legislature be
sure of something more than speech, unless he is incited by the hope
of action, and chastened by the chance of responsibility, a first-rate
man will not care to take the place, and will not do much if he does
take it. To belong to a debating society adhering to an executive
(and this is no inapt description of a congress under a presidential
constitution) is not an object to stir a noble ambition, and is a
position to encourage idleness. The members of a parliament

excluded from office can never be comparable, much less equal, to those of a parliament not excluded from office. The presidential government, by its nature, divides political life into two halves, an executive half and a legislative half; and, by so dividing it, makes neither half worth a man having—worth his making it a continuous career—worthy to absorb, as cabinet government absorbs, his whole soul. The statesmen from whom a nation chooses under a presidential system are much inferior to those from whom it chooses under a cabinet system, while the selecting apparatus is also far less discerning.

All these advantages are more important at critical periods, because government itself is more important. A formed public opinion, a respectable, able, and disciplined legislature, a well-chosen executive, a parliament and an administration not thwarting each other, but co-operating with each other, are of greater consequence when great affairs are in progress than when small affairs are in progress—when there is much to do than when there is little to do. But in addition to this, a parliamentary or cabinet constitution possesses an additional and special advantage in very dangerous times. It has what we may call a reserve of power fit for and needed by extreme exigencies.

The principle of popular government is that the supreme power, the determined efficacy in matters political, resides in the people—not necessarily or commonly in the whole people, in the numerical majority, but in a *chosen* people, a picked and selected people. It is so in England; it is so in all free countries. Under a cabinet constitution at a sudden emergency this people can choose a ruler for the occasion. It is quite possible and even likely that he would not be ruler *before* the occasion. The great qualities, the imperious will, the rapid energy, the eager nature fit for a great crisis are not required—are impediments—in common times. A Lord Liverpool is better in every-day politics than a Chatham—a Louis Philippe far better than a Napoleon.* By the structure of the world we often want, at the sudden occurrence of a grave tempest, to change the helmsman—to replace the pilot of the calm by the pilot of the storm. In England we have had so few catastrophes since our constitution attained maturity, that we hardly appreciate this latent excellence. We have not needed a Cavour* to rule a revolution—a representative man above all men fit for a great occasion, and by a natural, legal mode brought in to rule. But even in England, at what was the nearest to a great sudden crisis which we have had of late years—at the Crimean difficulty*—we used this inherent power. We abolished the Aberdeen cabinet, the ablest we have had, perhaps, since the Reform Act*—a cabinet not only adapted, but eminently adapted for every sort of difficulty save the one it had to meet—which abounded in pacific discretion, and was wanting only in the 'demonic element;' we chose a statesman who had the sort of merit then wanted, who, when he feels the steady power of England behind him, will advance without reluctance, and will strike without restraint. As was said at the time, 'We turned out the Quaker, and put in the pugilist.'

But under a presidential government you can do nothing of the kind. The American government calls itself a government of the supreme people; but at a quick crisis, the time when a sovereign power is most needed, you cannot *find* the supreme people. You have got a Congress elected for one fixed period, going out perhaps by fixed instalments, which cannot be accelerated or retarded—you have a President chosen for a fixed period, and immovable during that period: all the arrangements are for *stated* times. There is no *elastic* element, everything is rigid, specified, dated. Come what may, you can quicken nothing and can retard nothing. You have bespoken your government in advance, and whether it suits you or not, whether it works well or works ill, whether it is what you want or not, by law you must keep it. In a country of complex foreign relations it would mostly happen that the first and most critical year of every war would be managed by a peace premier, and the first and most critical years of peace by a war premier. In each case the period of transition would be irrevocably governed by a man selected not for what he was to introduce, but what he was to change—for the policy he was to abandon, not for the policy he was to administer.

The whole history of the American civil war—a history which has thrown an intense light on the working of a presidential government at the time when government is most important—is but a vast continuous commentary on these reflections. It would, indeed, be absurd to press against presidential government *as such* the singular defect by which Vice-President Johnson has become President* by which a man elected to a sinecure is fixed in what is for the moment the most important administrative part in the political world. This defect, though most characteristic of the expectations[1] of the framers of the constitution and of its working, is but an accident of this particular case of presidential government, and no necessary ingredient in that government itself. But the first election of Mr Lincoln* is liable to no such objection. It was a characteristic instance of the natural working of such a government upon a great occasion. And what was that working, for it may be summed up in a word, and it is easy to say it was government by an *unknown quantity*. Hardly anyone in America had any living idea what Mr Lincoln was like, or any definite notion what he would do. The leading statesmen under the system of cabinet government are not only household words, but household *ideas*. A conception not, perhaps, in all respects a true, but a most vivid conception, what Mr Gladstone is like, or what Lord Palmerston is like, runs through society. We have simply no notion what it would be to be left with the visible sovereignty in the hands of an unknown man. The notion of employing a man of unknown smallness at a crisis of unknown greatness is to our minds ludicrous. Mr Lincoln, it is true, happened to be a man, if not of eminent ability, yet of eminent justness. There was an inner depth of Puritan nature which came out under suffering, and was very attractive. But success in a lottery is no argument for lotteries. What were the chances against a person of Lincoln's antecedents, elected as he was, proving to be what he was?

Such an incident is, however, natural to a presidential government. The President is elected by processes which forbid the election of known men, except at peculiar conjunctures, and in moments when public opinion is excited and despotic; and consequently, if a crisis comes upon us soon after he is elected, inevitably we have government by an unknown quantity—the superintendence of that crisis by what our great satirist* would have called 'Statesman X.' Even in quiet times, government by a president is, for the several various reasons which have been stated, inferior to government by a cabinet; but the difficulty of quiet times is nothing as compared with the difficulty of unquiet times. The comparative deficiencies of the

---

[1] The framers of the constitution expected that the *vice*-president would be elected by the Electoral College as the second wisest man in the country. The vice-presidentship being a sinecure, a second-rate man agreeable to the wire-pullers is always smuggled in. The chance of succession to the presidentship is too distant to be thought of.

regular, common operation of a presidential government, are far less than the comparative deficiencies in time of sudden trouble—the want of elasticity, the impossibility of a dictatorship, the total absence of a *revolutionary reserve*.

This contrast explains why the characteristic quality of cabinet governments—the fusion of the executive power with the legislative power—is of such cardinal importance. I shall proceed to show what nations can have it, and what is the form under which it exists in England.

2

THE PRE-REQUISITES OF CABINET GOVERNMENT, AND THE PECULIAR FORM WHICH THEY HAVE ASSUMED IN ENGLAND

CABINET government is rare because its pre-requisites are many. It requires the co-existence of several national characteristics which are not often found together in the world, and which should be perceived more distinctly than they often are. It is fancied that the possession of a certain intelligence, and a few simple virtues, are the sole requisites. These mental and moral qualities are necessary, but much else is necessary also. A cabinet government is the government of a committee elected by the legislature, and there are therefore a double set of conditions to it: first, those which are essential to all elective governments as such; and second, those which are requisite to this particular elective government. There are pre-requisites for the genus, and additional ones for the species.

The first pre-requisite of elective government is the *mutual confidence* of the electors. We are so accustomed to submit to be ruled by elected ministers, that we are apt to fancy all mankind would readily be so too. Knowledge and civilisation have at least made this progress, that we instinctively, without argument, almost without consciousness, allow a certain number of specified persons to choose our rulers for us. It seems to us the simplest thing in the world. But it is one of the gravest things.

The peculiar marks of semi-barbarous people are diffused distrust and indiscriminate suspicion. People, in all but the most favoured times and places, are rooted to the places where they were born, think the thoughts of those places, can endure no other thoughts. The next parish even is suspected. Its inhabitants have different usages, almost imperceptibly different, but yet different; they speak a varying accent; they use a few peculiar words; tradition says that their faith is dubious. And if the next parish is a little suspected, the next county is much more suspected. Here is a definite beginning of new maxims, new thoughts, new ways: the immemorial boundary mark begins in feeling a strange world. And if the next county is dubious, a remote county is untrustworthy. 'Vagrants come from thence' men know, and they know nothing else. The inhabitants of the north speak a dialect different from the dialect of the south: they have other laws, another aristocracy, another life. In ages when distant territories are blanks in the mind, when neighbourhood is a sentiment, when locality is a passion, concerted co-operation between remote regions is impossible even on trivial matters. Neither would rely enough upon good faith, good sense, and good judgment of the other. Neither could enough calculate on the other.

And if such co-operation is not to be expected in trivial matters, it is not to be thought of in the most vital matter of government—the choice of the executive ruler. To fancy that Northumberland in the thirteenth century would have consented to ally itself with Somersetshire for the choice of a chief magistrate is absurd; it would scarcely have allied itself to choose a hangman. Even now, if it were palpably explained, neither district would like it. But no one says at a county election, 'The object of this present meeting is to choose our delegate to what the Americans call the "Electoral College," to the assembly which names our first magistrate—our substitute for their president. Representatives from this county will meet representatives from other counties, from cities and boroughs, and proceed to choose our rulers.' Such bald exposition would have been impossible in old times; it would be considered queer, eccentric, if it were used now. Happily, the process of election is so indirect and hidden, and the introduction of that process was so gradual and latent, that we scarcely perceive the immense political trust we repose in each other. The best mercantile credit seems to those who give it, natural, simple, obvious; they do not argue about it, or think about it. The best political credit is analogous; we trust our countrymen without remembering that we trust them.

A second and very rare condition of an elective government is a *calm* national mind—a tone of mind sufficiently stable to bear the necessary excitement of conspicuous revolutions. No barbarous, no semi-civilised nation has ever possessed this. The mass of uneducated men could not now in England be told 'go to, choose your rulers;' they would go wild; their imaginations would fancy unreal dangers, and the attempt at election would issue in some forcible usurpation. The incalculable advantage of august institutions in a free state is, that they prevent this collapse. The excitement of choosing our rulers is prevented by the apparent existence of an unchosen ruler. The poorer and more ignorant classes—those who would most feel excitement, who would most be misled by excitement—really believe that the Queen governs. You could not explain to them the recondite difference between 'reigning' and 'governing;' the words necessary to express it do not exist in their dialect; the ideas necessary to comprehend it do not exist in their minds. The separation of principal power from principal station is a refinement which they could not even conceive. They fancy they are governed by an hereditary queen, a queen by the grace of God, when they are really governed by a cabinet and a parliament—men like themselves, chosen by themselves. The conspicuous dignity awakens the sentiment of reverence, and men, often very undignified, seize the occasion to govern by means of it.

Lastly. The third condition of all elective government is what I may call *rationality*, by which I mean a power involving intelligence, but yet distinct from it. A whole people electing its rulers must be able to form a distinct conception of distant objects. Mostly, the 'divinity' that surrounds a king altogether prevents anything like a steady conception of him. You fancy that the object of your loyalty is as much elevated above you by intrinsic nature as he is by extrinsic position; you deify him in sentiment, as once men deified him in doctrine. This illusion has been and still is of incalculable benefit to the human race. It prevents, indeed, men from choosing their rulers; you cannot invest with that loyal illusion a man who was yesterday what you are, who tomorrow may be so again, whom you chose to be what he is. But though this superstition prevents the election of rulers, it renders possible the existence of unelected rulers. Untaught people fancy that their king, crowned with the holy crown, anointed with the oil of Rheims—descended of the House of Plantagenet—is a different sort of being from any one not descended of the Royal House—not crowned—not anointed. They believe that there is *one* man whom by mystic right they should obey; and therefore they do obey him. It is only in later times, when the world is wider, its experience larger, and its thought colder, that the plain rule of a palpably chosen ruler is even possible.

These conditions narrowly restrict elective government. But the pre-requisites of a cabinet government are rarer still; it demands not only the conditions I have mentioned, but the possibility likewise of a good legislature—a legislature competent to elect a sufficient administration.

Now a competent legislature is very rare. *Any* permanent legislature at all, any constantly acting mechanism for enacting and repealing laws, is, though it seems to us so natural, quite contrary to the inveterate conceptions of mankind. The great majority of nations conceive of their law, either as something Divinely given, and therefore unalterable, or as a fundamental habit, inherited from the past to be transmitted to the future. The English Parliament, of which the prominent functions are now legislative, was not all so once. It was rather a *preservative* body. The custom of the realm— the aboriginal transmitted law—the law which was in the breast of the judges, could not be altered without the consent of parliament, and therefore everybody felt sure it would not be altered except in grave, peculiar, and anomalous cases. The *valued* use of parliament was not half so much to alter the law, as to prevent the laws being altered. And such too was its real use. In early societies it matters much more that the law should be fixed than that it should be good. Any law which the people of ignorant times enact is sure to involve many misconceptions, and to cause many evils. Perfection in legislation is not to be looked for, and is not, indeed, much wanted in a rude, painful, confined life. But such an age covets fixity. That men should enjoy the fruits of their labour, that the law of property should be known, that the law of marriage should be known, that the whole course of life should be kept in a calculable track, is the *summum bonum** of early ages, the first desire of semi-civilised mankind. In that age men do not want to have their laws adapted, but to have their laws steady. The passions are so powerful, force so eager, the social bond so weak, that the august spectacle of an all but unalterable law is necessary to preserve it. In the early stages of human society all change is thought an evil. And *most* change is an evil. The conditions of life are so simple and so unvarying that any decent sort of rules suffice, so long as men know what they are. Custom is the first check on tyranny; that fixed routine of social life at which modern innovations chafe, and by which modern improvement is impeded, is the primitive check on base power. The perception of political expediency has hardly begun; the sense of abstract justice is weak and vague, and a rigid adherence to the fixed mould of transmitted usage is essential to an unmarred, unspoiled, unbroken life.

In such an age a legislature continuously sitting, always making laws, always repealing laws, would have been both an anomaly and a nuisance. But in the present state of the civilised part of the world such difficulties are obsolete. There is a diffused desire in civilised communities for an *adjusting* legislation; for a legislation which should adapt the inherited laws to the new wants of a world which now changes every day. It has ceased to be necessary to maintain bad laws, because it is necessary to have some laws. Civilisation is robust enough to bear the incision of legal improvements. But taking history at large, the rarity of cabinets is mostly due to the greater rarity of continuous legislatures.

Other conditions, however, limit even at the present day the area of a cabinet government. It must be possible to have not only a legislature, but to have a competent legislature—a legislature willing to elect and willing to maintain an efficient executive. And this is no easy matter. It is indeed true that we need not trouble ourselves to look for that elaborate and complicated organisation which partially exists in the House of Commons, and which is more fully and freely expanded in plans for improving the House of Commons. We are not now concerned with perfection or excellence; we seek only for simple fitness and bare competency.

The conditions of fitness are two. First, you must get a good legislature; and next, you must keep it good. And these are by no means so nearly connected as might be thought at first sight. To keep a legislature efficient, it must have a sufficient supply of substantial business. If you employ the best sort of men to do nearly nothing, they will quarrel with each other about that nothing. Where great questions end, little parties begin. And a very happy community, with few new laws to make, few old bad laws to repeal, and but simple foreign relations to adjust, has great difficulty in employing a legislature. There is nothing for it to enact, and nothing for it to settle. Accordingly, there is great danger that the legislature, being debarred from all other kind of business, may take to quarrelling about its elective business; that controversies as to ministries may occupy all its time, and yet that time be perniciously employed; that a constant succession of feeble administrations, unable to govern and unfit to govern, may be substituted for the proper result of cabinet government,—a sufficient body of men long enough in power to evince their sufficiency. The exact amount of non-elective business necessary for a parliament which is to elect the executive cannot, of course, be formally stated. There are no numbers and no statistics in the theory of constitutions. All we can say is, that a parliament with little business, which is to be as efficient as a parliament with much business, must be in all other respects much better. An indifferent parliament may be much improved by the steadying effect of grave affairs; but a parliament which has no such affairs must be intrinsically excellent, or it will fail utterly.

But the difficulty of keeping a legislature good, is evidently secondary to the difficulty of first getting it. There are two kinds of nations which can elect a good parliament. The first is a nation in which the mass of the people are intelligent, and in which they are comfortable. Where there is no honest poverty, where education is diffused, and political intelligence is common, it is easy for the mass of the people to elect a fair legislature. The ideal is roughly realised in the North American colonies of England, and in the whole free States of the Union. In these countries there is no such thing as honest poverty; physical comfort, such as the poor cannot imagine here, is there easily attainable by healthy industry. Education is diffused much, and is fast spreading. Ignorant emigrants from the Old World often prize the intellectual advantages of which they are themselves destitute, and are annoyed at their inferiority in a place where rudimentary culture is so common. The greatest difficulty of such new communities is commonly geographical. The population is mostly scattered; and where population is sparse, discussion is difficult. But in a country very large, as we reckon in Europe, a people really intelligent, really educated, really comfortable, would soon form a good opinion. No one can doubt that the New England States, if they were a separate community, would have an education, a political capacity, and an intelligence such as the numerical majority of no people, equally numerous, has ever possessed. In a state of this sort, where all the community is fit to choose a sufficient legislature, it is possible, it is almost easy, to create that legislature. If the New England States possessed a cabinet government as a separate nation, they would be as renowned in the world for political sagacity as they now are for diffused happiness.

The structure of these communities is indeed based on the principle of equality, and it is impossible that *any* such community can wholly satisfy the severe requirements of a political theorist. In every old community its primitive and guiding assumption is at war with truth. By its theory all people are entitled to the same political power, and they can only be so entitled on the ground that in politics they are equally wise. But at the outset of an agricultural colony this postulate is as near the truth as politics want. There are in such communities no large properties, no great capitals, no refined classes,—every one is comfortable and homely, and no one is at all more. Equality is not artificially established in a new colony; it establishes itself. There is a story that among the first settlers in Western Australia, some, who were rich, took out labourers at their own expense, and also carriages to ride in. But soon they had to try if they could live in the carriages. Before the masters' houses were built, the labourers had gone off,—they were building houses and cultivating land for themselves, and the masters were left to their carriages. Whether this exact thing happened I do not know, but this sort of thing has happened a thousand times. There have been a whole series of attempts to transplant to the colonies a graduated English society. But they have always failed at the first step. The rude classes at the bottom felt that they were equal to or better than the delicate classes at the top; they shifted for themselves, and left the 'gentlefolks' to shift for themselves; the base of the elaborate pyramid spread abroad, and the apex tumbled in and perished. In the early ages of an agricultural colony, whether you have political democracy or not, social democracy you must have, for nature makes it, and not you. But in time wealth grows and inequality begins. A and his children are industrious, and prosper; B and his children are idle, and fail. If manufactures on a considerable scale are established—and most young communities strive even by protection to establish them—the tendency to inequality is intensified. The capitalist becomes a unit with much, and his labourers a crowd with little. After generations of education, too, there arise varieties of culture—there will be an upper thousand, or ten thousand, of highly cultivated people in the midst of a great nation of moderately educated people. In theory it is desirable that this highest class of wealth and leisure should have an influence far out of proportion to its mere number: a perfect constitution would find for it a delicate expedient to make its fine thought tell upon the surrounding cruder thought. But as the world goes, when the whole of the population is as instructed and as intelligent as in the case I am supposing, we need not care much about this. Great communities have scarcely ever—never save for transient moments—been ruled by their highest thought. And if we can get them ruled by a decent capable thought, we may be well enough contented with our work. We have done more than could be expected, though not all which could be desired. At any rate, an isocratic polity—a polity where every one votes, and where every one votes alike—is, in a community of sound education and diffused intelligence, a conceivable case of cabinet government. It satisfies the essential condition; there is a people able to elect a parliament able to choose.

But suppose the mass of the people are not able to elect,—and this is the case with the numerical majority of all but the rarest nations,—how is a cabinet government to be then possible? It is only possible in what I may venture to call *deferential* nations. It has been thought strange, but there *are* nations in which the numerous unwiser part wishes to be ruled by the less numerous wiser part. The numerical majority—whether by custom or by choice, is immaterial—is ready, is eager to delegate its power of choosing its ruler to a certain select minority. It abdicates in favour of its *élite*, and consents to obey whoever that *élite* may confide in. It acknowledges as its secondary electors—as the choosers of its government—an educated minority, at once competent and unresisted; it has a kind of loyalty to some superior persons who are fit to choose a good government, and whom no other class opposes. A nation in such a happy state as this has obvious advantages for constructing a cabinet government. It has the best people to elect a legislature, and therefore it may fairly be expected to choose a good legislature—a legislature competent to select a good administration.

England is the type of deferential countries, and the manner in which it is so, and has become so, is extremely curious. The middle classes—the ordinary majority of educated men—are in the present day the despotic power in England. 'Public opinion' now-a-days, 'is the opinion of the bald-headed man at the back of the omnibus.' It is *not* the opinion of the aristocratical classes as such; or of the most educated or refined classes as such; it is simply the opinion of the ordinary mass of educated, but still commonplace mankind. If you look at the mass of the constituencies, you will see that they are not very interesting people; and perhaps if you look behind the scenes and see the people who manipulate and work the constituencies, you will find that these are yet more uninteresting. The English constitution in its palpable form is this—the mass of the people yield obedience to a select few; and when you see this select few, you perceive that though not of the lowest class, nor of an unrespectable class, they are yet of a heavy sensible class—the last people in the world to whom, if they were drawn up in a row, an immense nation would ever give an exclusive preference.

In fact, the mass of the English people yield a deference rather to something else than to their rulers. They defer to what we may call the *theatrical show* of society. A certain state passes before them; a certain pomp of great men; a certain spectacle of beautiful women; a wonderful scene of wealth and enjoyment is displayed, and they are coerced by it. Their imagination is bowed down; they feel they are not equal to the life which is revealed to them. Courts and aristocracies have the great quality which rules the multitude, though philosophers can see nothing in it—visibility. Courtiers can do what others cannot. A common man may as well try to rival the actors on the stage in their acting, as the aristocracy in *their* acting. The higher world, as it looks from without, is a stage on which the actors walk their parts much better than the spectators can. This play is played in every district. Every rustic feels that his house is not like my lord's house; his life like my lord's life; his wife like my lady. The climax of the play is the Queen: nobody supposes that their house is like the court; their life like her life; her orders like their orders. There is in England a certain charmed spectacle which imposes on the many, and guides their fancies as it will. As a rustic on coming to London, finds himself in presence of a great show and vast exhibition of inconceivable mechanical things, so by the structure of our society he finds himself face to face with a great exhibition of political things which he could not have imagined, which he could not make—to which he feels in himself scarcely anything analogous.

Philosophers may deride this superstition, but its results are inestimable. By the spectacle of this august society, countless ignorant men and women are induced to obey the few nominal electors—the £10 borough renters, and the £50 county renters*—who have nothing imposing about them, nothing which would attract the eye or fascinate the fancy. What impresses men is not mind, but the result of mind. And the greatest of these results is this wonderful spectacle of society, which is ever new, and yet ever the same; in which accidents pass and essence remains; in which one generation dies and another succeeds, as if they were birds in a cage, or animals in a menagerie; of which it seems almost more than a metaphor to treat the parts as limbs of a perpetual living thing, so silently do they seem to change, so wonderfully and so perfectly does the conspicuous life of the new year take the place of the conspicuous life of last year. The apparent rulers of the English nation are like the most imposing personages of a splendid procession: it is by them the mob are influenced; it is they whom the spectators cheer. The real rulers are secreted in second-rate carriages; no one cares for them or asks about them, but they are obeyed implicitly and unconsciously by reason of the splendour of those who eclipsed and preceded them.

It is quite true that this imaginative sentiment is supported by a sensation of political satisfaction. It cannot be said that the mass of the English people are well off. There are whole classes who have not a conception of what the higher orders call comfort; who have not the pre-requisites of moral existence; who cannot lead the life that becomes a man. But the most miserable of these classes do not impute their misery to politics. If a political agitator were to lecture to the peasants of Dorsetshire, and try to excite political dissatisfaction, it is much more likely that he would be pelted than that he would succeed. Of parliament these miserable creatures know scarcely anything; of the cabinet they never heard. But they would say that, 'for all they have heard, the Queen is very good;' and rebelling against the structure of society is to their minds rebelling against the Queen, who rules that society, in whom all its most impressive part—the part that they know—culminates. The mass of the English people are politically contented as well as politically deferential.

A deferential community, even though its lowest classes are not intelligent, is far more suited to a cabinet government than any kind of democratic country, because it is more suited to political excellence. The highest classes can rule in it; and the highest classes must, as such, have more political ability than the lower classes. A life of labour, an incomplete education, a monotonous occupation, a career in which the hands are used much and the judgment is used little, cannot create as much flexible thought, as much applicable intelligences as a life of leisure, a long culture, a varied experience, an existence by which the judgment is incessantly exercised, and by which it may be incessantly improved. A country of respectful poor, though far less happy than where there are no poor to be respectful, is nevertheless far more fitted for the best government. You can use the best classes of the respectful country; you can only use the worst where every man thinks he is as good as every other.

It is evident that no difficulty can be greater than that of founding a deferential nation. Respect is traditional; it is given not to what is proved to be good, but to what is known to be old. Certain classes in certain nations retain by common acceptance a marked political preference, because they have always possessed it, and because they inherit a sort of pomp which seems to make them worthy of it. But in a new colony, in a community where merit *may* be equal, and where there *cannot* be traditional marks of merit and fitness, it is obvious that a political deference can be yielded to higher culture, only upon proof, first of its existence, and next of its political value. But it is nearly impossible to give such a proof so as to satisfy persons of less culture. In a future and better age of the world it may be effected; but in this age the requisite premises scarcely exist; if the discussion be effectually open, if the debate be fairly begun, it is hardly possible to obtain a rational, an argumentative acquiescence in the rule of the cultivated few. As yet the few rule by their hold, not over the reason of the multitude, but over their imaginations, and their habits; over their fancies as to distant things they do not know at all, over their customs as to near things which they know very well.

A deferential community in which the bulk of the people are ignorant, is therefore in a state of what is called in mechanics unstable equilibrium. If the equilibrium is once disturbed there is no tendency to return to it, but rather to depart from it. A cone balanced on its point is in unstable equilibrium, for if you push it ever so little it will depart farther and farther from its position and fall to the earth. So in communities where the masses are ignorant but respectful; if you once permit the ignorant class to begin to rule you may bid farewell to deference for ever. Their demagogues will inculcate, their newspapers will recount, that the rule of the existing dynasty (the people) is better than the rule of the fallen dynasty (the aristocracy). A people very rarely hears two sides of a subject in which it is much interested; the popular organs take up the side which is acceptable, and none but the popular organs in fact reach the people. A people *never* hears censure of itself. No one will tell it that the educated minority whom it dethroned governed better or more wisely than it governs. A democracy will never, save after an awful catastrophe, return what has once been conceded to it, for to do so would be to admit an inferiority in itself, of which, except by some almost unbearable misfortune, it could never be convinced.

3

THE MONARCHY

THE use of the Queen, in a dignified capacity, is incalculable. Without her in England, the present English Government would fail and pass away. Most people when they read that the Queen walked on the slopes at Windsor—that the Prince of Wales went to the Derby—have imagined that too much thought and prominence were given to little things. But they have been in error; and is it nice to trace how the actions of a retired widow and an unemployed youth become of such importance?

The best reason why Monarchy is a strong government is, that it is an intelligible government. The mass of mankind understand it, and they hardly anywhere in the world understand any other. It is often said that men are ruled by their imaginations; but it would be truer to say they are governed by the weakness of their imaginations. The nature of a constitution, the action of an assembly, the play of parties, the unseen formation of a guiding opinion, are complex facts, difficult to know, and easy to mistake. But the action of a single will, the fiat of a single mind, are easy ideas; anybody can make them out, and no one can ever forget them. When you put before the mass of mankind the question, 'Will you be governed by a king, or will you be governed by a constitution?' the inquiry comes out thus—'Will you be governed in a way you understand, or will you be governed in a way you do not understand?' The issue was put to the French people; they were asked, 'Will you be governed by Louis Napoleon, or will you be governed by an assembly?' The French people said, 'We will be governed by the one man we can imagine, and not by the many people we cannot imagine.'

The best mode of comprehending the nature of the two governments, is to look at a country in which the two have within a comparatively short space of years succeeded each other.

'The political condition,' says Mr Grote,* 'which Grecian legend everywhere presents to us, is in its principal features strikingly different from that which had become universally prevalent among the Greeks in the time of the Peloponnesian war. Historical oligarchy, as well as democracy, agreed in requiring a certain established system of government, comprising the three elements of specialised functions, temporary functionaries, and ultimate responsibility (under some forms or other) to the mass of qualified citizens—either a Senate or an Ecclesia, or both. There were, of course, many and capital distinctions between one government and another, in respect to the qualification of the citizen, the attributes and efficiency of the general assembly, the admissibility to power, &c; and men might often be dissatisfied with the way in which these questions were determined in their own city. But in the mind of every man, some determining rule or system—something like what in modern times is called a *constitution*—was indispensable to any government entitled to be called legitimate, or capable of creating in the mind of a Greek a feeling of moral obligation to obey it. The functionaries who exercised authority under it might be more or less competent or popular; but his personal feelings towards them were commonly lost in his attachment or aversion to the general system. If any energetic man could by audacity or craft break down the constitution, and render himself permanent ruler according to his own will and pleasure, even though he might govern well, he could never inspire the people with any sentiment of duty towards him: his sceptre was illegitimate from the beginning, and even the taking of his life, far from being interdicted by that moral feeling which condemned the shedding of blood in other cases, was considered meritorious: he could not even be mentioned in the language except by a name (τύραννος, *despot*) which branded him as an object of mingled fear and dislike.

'If we carry our eyes back from historical to legendary Greece, we find a picture the reverse of what has been here sketched. We discern a government in which there is little or no scheme or system,—still less any idea of responsibility to the governed,—but in which the main-spring of obedience on the part of the people consists in their personal feeling and reverence towards the chief. We remark, first and foremost, the King; next, a limited number of subordinate kings or chiefs; afterwards, the mass of armed freemen, husbandmen, artisans, freebooters, &c.; lowest of all, the free labourers for hire and the bought slaves. The King is not distinguished by any broad, or impassable boundary from the other chiefs, to each of whom the title *Basileus* is applicable as well as to himself: his supremacy has been inherited from his ancestors, and passes by inheritance, as a general rule, to his eldest son, having been conferred upon the family as a privilege by the favour of Zeus. In war, he is the leader, foremost in personal prowess, and directing all military movements; in peace, he is the general protector of the injured and oppressed; he offers up moreover those public prayers and sacrifices which are intended to obtain for the whole people the favour of the gods. An ample domain is assigned to him as an appurtenance of his lofty position, and the produce of his fields and his cattle is consecrated in part to an abundant, though rude hospitality. Moreover he receives frequent presents, to avert his enmity, to conciliate his favour, or to buy off his exactions; and when plunder is taken from the enemy, a large previous share, comprising probably the most alluring female captive, is reserved for him apart from the general distribution.

'Such is the position of the King in the heroic times of Greece,— the only person (if we except the heralds and priests, each both special and subordinate) who is then presented to us as clothed with any individual authority,—the person by whom all the executive functions, then few in number, which the society requires, are either performed or directed. His personal ascendancy—derived from divine countenance bestowed both upon himself individually and upon his race, and probably from accredited divine descent—is the salient feature in the picture: the people hearken to his voice, embrace his propositions, and obey his orders: not merely resistance, but even criticism upon his acts, is generally exhibited in an odious point of view, and is indeed never heard of except from some one or more of the subordinate princes.'

The characteristic of the English Monarchy is that it retains the feelings by which the heroic kings governed their rude age, and has added the feelings by which the constitutions of later Greece ruled in more refined ages. We are a more mixed people than the Athenians, or probably than any political Greeks. We have progressed more unequally. The slaves in ancient times were a separate order; not ruled by the same laws, or thoughts, as other men. It was not necessary to think of them in making a constitution: it was not necessary to improve them in order to make a constitution possible. The Greek legislator had not to combine in his polity men like the labourers of Somersetshire, and men like Mr Grote. He had not to deal with a community in which primitive barbarism lay as a recognised basis to acquired civilisation. *We have.* We have no slaves to keep down by special terrors and independent legislation. But we have whole classes unable to comprehend the idea of a constitution—unable to feel the least attachment to impersonal laws. Most do indeed vaguely know that there are some other institutions besides the Queen, and some rules by which she governs. But a vast number like their minds to dwell more upon her than on anything else, and therefore she is inestimable. A Republic has only difficult ideas in government; a Constitutional Monarchy has an easy idea too; it has a comprehensible element for the vacant many, as well as complex laws and notions for the inquiring few.

A *family* on the throne is an interesting idea also. It brings down the pride of sovereignty to the level of petty life. No feeling could seem more childish than the enthusiasm of the English at the marriage of the Prince of Wales.* They treated as a great political event, what, looked at as a matter of pure business, was very small indeed. But no feeling could be more like common human nature, as it is, and as it is likely to be. The women—one half the human race at least—care fifty times more for a marriage than a ministry. All but a few cynics like to see a pretty novel touching for a moment the dry scenes of the grave world. A princely marriage is the brilliant edition of a universal fact, and as such, it rivets mankind. We smile at the *Court Circular*;* but remember how many people read the *Court Circular*! Its use is not in what it says, but in those to whom it speaks. They say that the Americans were more pleased at the Queen's letter to Mrs Lincoln* than at any act of the English Government. It was a spontaneous act of intelligible feeling in the midst of confused and tiresome business. Just so a royal family sweetens politics by the seasonable addition of nice and pretty events. It introduces irrelevant facts into the business of government, but they are facts which speak to 'men's bosoms,' and employ their thoughts.

To state the matter shortly, Royalty is a government in which the attention of the nation is concentrated on one person doing interesting actions. A Republic is a government in which that attention is divided between many, who are all doing uninteresting actions. Accordingly, so long as the human heart is strong and the human reason weak, Royalty will be strong because it appeals to diffused feeling, and Republics weak because they appeal to understanding.

Secondly. The English Monarchy strengthens our government with the strength of religion. It is not easy to say why it should be so.

Every instructed theologian would say that it was the duty of a person born under a Republic as much to obey that Republic as it is the duty of one born under a Monarchy to obey the monarch. But the mass of the English people do not think so; they agree with the oath of allegiance; they say it is their duty to obey the 'Queen;' and they have but hazy notions as to obeying laws without a queen. In former times, when our constitution was incomplete, this notion of local holiness in one part was mischievous. All parts were struggling, and it was necessary each should have its full growth. But superstition said one should grow where it would, and no other part should grow without its leave. The whole cavalier party said it was their duty to obey the king, whatever the king did. There was to be 'passive obedience' to him, and there was no religious obedience due to any one else. He was the 'Lord's anointed,' and no one else had been anointed at all. The parliament, the laws, the press were human institutions; but the Monarchy was a Divine institution. An undue advantage was given to a part of the constitution, and therefore the progress of the whole was stayed.

After the Revolution* this mischievous sentiment was much weaker. The change of the line of sovereigns was at first conclusive. If there was a mystic right in any one, that right was plainly in James II; if it was an English duty to obey any one whatever he did, he was the person to be so obeyed; if there was an inherent inherited claim in any king, it was in the Stuart king to whom the crown had come by descent, and not in the Revolution king to whom it had come by vote of Parliament. All through the reign of William III there was (in common speech) one king whom man had made, and another king whom God had made. The king who ruled had no consecrated loyalty to build upon; although he ruled in fact, according to sacred theory there was a king in France who ought to rule. But it was very hard for the English people, with their plain sense and slow imagination, to keep up a strong sentiment of veneration for a foreign adventurer. He lived under the protection of a French king; what he did was commonly stupid, and what he left undone was very often wise. As soon as Queen Anne began to reign there was a change of feeling; the old sacred sentiment began to cohere about her. There were indeed difficulties which would have baffled most people; but an Englishman whose heart is in the matter is not easily baffled. Queen Anne had a brother living and a father living, and by every rule of descent, their right was better than hers. But many people evaded both claims. They said James II had 'run away,' and so abdicated, though he only ran away because he was in duresse and was frightened, and though he claimed the allegiance of his subjects day by day. The Pretender,* it was said, was not legitimate, though the birth was proved by evidence which any Court of Justice would have accepted. The English people were 'out of' a sacred monarch, and so they tried very hard to make a new one. Events, however, were too strong for them. They were ready and eager to take Queen Anne as the stock of a new dynasty; they were ready to ignore the claims of her father and the claims of her brother, but they could not ignore the fact that at the critical period she had no children. She had once had thirteen, but they all died in her lifetime, and it was necessary either to revert to the Stuarts or to make a new king by Act of Parliament.

According to the Act of Settlement passed by the Whigs, the crown was settled on the descendants of the 'Princess Sophia' of Hanover, a younger daughter of a daughter of James I. There were before her James II, his son, the descendants of a daughter of Charles I, and elder children of her own mother. But the Whigs passed these over because they were Catholics, and selected the Princess Sophia, who, if she was anything, was a Protestant. Certainly this selection was statesman-like, but it could not be very popular. It was quite impossible to say that it was the duty of the English people to obey the House of Hanover upon any principles which do not concede the right of the people to choose their rulers, and which do not degrade monarchy from its solitary pinnacle of majestic reverence, and make it one only among many expedient institutions. If a king is a useful public functionary who may be changed, and in whose place you may make another, you cannot regard him with mystic awe and wonder; and if you are bound to worship him, of course you cannot change him. Accordingly, during the whole reigns of George I and George II the sentiment of religious loyalty altogether ceased to support the Crown. The prerogative of the king had no strong party to support it; the Tories, who naturally would support it, disliked the actual king; and the Whigs, according to their creed, disliked the king's office. Until the accession of George III the most vigorous opponents of the crown were the country gentlemen, its natural friends, and the representatives of quiet rural districts, where loyalty is mostly to be found, if anywhere. But after the accession of George III the common feeling came back to the same point as in Queen Anne's time. The English were ready to take the new young prince as the beginning of a sacred line of sovereigns, just as they had been willing to take an old lady who was the second cousin of his great-great-grandmother. So it is now. If you ask the immense majority of the Queen's subjects by what right she rules, they would never tell you that she rules by Parliamentary right, by virtue of 6 Anne, c. 7.* They will say she rules by 'God's grace;' they believe that they have a mystic obligation to obey her. When her family came to the Crown it was a sort of treason to maintain the inalienable right of lineal sovereignty, for it was equivalent to saying that the claim of another family was better than hers; but now, in the strange course of human events, that very sentiment has become her surest and best support.

But it would be a great mistake to believe that at the accession of George III the instinctive sentiment of hereditary loyalty at once became as useful as now. It began to be powerful, but it hardly began to be useful. There was so much harm done by it as well as so much good, that it is quite capable of being argued whether on the whole it was beneficial or hurtful. Throughout the greater part of his life George III was a kind of 'consecrated obstruction.' Whatever he did had a sanctity different from what any one else did, and it perversely happened that he was commonly wrong. He had as good intentions as any one need have, and he attended to the business of his country, as a clerk with his bread to get attends to the business of his office. But his mind was small, his education limited, and he lived in a changing time. Accordingly he was always resisting what ought to be, and prolonging what ought not to be. He was the sinister but sacred assailant of half his ministries; and when the French revolution excited the horror of the world, and proved democracy to be 'impious,' the piety of England concentrated upon him, and gave him tenfold strength. The monarchy by its religious sanction now confirms all our political order; in George III's time it confirmed little except itself. It gives now a vast strength to the entire constitution, by enlisting on its behalf the credulous obedience of enormous masses; then it lived aloof, absorbed all the holiness into itself, and turned over all the rest of the polity to the coarse justification of bare expediency.

A principal reason why the monarchy so well consecrates our whole state is to be sought in the peculiarity many Americans and many utilitarians* smile at. They laugh at this 'extra,' as the Yankee called it, at the solitary transcendent element. They quote Napoleon's saying,* 'that he did not wish to be fatted in idleness,' when he refused to be grand elector in Sièyes' constitution, which was an office copied, and M. Thiers says, well copied, from constitutional monarchy. But such objections are totally wrong. No doubt it was absurd enough in the Abbé Sièyes to propose that a new institution, inheriting no reverence, and made holy by no religion, should be created to fill the sort of post occupied by a constitutional king in nations of monarchical history. Such an institution, far from being so august as to spread reverence around it, is too novel and artificial to get reverence for itself; if, too, the absurdity could anyhow be augmented, it was so by offering an office of inactive uselessness and pretended sanctity to Napoleon, the most active man in France, with the greatest genius for business, only not sacred, and exclusively fit for action. But the blunder of Sièyes brings the excellence of real monarchy to the best light. When a monarch can bless, it is best that he should not be touched. It should be evident that he does no wrong. He should not be brought too closely to real measurement. He should be aloof and solitary. As the functions of English royalty are for the most part latent, it fulfils this condition. It seems to order, but it never seems to struggle. It is commonly hidden like a mystery, and sometimes paraded like a pageant, but in neither case is it contentious. The nation is divided into parties, but the Crown is of no party. Its apparent separation from business is that which removes it both from enmities and from desecration, which preserves its mystery, which enables it to combine the affection of conflicting parties,—to be a visible symbol of unity to those still so imperfectly educated as to need a symbol.

Thirdly. The Queen is the head of our society. If she did not exist the Prime Minister would be the first person in the country. He and his wife would have to receive foreign ministers, and occasionally foreign princes, to give the first parties in the country; he and she would be at the head of the pageant of life; they would represent England in the eyes of foreign nations; they would represent the Government of England in the eyes of the English.

It is very easy to imagine a world in which this change would not be a great evil. In a country where people did not care for the outward show of life, where the genius of the people was untheatrical, and they exclusively regarded the substance of things, this matter would be trifling. Whether Lord and Lady Derby* received the foreign ministers, or Lord and Lady Palmerston, would be a matter of indifference; whether they gave the nicest parties would be important only to the persons at those parties. A nation of unimpressible philosophers would not care at all how the externals of life were managed. Who is the showman is not material unless you care about the show.

But of all nations in the world the English are perhaps the least a nation of pure philosophers. It would be a very serious matter to us to change every four or five years the visible head of our world. We are not now remarkable for the highest sort of ambition; but we are remarkable for having a great deal of the lower sort of ambition and envy. The House of Commons is thronged with people who get there merely for 'social purposes,' as the phrase goes; that is, that they and their families may go to parties else impossible. Members of Parliament are envied by thousands merely for this frivolous glory, as a thinker calls it. If the highest post in conspicuous life were thrown open to public competition, this low sort of ambition and envy would be fearfully increased. Politics would offer a prize too dazzling for mankind; clever base people would strive for it, and stupid base people would envy it. Even now a dangerous distinction is given by what is exclusively called public life. The newspapers describe daily and incessantly a certain conspicuous existence; they comment on its characters, recount its details, investigate its motives, anticipate its course. They give a precedence and a dignity to that world which they do not give to any other. The literary world, the scientific world, the philosophic world, not only are not comparable in dignity to the political world, but in comparison are hardly worlds at all. The newspaper makes no mention of them, and could not mention them. As are the papers, so are the readers; they, by irresistible sequence and association, believe that those people who constantly figure in the papers are cleverer, abler, or at any rate, somehow higher, than other people. 'I wrote books,' we have heard of a man saying, 'for twenty years, and I was nobody; I got into Parliament, and before I had taken my seat I had become somebody.' English politicians are the men who fill the thoughts of the English public; they are the actors on the scene, and it is hard for the admiring spectators not to believe that the admired actor is greater than themselves. In this present age and country it would be very dangerous to give the slightest addition to a force already perilously great. If the highest social rank was to be scrambled for in the House of Commons, the number of social adventurers there would be incalculably more numerous, and indefinitely more eager.

A very peculiar combination of causes has made this characteristic one of the most prominent in English society. The middle ages left all Europe with a social system headed by Courts. The government was made the head of all society, all intercourse, and all life; every thing paid allegiance to the sovereign, and everything ranged itself round the sovereign —what was next to be greatest, and what was farthest least. The idea that the head of the government is the head of society is so fixed in the ideas of mankind that only a few philosophers regard it as historical and accidental, though when the matter is examined, that conclusion is certain and even obvious.

In the first place, society as society does not naturally need a head at all. Its constitution, if left to itself, is not monarchical, but aristocratical. Society, in the sense we are now talking of, is the union of people for amusement and conversation. The making of marriages goes on in it, as it were, incidentally, but its common and main concern is talking and pleasure. There is nothing in this which needs a single supreme head; it is a pursuit in which a single person does not of necessity dominate. By nature it creates an 'upper ten thousand;'* a certain number of persons and families possessed of equal culture, and equal faculties, and equal spirit, get to be on a level— and that level a high level. By boldness, by cultivation, by 'social science' they raise themselves above others; they become the 'first families,' and all the rest come to be below them. But they tend to be much about a level among one another; no one is recognised by all or by many others as superior to them all. This is society as it grew up in Greece or Italy, as it grows up now in any American or colonial town. So far from the notion of a 'head of society' being a necessary notion, in many ages it would scarcely have been an intelligible notion. You could not have made Socrates* understand it. He would have said, 'If you tell me that one of my fellows is chief magistrate, and that I am bound to obey him, I understand you, and you speak well; or that another is a priest, and that he ought to offer sacrifices to the gods which I or any one not a priest ought not to offer, again I understand and agree with you. But if you tell me that there is in some citizen a hidden charm by which his words become better than my words, and his house better than my house, I do not follow you, and should be pleased if you will explain yourself.'

And even if a head of society were a natural idea, it certainly would not follow that the head of the civil government should be that head. Society as such has no more to do with civil polity than with ecclesiastical. The organisation of men and women for the purpose of amusement is not necessarily identical with their organisation for political purposes, any more than with their organisation for religious purposes; it has of itself no more to do with the State than it has with the Church. The faculties which fit a man to be a great ruler are not those of society; some great rulers have been unintelligible like Cromwell, or brusque like Napoleon, or coarse and barbarous like Sir Robert Walpole. The light nothings of the drawing-room and the grave things of office are as different from one another as two human occupations can be. There is no naturalness in uniting the two; the end of it always is, that you put a man at the head of society who very likely is remarkable for social defects, and is not eminent for social merits.

The best possible commentary on these remarks is the 'History of English Royalty.' It has not been sufficiently remarked that a change has taken place in the structure of our society exactly analogous to the change in our polity. A Republic has insinuated itself beneath the folds of a Monarchy. Charles II was really the head of society; Whitehall, in his time, was the centre of the best talk, the best fashion, and the most curious love affairs of the age. He did not contribute good morality to society, but he set an example of infinite agreeableness. He concentrated around him all the light part of the high world of London, and London concentrated around it all the light part of the high world of England. The Court was the focus where everything fascinating gathered, and where everything exciting centred. Whitehall was an unequalled club, with female society of a very clever and sharp sort superadded. All this, as we know, is now altered. Buckingham Palace is as unlike a club as any place is likely to be. The Court is a separate part, which stands aloof from the rest of the London world, and which has but slender relations with the more amusing part of it. The two first Georges were men ignorant of English, and wholly unfit to guide and lead English society. They both preferred one or two German ladies of bad character to all else in London. George III had no social vices, but he had no social pleasures. He was a family man, and a man of business, and sincerely preferred a leg of mutton and turnips after a good day's work, to the best fashion and the most exciting talk. In consequence, society in London, though still, in form, under the domination of a Court, assumed in fact its natural and oligarchical structure. It too has become an 'upper ten thousand;' it is no more monarchical in fact than the society of New York. Great ladies give the tone to it with little reference to the particular Court world. The peculiarly masculine world of the clubs and their neighbourhood has no more to do in daily life with Buckingham Palace than with the Tuileries. Formal ceremonies of presentation and attendance are retained. The names of levée and drawing-room still sustain the memory of the time when the king's bed-chamber and the queen's 'withdrawing room' were the centres of London life, but they no longer make a part of social enjoyment; they are a sort of ritual in which now-a-days almost every decent person can if he likes take part. Even Court balls, where pleasure is at least supposed to be possible, are lost in a London July. Careful observers have long perceived this, but it was made palpable to every one by the death of the Prince Consort. Since then the Court has been always in a state of suspended animation, and for a time it was quite annihilated. But everything went on as usual. A few people who had no daughters and little money made it an excuse to give fewer parties, and if very poor, stayed in the country, but upon the whole the difference was not perceptible. The queen bee was taken away, but the hive went on.

Refined and original observers have of late objected to English royalty that it is not splendid enough. They have compared it with the French Court, which is better in show, which comes to the surface everywhere so that you cannot help seeing it, which is infinitely and beyond question the most splendid thing in France. They have said, 'that in old times the English Court took too much of the nation's money, and spent it ill; but now, when it could be trusted to spend well, it does not take enough of the nation's money. There are arguments for not having a Court, and there are arguments for having a splendid Court; but there are no arguments for having a mean Court. It is better to spend a million in dazzling when you wish to dazzle, than three-quarters of a million in trying to dazzle and yet not dazzling.' There may be something in this theory; it may be that the Court of England is not quite as gorgeous as we might wish to see it. But no comparison must ever be made between it and the French Court. The Emperor represents a different idea from the Queen. He is not the head of the State; he *is* the State. The theory of his Government is that every one in France is equal, and that the Emperor embodies the principle of equality. The greater you make him, the less, and therefore the more equal, you make all others. He is magnified that others may be dwarfed. The very contrary is the principle of English royalty. As in politics it would lose its principal use if it came forward into the public arena, so in society if it advertised itself it would be pernicious. We have voluntary show enough already in London; we do not wish to have it encouraged and intensified, but quieted and mitigated. Our Court is but the head of an unequal, competing, aristocratic society: its splendour would not keep others down, but incite others to come on. It is of use so long as it keeps others out of the first place, and is guarded and retired in that place. But it would do evil if it added a new example to our many examples of showy wealth—if it gave the sanction of its dignity to the race of expenditure.

Fourthly. We have come to regard the crown as the head of our *morality*. The virtues of Queen Victoria and the virtues of George III have sunk deep into the popular heart. We have come to believe that it is natural to have a virtuous sovereign, and that the domestic virtues are as likely to be found on thrones as they are eminent when there. But a little experience and less thought show that royalty cannot take credit for domestic excellence. Neither George I, nor George II, nor William IV, were patterns of family merit; George IV was a model of family demerit. The plain fact is, that to the disposition of all others most likely to go wrong, to an excitable disposition, the place of a constitutional king has greater temptations than almost any other, and fewer suitable occupations than almost any other. All the world and all the glory of it, whatever is most attractive, whatever is most seductive, has always been offered to the Prince of Wales of the day, and always will be. It is not rational to expect the best virtue where temptation is applied in the most trying form at the frailest time of human life. The occupations of a constitutional monarch are grave, formal, important, but never exciting;

they have nothing to stir eager blood, awaken high imagination, work off wild thoughts. On men like George III, with a predominant taste for business occupations, the routine duties of constitutional royalty have doubtless a calm and chastening effect. The insanity with which he struggled, and in many cases struggled very successfully, during many years, would have burst out much oftener but for the sedative effect of sedulous employment. But how few princes have ever felt the anomalous impulse for real work; how uncommon is that impulse anywhere; how little are the circumstances of princes calculated to foster it; how little can it be relied on as an ordinary breakwater to their habitual temptations! Grave and careful men may have domestic virtues on a constitutional throne, but even these fail sometimes, and to imagine that men of more eager temperaments will commonly produce them is to expect grapes from thorns and figs from thistles.

Lastly. Constitutional royalty has the function which I insisted on at length in my last essay, and which, though it is by far the greatest, I need not now enlarge upon again. It acts as a *disguise*. It enables our real rulers to change without heedless people knowing it. The masses of Englishmen are not fit for an elective government; if they knew how near they were to it, they would be surprised, and almost tremble.

In ultimate analysis, perhaps identical with this disguise is the value of constitutional royalty in times of transition. The greatest of all helps to the substitution of a cabinet government for a preceding absolute monarchy, is the accession of a king favourable to such a government, and pledged to it. Cabinet government, when new, is weak in time of trouble. The prime minister—the chief on whom everything depends, who must take responsibility if any one is to take it, who must use force if any one is to use it—is not fixed in power. He holds his place, by the essence of the government, with some uncertainty. Among a people well-accustomed to such a government such a functionary may be bold; he may rely, if not on the parliament, on the nation which understands and values him. But when that government has only recently been introduced, it is difficult for such a minister to be as bold as he ought to be. He relies too much on human reason, and too little on human instinct. The traditional strength of the hereditary monarch is at these times of incalculable use. It would have been impossible for England to get through the first years after 1688 but for the singular ability of William III; it would have been impossible for Italy to have attained and kept her freedom without the help of Victor Emmanuel; neither the work of Cavour nor the work of Garibaldi were more necessary than his.* But the failure of Louis Philippe* to use his reserve power as constitutional monarch, is the most instructive proof how great that reserve power is. In February, 1848, Guizot was weak because his tenure of office was insecure. Louis Philippe should have made that tenure certain. Parliamentary reform might afterwards have been conceded to instructed opinion, but nothing ought to have been conceded to the mob. The Parisian populace ought to have been put down, as Guizot wished. If Louis Philippe had been a fit king to introduce free government, he would have strengthened his ministers when they were the instruments of order, even if he afterwards discarded them when order was safe, and policy could be discussed. But he was one of the cautious men who are 'noted' to fail in old age: though of the largest experience, and of great ability, he failed, and lost his crown for want of petty and momentary energy, which at such a crisis a plain man would have at once put forth.

Such are the principal modes in which the institution of royalty by its august aspect influences mankind, and in the English state of civilisation they are invaluable. Of the actual business of the sovereign—the real work the Queen does—I shall speak in my next paper.

4

THE MONARCHY (CONTINUED)

THE House of Commons has inquired into most things, but has never had a committee on the 'Queen.' There is no authentic blue-book to say what she does. Such an investigation cannot take place; but if it could, it would probably save her much vexatious routine, and many toilsome and unnecessary hours.

The popular theory of the English Constitution involves two errors as to the sovereign. First, in its oldest form, at least, it considers him as an 'Estate of the Realm,' a separate co-ordinate with the House of Lords and the House of Commons. This and much else the sovereign once was, but this he is no longer. That authority could only be exercised by a monarch with a legislative veto. He should be able to reject bills, if not as the House of Commons rejects them, at least as the House of Peers rejects them. But the Queen has no such veto. She must sign her own death-warrant if the two Houses unanimously send it up to her. It is a fiction of the past to ascribe to her legislative power. She has long ceased to have any. Secondly, the ancient theory holds that the Queen is the executive. The American Constitution was made upon a most careful argument, and most of that argument assumes the king to be the administrator of the English Constitution, and an unhereditary substitute for him—viz., a president—to be peremptorily necessary. Living across the Atlantic, and misled by accepted doctrines, the acute framers of the Federal Constitution, even after the keenest attention, did not perceive the Prime Minister to be the principal executive of the British Constitution, and the sovereign a cog in the mechanism. There is, indeed, much excuse for the American legislators in the history of that time. They took their idea of our constitution from the time when they encountered it. But in the so-called government of Lord North,* George III was the government. Lord North was not only his appointee, but his agent. The minister carried on a war which he disapproved and hated, because it was a war which his sovereign approved and liked. Inevitably, therefore, the American Convention believed the king, from whom they had suffered, to be the real executive, and not the minister, from whom they had not suffered.

If we leave literary theory, and look to our actual old law, it is wonderful how much the sovereign can do. A few years ago the Queen very wisely attempted to make life Peers,* and the House of Lords very unwisely, and contrary to its own best interests, refused to admit her claim. They said her power had decayed into non-existence; she once had it, they allowed, but it had ceased by long disuse. If any one will run over the pages of Comyn's 'Digest,'* or any other such book, title 'Prerogative,' he will find the Queen has a hundred such powers which waver between reality and desuetude, and which would cause a protracted and very interesting legal argument if she tried to exercise them. Some good lawyer ought to write a careful book to say which of these powers are really usable, and which are obsolete. There is no authentic explicit information as to what the Queen can do, any more than of what she does.

In the bare superficial theory of free institutions this is undoubtedly a defect. Every power in a popular government ought to be known. The whole notion of such a government is that the political people—the governing people—rules as it thinks fit. All the acts of every administration are to be canvassed by it; it is to watch if such acts seem good, and in some manner or other to interpose if they seem not good. But it cannot judge if it is kept in ignorance; it cannot interpose if it does not know. A secret prerogative is an anomaly—perhaps the greatest of anomalies. That secrecy is, however, essential to the utility of English royalty as it now is. Above all things our royalty is to be reverenced, and if you begin to poke about it you cannot reverence it. When there is a select committee on the Queen, the charm of royalty will be gone. Its mystery is its life. We must not let in daylight upon magic. We must not bring the Queen into the combat of politics or she will cease to be reverenced by all combatants; she will become one combatant among many. The existence of this secret power is, according to abstract theory, a defect in our constitutional polity, but it is a defect incident to a civilisation such as ours, where august and therefore unknown powers are needed, as well as known and serviceable powers.

If we attempt to estimate the working of this inner power by the evidence of those, whether dead or living, who have been brought in contact with it, we shall find a singular difference. Both the courtiers of George III and the courtiers of Queen Victoria are agreed as to the magnitude of the royal influence. It is with both an accepted secret doctrine that the Crown does more than it seems. But there is a wide discrepancy in opinion as to the quality of that action. Mr Fox did not scruple to describe the hidden influence of George III as the undetected agency 'of an infernal spirit.'* The action of the Crown at that period was the dread and terror of Liberal politicians. But now the best Liberal politicians say, '*We* shall never know, but when history is written our children may know, what we owe to the Queen and Prince Albert.' The mystery of the constitution, which used to be hated by our calmest, most thoughtful, and instructed statesmen, is now loved and reverenced by them.

Before we try to account for this change, there is one part of the duties of the Queen which should be struck out of the discussion. I mean the formal part. The Queen has to assent to and sign countless formal documents, which contain no matter of policy, of which the purport is insignificant, which any clerk could sign as well. One great class of documents George III used to read before he signed them, till Lord Thurlow* told him, 'It was nonsense his looking at them, for he could not understand them.' But the worst case is that of commissions in the army. Till an Act passed only three years since the Queen used to sign *all* military commissions,* and she still signs all fresh commissions. The inevitable and natural consequence is that such commissions were, and to some extent still are, in arrears by thousands. Men have often been known to receive their commissions for the first time years after they have left the service. If the Queen had been an ordinary officer she would long since have complained, and long since have been relieved of this slavish labour. A cynical statesman is said to have defended it on the ground 'that you *may* have a fool for a sovereign, and then it would be desirable he should have plenty of occupation in which he can do no harm.' But it is in truth childish to heap formal duties of business upon a person who has of necessity so many formal duties of society. It is remnant of the old days when George III would know everything, however trivial, and assent to everything, however insignificant. These labours of routine may be dismissed from the discussion. It is not by them that the sovereign acquires his authority either for evil or for good.

The best mode of testing what we owe to the Queen is to make a vigorous effort of the imagination, and see how we should get on without her. Let us strip cabinet government of all its accessories, let us reduce it to its two necessary constituents,—a representative assembly—a House of Commons—and a cabinet appointed by that assembly,—and examine how we should manage with them only. We are so little accustomed to analyse the constitution; we are so used to ascribe the whole effect of the constitution to the whole constitution, that a great many people will imagine it to be impossible that a nation should thrive or even live with only these two simple elements. But it is upon that possibility that the general imitability of the English Government depends. A monarch that can be truly reverenced, a House of Peers that can be really respected, are historical accidents nearly peculiar to this one island, and entirely peculiar to Europe. A new country, if it is to be capable of a cabinet government, if it is not to degrade itself to presidential government, must create that cabinet out of its native resources—must not rely on these old world *débris*.

Many modes might be suggested by which a parliament might do in appearance what our Parliament does in reality, viz., appoint a premier. But I prefer to select the simplest of all modes. We shall then see the bare skeleton of this polity, perceive in what it differs from the royal form, and be quite free from the imputation of having selected an unduly charming and attractive substitute.

Let us suppose the House of Commons—existing alone and by itself—to appoint the Premier quite simply, just as the shareholders of a railway choose a director. At each vacancy, whether caused by death or resignation, let any member or members have the right of nominating a successor; after a proper interval such as the time now commonly occupied by a ministerial crisis, ten days or a fortnight, let the members present vote for the candidate they prefer; then let the Speaker count the votes, and the candidate with the greatest number be premier. This mode of election would throw the whole choice into the hands of party organisation, just as our present mode does, except in so far as the Crown interferes with it; no outsider would ever be appointed, because the immense number of votes which every great party brings into the field would far outnumber every casual and petty minority. The premier should not be appointed for a fixed time, but during good behaviour or the pleasure of Parliament. *Mutatis mutandis*, subject to the differences now to be investigated, what goes on now would go on then. The premier then, as now, must resign upon a vote of want of confidence, but the volition of parliament would then be the overt and single force in the selection of a successor, whereas it is now the predominant though latent force.

It will help the discussion very much if we divide it into three parts. The whole course of a representative government has three stages—first, when a ministry is appointed; next, during its continuance; last, when it ends. Let us consider what is the exact use of the Queen at each of these stages, and how our present form of government differs in each, whether for good or for evil, from that simpler form of cabinet government which might exist without her.

At the beginning of an administration there would not be much difference between the royal and unroyal species of cabinet governments when there were only two great parties in the State, and when the greater of those parties was thoroughly agreed within itself who should be its parliamentary leader, and who therefore should be its premier. The sovereign must now accept that recognised leader; and if the choice were directly made by the House of Commons, the House must also choose him; its supreme section, acting compactly and harmoniously, would sway its decisions without substantial resistance, and perhaps without even apparent competition. A predominant party, rent by no intestine demarcation, would be despotic. In such a case cabinet government would go on without friction whether there was a Queen or whether there was no Queen. The best sovereign could then achieve no good, and the worst effect no harm.

But the difficulties are far greater when the predominant party is not agreed who should be its leader. In the royal form of cabinet government the sovereign then has sometimes a substantial selection; in the unroyal, who would choose? There must be a meeting at 'Willis's Rooms;'* there must be that sort of interior despotism of the majority over the minority within the party, by which Lord John Russell in 1859 was made to resign his pretensions to the supreme government, and to be content to serve as a subordinate to Lord Palmerston. The tacit compression which a party anxious for office would exercise over leaders who divided its strength, would be used and must be used. Whether such a party would always choose precisely the best man may well be doubted. In a party once divided it is very difficult to secure a unanimity in favour of the very person whom a disinterested by-stander would recommend. All manner of jealousies and enmities are immediately awakened, and it is always difficult, often impossible, to get them to sleep again. But though such a party might not select the very best leader, they have the strongest motives to select a very good leader. The maintenance of their rule depends on it. Under a presidential constitution the preliminary caucuses which choose the president need not care as to the ultimate fitness of the man they choose. They are solely concerned with his attractiveness as a candidate; they need not regard his efficiency as a ruler. If they elect a man of weak judgment, he will reign his stated term;—even though he show the best judgment, at the end of that term there will be by constitutional destiny another election. But under a ministerial government there is no such fixed destiny. The government is a removable government; its tenure depends upon its conduct. If a party in power were so foolish as to choose a weak man for its head, it would cease to be in power. Its judgment is its life. Suppose in 1859 that the Whig party had determined to set aside both Earl Russell and Lord Palmerston, and to choose for its head an incapable nonentity, the Whig party would probably have been exiled from office at the Schleswig-Holstein difficulty.* The nation would have deserted them, and Parliament would have deserted them, too; neither would have endured to see a secret negotiation, on which depended the portentous alternative of war or peace, in the hands of a person who was thought to be weak—who had been promoted because of his mediocrity—whom his own friends did not respect. A ministerial government, too, is carried on in the face of day. Its life is in debate. A president may be a weak man; yet if he keep good ministers to the end of his administration, he may not be found out—it may still be a dubious controversy whether he is wise or foolish. But a prime minister must show what he is. He must meet the House of Commons in debate; he must be able to guide that assembly in the management of its business, to gain its ear in every emergency, to rule it in its hours of excitement. He is conspicuously submitted to a searching test, and if he fails he must resign.

Nor would any party like to trust to a weak man the great power which a cabinet government commits to its premier. The premier, though elected by parliament, can dissolve parliament. Members would be naturally anxious that the power which might destroy their coveted dignity should be lodged in fit hands. They dare not place in unfit hands a power which, besides hurting the nation, might altogether ruin them. We may be sure, therefore, that whenever the predominant party is divided, the *un*-royal form of cabinet government would secure for us a fair and able parliamentary leader,—that it would give us a good premier, if not the very best. Can it be said that the royal form does more?

In one case I think it may. If the constitutional monarch be a man of singular discernment, of unprejudiced disposition, and great political knowledge, he may pick out from the ranks of the divided party its very best leader, even at a time when the party, if left to itself, would not nominate him. If the sovereign be able to play the part of that thoroughly intelligent but perfectly disinterested spectator who is so prominent in the works of certain moralists, he may be able to choose better for his subjects than they would choose for themselves. But if the monarch be not so exempt from prejudice, and have not this nearly miraculous discernment, it is not likely that he will be able to make a wiser choice than the choice of the party itself. He certainly is not under the same motive to choose wisely. His place is fixed whatever happens, but the failure of an appointing party depends on the capacity of their appointee.

There is great danger, too, that the judgment of the sovereign may be prejudiced. For more than forty years the personal antipathies of George III materially impaired successive administrations. Almost at the beginning of his career* he discarded Lord Chatham; almost at the end he would not permit Mr Pitt to coalesce with Mr Fox. He always preferred mediocrity; he generally disliked high ability; he always disliked great ideas. If constitutional monarchs be ordinary men of restricted experience and common capacity (and we have no right to suppose that *by miracle* they will be more), the judgment of the sovereign will often be worse than the judgment of the party, and he will be very subject to the chronic danger of preferring a respectful common-place man, such as Addington,* to an independent first-rate man, such as Pitt.

We shall arrive at the same sort of mixed conclusion if we examine the choice of a premier under both systems in the critical case of cabinet government—the case of three parties. This is the case in which that species of government is most sure to exhibit its defects, and least likely to exhibit its merits. The defining characteristic of that government is the choice of the executive ruler by the legislative assembly: but when there are three parties a satisfactory choice is impossible. A really good selection is a selection by a large majority which trusts those it chooses. But when there are three parties there is no such trust. The numerically weakest has the casting vote. It can determine which candidate shall be chosen. But it does so under a penalty. It forfeits the right of voting for its own candidate. It settles which of other people's favourites shall be chosen, on condition of abandoning its own favourite. A choice based on such self-denial can never be a firm choice: it is a choice at any moment liable to be revoked. The events of 1858,* though not a perfect illustration of what I mean, are a sufficient illustration. The Radical party, acting apart from the moderate Liberal party, kept Lord Derby in power. The ultra-movement party thought it expedient to combine with the non-movement party. As one of them coarsely but clearly put it, '*We* get more of our way under these men than under the other men;' he meant that, in his judgment, the Tories would be more obedient to the Radicals than the Whigs. But it is obvious that a union of opposites so marked could not be durable. The Radicals bought it by choosing the men whose principles were most adverse to them; the Conservatives bought it by agreeing to measures whose scope was most adverse to them. After a short interval the Radicals returned to their natural alliance and their natural discontent with the moderate Whigs. They used their determining vote first for a government of one opinion and then for a government of the contrary opinion.

I am not blaming this policy. I am using it merely as an illustration. I say that if we imagine this sort of action greatly exaggerated and greatly prolonged, parliamentary government becomes impossible. If there are three parties, no two of which will steadily combine for mutual action, but of which the weakest gives a rapidly oscillating preference to the two others, the primary condition of a cabinet polity is not satisfied. We have not a parliament fit to choose; we cannot rely on the selection of a sufficiently permanent executive, because there is no fixity in the thoughts and feelings of the choosers.

Under every species of cabinet government, whether the royal or the unroyal, this defect can be cured in one way only. The moderate people of every party must combine to support the government which, on the whole, suits every party best. This is the mode in which Lord Palmerston's administration has been lately maintained: a ministry in many ways defective, but more beneficially vigorous abroad, and more beneficially active at home, than the vast majority of English ministries. The moderate Conservatives and the moderate Radicals have maintained a steady government by a sufficient coherent union with the moderate Whigs. Whether there is a king or no king, this preservative self-denial is the main force on which we must rely for the satisfactory continuance of a parliamentary government at this its period of greatest trial. Will that moderation be aided or impaired by the addition of a sovereign? Will it be more effectual under the royal sort of ministerial government, or will it be less effectual?

If the sovereign has a genius for discernment, the aid which he can give at such a crisis will be great. He will select for his minister, and if possible maintain as his minister, the statesman upon whom the moderate party will ultimately fix their choice, but for whom at the outset it is blindly searching; being a man of sense, experience, and tact, he will discern which is the combination of equilibrium, which is the section with whom the milder members of the other sections will at last ally themselves. Amid the shifting transitions of confused parties, it is probable that he will have many opportunities of exercising a selection. It will rest with him to call either on A B to form an administration, or upon X Y, and either may have a chance of trial. A disturbed state of parties is inconsistent with fixity, but it abounds in momentary tolerance. Wanting something, but not knowing with precision what, it will accept for a brief period anything, to see whether it may be that unknown something,—to see what it will do. During the long succession of weak governments which begins with the resignation of the Duke of Newcastle* in 1762 and ends with the accession of Mr Pitt in 1784, the vigorous will of George III was an agency of the first magnitude. If at a period of complex and protracted division of parties, such as are sure to occur often and last long in every enduring parliamentary government, the extrinsic force of royal selection were always exercised discreetly, it would be a political benefit of incalculable value.

But will it be so exercised? A constitutional sovereign must in the common course of government be a man of but common ability. I am afraid, looking to the early acquired feebleness of hereditary dynasties, that we must expect him to be a man of inferior ability. Theory and experience both teach that the education of a prince can be but a poor education, and that a royal family will generally have less ability than other families. What right have we then to expect the perpetual entail on any family of an exquisite discretion, which if it be not a sort of genius, is at least as rare as genius.

Probably in most cases the greatest wisdom of a constitutional king would show itself in well considered inaction. In the confused interval between 1857 and 1859, the Queen and Prince Albert were far too wise to obtrude any selection of their own. If they had chosen, perhaps they would not have chosen Lord Palmerston. But they saw, or may be believed to have seen, that the world was settling down without them, and that by interposing an extrinsic agency, they would but delay the beneficial crystallisation of intrinsic forces. There is, indeed, a permanent reason which would make the wisest king, and the king who feels most sure of his wisdom, very slow to use that wisdom. The responsibility of parliament should be felt by parliament. So long as parliament thinks it is the sovereign's business to find a government, it will be sure not to find a government itself. The royal form of ministerial government is the worst of all forms if it erect the subsidiary apparatus into the principal force, if it induce the assembly which ought to perform paramount duties to expect someone else to perform them.

It should be observed, too, in fairness to the unroyal species of cabinet government, that it is exempt from one of the greatest and most characteristic defects of the royal species. Where there is no court, there can be no evil influence from a court. What these influences are everyone knows; though no one, hardly the best and closest observer, can say with confidence and precision how great their effect is. Sir Robert Walpole, in language too coarse for our modern manners, declared after the death of Queen Caroline, that he would pay no attention to the king's daughters ('those girls,' as he called them), but would rely exclusively on Madame de Walmoden,* the king's mistress. 'The king,' says a writer in George IV's time, 'is in our favour, and what is more to the purpose, the Marchioness of Conyngham* is so too.' Everybody knows to what sort of influences several Italian changes of government since the unity of Italy have been attributed. These sinister agencies are likely to be most effective just when everything else is troubled, and when, therefore, they are particularly dangerous. The wildest and wickedest king's mistress would not plot against an invulnerable administration. But very many will intrigue when parliament is perplexed, when parties are divided, when alternatives are many, when many evil things are possible, when cabinet government must be difficult.

It is very important to see that a good administration can be started without a sovereign, because some colonial statesmen have doubted it. 'I can conceive,' it has been said, 'that a ministry would go on well enough without a governor when it was launched, but I do not see how to launch it.' It has even been suggested that a colony which broke away from England, and had to form its own government, might not unwisely choose a governor for life, and solely trusted with selecting ministers, something like the Abbé Sièyes's grand elector. But the introduction of such an officer into such a colony would in fact be the voluntary erection of an artificial encumbrance to it. He would inevitably be a party man. The most dignified post in the State must be an object of contest to the great sections into which every active political community is divided. These parties mix in everything and meddle in everything; and they neither would nor could permit the most honoured and conspicuous of all stations to be filled, except at their pleasure. They know, too, that the grand elector, the great chooser of ministries might be, at a sharp crisis, either a good friend or a bad enemy. The strongest party would select someone who would be on their side when he had to take a side, who should incline to them when he did incline, who should be a constant auxiliary to them, and a constant impediment to their adversaries. It is absurd to choose by contested party election an impartial chooser of ministers.

But it is during the continuance of a ministry, rather than at its creation, that the functions of the sovereign will mainly interest most persons, and that most people will think them to be of the gravest importance. I own I am myself of that opinion. I think it may be shown that the post of sovereign over an intelligent and political people under a constitutional monarchy is the post which a wise man would choose above any other—where he would find the intellectual impulses best stimulated and the worst intellectual impulses best controlled.

On the duties of the Queen during an administration we have an invaluable fragment from her own hand. In 1851 Louis Napoleon had his *coup d'état*;* in 1852 Lord John Russell had his; he expelled Lord Palmerston. By a most useful breach of etiquette he read in the House a royal memorandum on the duties of his rivals. It is as follows:—'The Queen requires, first, that Lord Palmerston will distinctly state what he proposes in a given case in order that the Queen may know as distinctly to what she is giving her royal sanction. Secondly, having once given her sanction to such a measure that it be not arbitrarily altered or modified by the minister. Such an act she must consider as failing in sincerity towards the Crown, and justly to be visited by the exercise of her constitutional right of dismissing that minister. She expects to be kept informed of what passes between him and foreign ministers before important decisions are taken based upon that intercourse; to receive the foreign despatches in good time; and to have the drafts for her approval sent to her in sufficient time to make herself acquainted with their contents before they must be sent off.'

In addition to the control over particular ministers, and especially over the foreign minister, the Queen has a certain control over the Cabinet. The first minister, it is understood, transmits to her authentic information of all the most important decisions, together with what the newspapers would do equally well, the more important votes in Parliament. He is bound to take care that she knows everything which there is to know as to the passing politics of the nation. She has by rigid usage a right to complain if she does not know of every great act of her ministry not only before it is done, but while there is yet time to consider it, while it is still possible that it may not be done.

To state the matter shortly, the sovereign has, under a constitutional monarchy such as ours, three rights—the right to be consulted, the right to encourage, the right to warn. And a king of great sense and sagacity would want no others. He would find that his having no others would enable him to use these with singular effect. He would say to his minister, 'The responsibility of these measures is upon you. Whatever you think best must be done. Whatever you think best shall have my full and effectual support. *But* you will observe that for this reason and that reason what you propose to do is bad; for this reason and that reason what you do not propose is better. I do not oppose, it is my duty not to oppose; but observe that I *warn*.' Supposing the king to be right, and to have what kings often have, the gift of effectual expression, he could not help moving his minister. He might not always turn his course, but he would always trouble his mind.

In the course of a long reign a sagacious king would acquire an experience with which few ministers could contend. The king could say, 'Have you referred to the transactions which happened during such and such an administration, I think about fourteen years ago? They afford an instructive example of the bad results which are sure to attend the policy which you propose. You did not at that time take so prominent a part in public life as you now do, and it is possible you do not fully remember all the events. I should recommend you to recur to them, and to discuss them with your older colleagues who took part in them. It is unwise to recommence a policy which so lately worked so ill.' The king would have the advantage which a permanent under-secretary has over his superior the parliamentary secretary. He took part in the proceedings of the previous parliamentary secretaries. These proceedings were part of his own life; occupied the best of his thoughts, gave him perhaps anxiety, perhaps pleasure, were commenced in spite of his dissuasion or were sanctioned by his approval. The parliamentary secretary vaguely remembers that something was done in the time of some of his predecessors, when he very likely did not know the least or care the least about that sort of public business. He has to begin by learning painfully and imperfectly what the permanent secretary knows by clear and instant memory. No doubt a parliamentary secretary always can, and sometimes does, silence his subordinate by the tacit might of his superior dignity. He says, 'I do not think there is much in all that. Many errors were committed at the time you refer to which we need not now discuss.' A pompous man easily sweeps away the suggestions of those beneath him. But though a minister may so deal with his subordinate he cannot so deal with his king. The social force of admitted superiority by which he overturned his under-secretary is now not with him but against him. He has no longer to regard the deferential hints of an acknowledged inferior, but to answer the arguments of a superior to whom he has himself to be respectful. George III in fact knew the forms of public business as well or better than any statesman of his time. If in addition to his capacity as a man of business and to his industry he had possessed the higher faculties of a discerning statesman, his influence would have been despotic. The old Constitution of England undoubtedly gave a sort of power to the Crown which our present Constitution does not give. While a majority in parliament was principally purchased, by royal patronage, the king was a party to the bargain either with his minister or without his minister. But even under our present constitution, a monarch like George III, with high abilities, would possess the greatest influence. It is known to all Europe that in Belgium King Leopold has exercised immense power by the use of such means as I have described.*

It is known, too, to every one conversant with the real course of the recent history of England, that Prince Albert really did gain great power in precisely the same way. He had the rare gifts of a constitutional monarch. If his life had been prolonged twenty years, his name would have been known to Europe as that of King Leopold is known. While he lived he was at a disadvantage. The statesmen who had most power in England were men of far greater experience than himself. He might, and no doubt did, exercise a great, if not a commanding, influence over Lord Malmesbury,* but he could not rule Lord Palmerston. The old statesman who governs England, at an age when most men are unfit to govern their own families, remembered a whole generation of statesmen who were dead before Prince Albert was born. The two were of different ages and different natures. The elaborateness of the German Prince—an elaborateness which has been justly and happily compared with that of Goethe— was wholly alien to the half-Irish, half-English statesman. The somewhat boisterous courage in minor dangers, and the obtrusive use of an always effectual, but not always refined, common-place, which are Lord Palmerston's defects, doubtless grated on Prince Albert, who had a scholar's caution and a scholar's courage. The facts will be known to our children's children, though not to us. Prince Albert did much, but he died ere he could have made his influence felt on a generation of statesmen less experienced than he was, and anxious to learn from him.

It would be childish to suppose that a conference between a minister and his sovereign can ever be a conference of pure argument. 'The divinity which doth hedge a king'* may have less sanctity than it had, but it still has much sanctity. No one, or scarcely any one, can argue with a cabinet minister in his own room as he would argue with another man in another room. He cannot make his own points as well; he cannot unmake as well the points presented to him. A monarch's room is worse. The best instance is Lord Chatham,* the most dictatorial and imperious of English statesmen, and almost the first English statesman who was borne into power against the wishes of the king and against the wishes of the nobility;—the first popular minister. We might have expected a proud tribune of the people to be dictatorial to his sovereign; to be to the king what he was to all others. On the contrary, he was the slave of his own imagination; there was a kind of mystic enchantment in vicinity to the monarch which divested him of his ordinary nature. 'The last peep into the king's closet,' said Mr Burke,* 'intoxicates him, and will to the end of his life.' A wit said that even at the levée, he bowed so low that you could see the tip of his hooked nose between his legs. He was in the habit of kneeling at the bedside of George III while transacting business. Now no man can *argue* on his knees. The same superstitious feeling which keeps him in that physical attitude will keep him in a corresponding mental attitude. He will not refute the bad arguments of the king as he will refute another man's bad arguments. He will not state his own best arguments effectively and incisively when he knows that the king would not like to hear them. In a nearly balanced argument the king must always have the better, and in politics many most important arguments are nearly balanced. Whenever there was much to be said for the king's opinion it would have its full weight; whatever was to be said for the minister's opinions would only have a lessened and an enfeebled weight.

The king, too, possesses a power, according to theory, for extreme use on a critical occasion, but which he can in law use on any occasion. He can dissolve; he can say to his minister in fact, if not in words, 'This parliament sent you here, but I will see if I cannot get another parliament to send some one else here.' George III well understood that it was best to take his stand at times and on points when it was perhaps likely, or at any rate not unlikely, the nation would support him. He always made a minister that he did not like tremble at the shadow of a possible successor. He had a cunning in such matters like the cunning of insanity. He had conflicts with the ablest men of his time, and he was hardly ever baffled. He understood best how to help a feeble argument by a tacit threat, and how best to address it to an habitual deference.

Perhaps such powers as these are what a wise man would most seek to exercise and least fear to possess. To wish to be a despot, 'to hunger after tyranny,' as the Greek phrase had it, marks in our day an uncultivated mind. A person who so wishes cannot have weighed what Butler calls the 'doubtfulness things are involved in.'* To be sure you are right, to impose your will or to wish to impose it with violence upon others,—to see your own ideas vividly and fixedly, and to be tormented till you can apply them in life and practice, not to like to hear the opinions of others, to be unable to sit down and weigh the truth they have, are but crude states of intellect in our present civilisation. We know, at least, that facts are many; that progress is complicated; that burning ideas (such as young men have) are mostly false and always incomplete. The notion of a far-seeing and despotic statesman, who can lay down plans for ages yet unborn, is a fancy generated by the pride of the human intellect to which facts give no support. The plans of Charlemagne died with him; those of Richelieu were mistaken; those of Napoleon gigantesque and frantic. But a wise and great constitutional monarch attempts no such vanities. His career is not in the air; he labours in the world of sober fact; he deals with schemes which can be effected—schemes which are desirable—schemes which are worth the cost. He says to the ministry his people send to him, to ministry after ministry, 'I think so and so; do you see if there is anything in it. I have put down my reasons in a certain memorandum, which I will give you. Probably it does not exhaust the subject, but it will suggest materials for your consideration.' By years of discussion with ministry after ministry, the best plans of the wisest king would certainly be adopted, and the inferior plans, the impracticable plans, rooted out and rejected. He could not be uselessly beyond his time, for he would have been obliged to convince the representatives, the characteristic men of his time. He would have the best means of proving that he was right on all new and strange matters, for he would have won to his side probably, after years of discussion, the chosen agents of the common-place world—men who were where they were, because they had pleased the men of the existing age, who will never be much disposed to new conceptions or profound thoughts. A sagacious and original constitutional monarch might go to his grave in peace if any man could. He would know that his best laws were in harmony with his age; that they suited the people who were to work them, the people who were to be benefited by them. And he would have passed a happy life. He would have passed a life in which he could always get his arguments heard, in which he could always make those who had the responsibility of action think of them before they acted,—in which he could know that the schemes which he had set at work in the world were not the casual accidents of an individual idiosyncrasy, which are mostly much wrong, but the likeliest of all things to be right—the ideas of one very intelligent man at last accepted and acted on by the ordinary intelligent many.

But can we expect such a king, or, for that is the material point, can we expect a lineal series of such kings? Every one has heard the reply of the Emperor Alexander to Madame de Stael,* who favoured him with a declamation in praise of beneficent despotism. 'Yes, Madame, but it is only a happy accident.' He well knew that the great abilities and the good intentions necessary to make an efficient and good despot never were continuously combined in any line of rulers. He knew that they were far out of reach of hereditary human nature. Can it be said that the characteristic qualities of a constitutional monarch are more within its reach? I am afraid it cannot. We found just now that the characteristic use of an hereditary constitutional monarch, at the outset of an administration, greatly surpassed the ordinary competence of hereditary faculties. I fear that an impartial investigation will establish the same conclusion as to his uses during the continuance of an administration.

If we look at history we shall find that it is only during the period of the present reign that in England the duties of a constitutional sovereign have ever been well performed. The first two Georges were ignorant of English affairs, and wholly unable to guide them whether well or ill; for many years in their time the Prime Minister, had over and above the labour of managing parliament, to manage the woman—sometimes the queen, sometimes the mistress—who managed the sovereign; George III interfered unceasingly, but he did harm unceasingly; George IV and William IV gave no steady continuing guidance, and were unfit to give it. On the Continent constitutional royalty has never lasted out of one generation. Louis Philippe, Victor Emmanuel, and Leopold are the founders of their dynasties; we must not reckon in constitutional monarchy any more than in despotic monarchy on the permanence in the descendants of the peculiar genius which founded the race. As far as experience goes, there is no reason to expect an hereditary series of useful limited monarchs.

If we look to theory, there is even less reason to expect it. A monarch is useful when he gives an effectual and beneficial guidance to his ministers. But these ministers are sure to be among the ablest men of their time. They will have had to conduct the business of parliament so as to satisfy it: they will have to speak so as to satisfy it.

The two together cannot be done save by a man of very great and varied ability. The exercise of the two gifts is sure to teach a man much of the world; and if it did not, a parliamentary leader has to pass through a magnificent training before he becomes a leader. He has to gain a seat in parliament; to gain the ear of parliament; to gain the confidence of parliament; to gain the confidence of his colleagues. No one can achieve these—no one, still more, can both achieve them and retain them—without a singular ability, nicely trained in the varied detail of life. What chance has an hereditary monarch, such as nature forces him to be, such as history shows he is, against men so educated and so born? He can but be an average man to begin with; sometimes he will be clever, but sometimes he will be stupid; in the long run he will be neither clever nor stupid: he will be the simple, common man who plods the plain routine of life from the cradle to the grave. His education will be that of one who has never had to struggle; who has always felt he has nothing to gain; who has had the first dignity given him; who has never seen common life as in truth it is. It is idle to expect an ordinary man born in the purple to have greater genius than an extraordinary man born out of the purple; to expect a man whose place has always been fixed to have a better judgement than one who has lived by his judgement; to expect a man whose career will be the same whether he is discreet or whether he is indiscreet to have the nice discretion of one who has risen by his wisdom, who will fall if he ceases to be wise.

The characteristic advantage of a constitutional king is the permanence of his place. This gives him the opportunity of acquiring a consecutive knowledge of complex transactions, but it gives only an opportunity. The king must use it. There is no royal road to political affairs: their detail is vast, disagreeable, complicated, and miscellaneous. A king, to be the equal of his ministers in discussion, must work as they work; he must be a man of business as they are men of business. Yet a constitutional prince is the man who is most tempted to pleasure, and the least forced to business. A despot must feel that he is the pivot of the State. The stress of his kingdom is upon him. As he is, so are his affairs. He may be seduced into pleasure; he may neglect all else; but the risk is evident. He will hurt himself. He may cause a revolution. If he becomes unfit to govern, some one else who is fit may conspire against him. But a constitutional king need fear nothing. He may neglect his duties, but he will not be injured. His place will be as fixed, his income as permanent, his opportunities of selfish enjoyment as full as ever. Why should he work? It is true he will lose the quiet and secret influence which in the course of years industry would gain for him; but an eager young man, on whom the world is squandering its luxuries and its temptations, will not be much attracted by the distant prospect of a moderate influence over dull matters. He may form good intentions; he may say, 'Next year I *will* read these papers; I will try and ask more questions; I will not let these women talk to me so.' But they will talk to him. The most hopeless idleness is that most smoothed with excellent plans. 'The Lord Treasurer,' says Swift,* 'promised he will settle it tonight, and so he will say a hundred nights.' We may depend upon it the ministry whose power will be lessened by the prince's attention, will not be too eager to get him to attend.

So it is if the prince come young to the throne; but the case is worse when he comes to it old or middle-aged. He is then unfit to work. He will then have spent the whole of youth and the first part of manhood in idleness, and it is unnatural to expect him to labour. A pleasure-loving lounger in middle life will not begin to work as George III worked, or as Prince Albert worked. The only fit material for a constitutional king is a prince who begins early to reign, —who in his youth is superior to pleasure,—who in his youth is willing to labour,—who has by nature a genius for discretion. Such kings are among God's greatest gifts, but they are also among His rarest.

An ordinary idle king on a constitutional throne will leave no mark on his time; he will do little good and as little harm; the royal form of cabinet government will work in his time pretty much as the unroyal. The addition of a cypher will not matter though it take precedence of the significant figures. But *corruptio optimi pessima*.* The most evil case of the royal form is far worse than the most evil case of the unroyal. It is easy to imagine, upon a constitutional throne, an active and meddling fool, who always acts when he should not, who never acts when he should, who warns his ministers against their judicious measures, who encourages them in their injudicious measures. It is easy to imagine that such a king should be the tool of others; that favourites should guide him; that mistresses should corrupt him; that the atmosphere of a bad court should be used to degrade free government.

We have had an awful instance of the dangers of constitutional royalty. We have had the case of a meddling maniac. During a great part of his life George III's reason was half upset by every crisis. Throughout his life he had an obstinacy akin to that of insanity. He was an obstinate and an evil influence; he could not be turned from what was inexpedient; by the aid of his station, he turned truer but weaker men from what was expedient. He gave an excellent moral example to his contemporaries, but he is an instance of those whose good dies with them, while their evil lives after them. He prolonged the American war, perhaps he caused the American war, so we inherit the vestiges of an American hatred; he forbad Mr Pitt's wise plans,* so we an inherit an Irish difficulty. He would not let us do right in time, so now our attempts at right are out of time and fruitless. Constitutional royalty under an active and half-insane king is one of the worst of governments. There is in it a secret power which is always eager, which is generally obstinate, which is often wrong, which rules ministers more than they know themselves, which overpowers them much more than the public believe, which is irresponsible because it is inscrutable, which cannot be prevented because it cannot be seen. The benefits of a good monarch are almost invaluable, but the evils of a bad monarch are almost irreparable.

We shall find these conclusions confirmed if we examine the powers and the duties of an English monarch at the break-up of an administration. But the power of dissolution and the prerogative of creating peers, the cardinal powers of that moment, are too important and involve too many complex matters to be sufficiently treated at the very end of a paper as long as this.

5

THE HOUSE OF LORDS

In my last essay I showed that it was possible for a constitutional monarch to be, when occasion served, of first-rate use both at the outset and during the continuance of an administration; but that on matter of fact it was not likely that he would be useful. The requisite ideas, habits, and faculties far surpass the usual competence of an average man, educated in the common manner of sovereigns. The same arguments are entirely applicable at the close of an administration. But at that conjuncture the two most singular prerogatives of an English king—the power of creating new peers and the power of dissolving the Commons—come into play; and we cannot duly criticise the use or misuse of these powers till we know what the peers are and what the House of Commons is.

The use of the House of Lords—or, rather, of the Order of the Lords in its dignified capacity—is very great. It does not attract so much reverence as the Queen, but it attracts very much. The office of an order of nobility is to impose on the common people—not necessarily to impose on them what is untrue, yet less what is hurtful; but still to impose on their quiescent imaginations what would not otherwise be there. The fancy of the mass of men is incredibly weak; it can see nothing without a visible symbol, and there is much that it can scarcely make out with a symbol. Nobility is the symbol of mind. It has the marks from which the mass of men always used to infer mind, and often still infer it. A common clever man who goes into a country place will get no reverence; but the 'old squire' will get reverence. Even after he is insolvent, when every one knows that his ruin is but a question of time, he will get five times as much respect from the common peasantry as the newly-made rich man who sits beside him. The common peasantry will listen to his nonsense more submissively than to the new man's sense. An old lord will get infinite respect. His very existence is so far useful that it awakens the sensation of obedience to a *sort* of mind—the coarse dull, contracted multitude, who could neither appreciate or perceive any other.

The order of nobility is of great use, too, not only in what it creates, but in what it prevents. It prevents the rule of wealth—the religion of gold. This is the obvious and natural idol of the Anglo-Saxon. He is always trying to make money; he reckons everything in coin; he bows down before a great heap, and sneers as he passes a little heap. He has a 'natural instinctive admiration of wealth for its own sake.' And within good limits the feeling is quite right. So long as we play the game of industry vigorously and eagerly (and I hope we shall long play it, for we must be very different from what we are if we do anything better), we shall of necessity respect and admire those who play successfully, and a little despise those who play unsuccessfully. Whether this feeling be right or wrong, it is useless to discuss; to a certain degree, it is involuntary: it is not for morals to settle whether we will have it or not; nature settles for us that, within moderate limits, we must have it. But the admiration of wealth in many countries goes far beyond this; it ceases to regard in any degree the skill of acquisition; it respects wealth in the hands of the inheritor just as much as in the hands of the maker; it is a simple envy and love of a heap of gold as a heap of gold. From this our aristocracy preserves us. There is no country where a 'poor devil of a millionaire is so ill off as in England.' The experiment is tried every day, and every day it is proved that money alone—money *pur et simple*—will not buy 'London Society.' Money is kept down, and, so to say, cowed by the predominant authority of a different power.

But it may be said that this is no gain; that worship for worship, the worship of money is as good as the worship of rank. Even granting that it were so, it is a great gain to society to have two idols; in the competition of idolatries, the true worship gets a chance. But it is not true that the reverence for rank—at least, for hereditary rank—is as base as the reverence for money. As the world has gone, manner has been half-hereditary in certain castes, and manner is one of the fine arts. It is the *style* of society; it is in the daily-spoken intercourse of human beings what the art of literary expression is in their occasional written intercourse. In reverencing wealth we reverence not a man, but an appendix to a man; in reverencing inherited nobility, we reverence the probable possession of a great faculty—the faculty of bringing out what is in one. The unconscious grace of life *may* be in the middle classes; finely-mannered persons are born everywhere, but it *ought* to be in the aristocracy; and a man must be born with a hitch in his nerves if he has not some of it. It is a physiological possession of the race, though it is sometimes wanting in the individual.

There is a third idolatry from which that of rank preserves us, and perhaps it is the worst of any—that of office. The basest deity is a subordinate *employé*, and yet just now in civilised governments it is the commonest. In France and all the best of the Continent it rules like a superstition. It is to no purpose that you prove that the pay of petty officials is smaller than mercantile pay; that their work is more monotonous than mercantile work; that their mind is less useful and their life more tame. They are still thought to be greater and better. They are *decorés*; they have a little red on the left breast of their coat, and no argument will answer that. In England, by the odd course of our society, what a theorist would desire, has in fact turned up. The great offices, whether permanent or parliamentary, which require mind now give social prestige, and almost only those. An Under-Secretary of State with £2,000 a-year is a much greater man than the director of a finance company with £5,000, and the country saves the difference. But except in a few offices like the Treasury, which were once filled with aristocratic people, and have an odour of nobility at second-hand, minor place is of no social use. A big grocer despises the exciseman; and what in many countries would be thought impossible, the exciseman envies the grocer. Solid wealth tells where there is no artificial dignity given to petty public functions. A clerk in the public service is 'nobody;' and you could not make a common Englishman see why he should be anybody.

But it must be owned that this turning of society into a political expedient has half spoiled it. A great part of the 'best' English people keep their mind in a state of decorous dulness. They maintain their dignity, they get obeyed; they are good and charitable to their dependants. But they have no notion of *play* of mind; no conception that the charm of society depends upon it. They think cleverness an antic, and have a constant though needless horror of being thought to have any of it. So much does this stiff dignity give the tone, that the few Englishmen capable of social brilliancy mostly secrete it. They reserve it for persons whom they can trust, and whom they know to be capable of appreciating its *nuances*. But a good government is well worth a great deal of social dulness. The dignified torpor of English society is inevitable if we give precedence—not to the cleverest classes, but to the oldest classes—and we have seen how useful that is.

The social prestige of the aristocracy is, as every one knows, immensely less than it was a hundred years or even fifty years since. Two great movements—the two greatest of modern society—have been unfavourable to it. The rise of industrial wealth in countless forms has brought in a competitor which has generally more mind, and which would be supreme were it not for awkwardness and intellectual *gêne*. Every day our companies, our railways, our debentures, and our shares, tend more and more to multiply these *surroundings* of the aristocracy, and in time they will hide it. And while this undergrowth has come up, the aristocracy have come down. They have less means of standing out than they used to have. Their power is in their theatrical exhibition, in their state. But society is every day becoming less stately. As our great satirist has observed,* 'The last Duke of St David's used to cover the north road with his carriages; landladies and waiters bowed before him. The present Duke sneaks away from a railway station, smoking a cigar, in a brougham.' The aristocracy cannot lead the old life if they would; they are ruled by a stronger power. They suffer from the tendency of all modern society to raise the average, and to lower—comparatively, and perhaps absolutely, to lower—the summit. As the picturesqueness, the featureliness of society diminishes, aristocracy loses the single instrument of its peculiar power.

If we remember the great reverence which used to be paid to nobility as such, we shall be surprised that the House of Lords, as an assembly, has always been inferior; that it was always just as now, not the first, but the second of our assemblies. I am not, of course, now speaking of the middle ages; I am not dealing with the embryo or the infant form of our Constitution; I am only speaking of its adult form. Take the times of Sir R. Walpole. He was Prime Minister because he managed the House of Commons; he was turned out because he was beaten on an election petition in that House; he ruled England because he ruled that House. Yet the nobility were then the governing power in England. In many districts the word of some lord was law. The 'wicked Lord Lowther,'* as he was called, left a name of terror in Westmoreland during the memory of men now living. A great part of the borough members and a great part of the county members were their nominees; an obedient, unquestioning deference was paid them. As individuals the peers were the greatest people; as a House the collected peers were but the second House.

Several causes contributed to create this anomaly, but the main cause was a natural one. The House of Peers has never been a House where the most important peers were most important. It could not be so. The qualities which fit a man for marked eminence, in a deliberative assembly, are not hereditary, and are not coupled with great estates. In the nation, in the provinces, in his own province, a Duke of Devonshire, or a Duke of Bedford, was a much greater man than Lord Thurlow.* They had great estates, many boroughs, innumerable retainers, followings like a court. Lord Thurlow had no boroughs, no retainers; he lived on his salary. Till the House of Lords met, the dukes were not only the greatest, but immeasurably the greatest. But as soon as the House met, Lord Thurlow became the greatest. He could speak, and the others could not speak. He could transact business in half an hour which they could not have transacted in a day, or could not have transacted at all. When some foolish peer, who disliked his domination, sneered at his birth, he had words to meet the case. He said it was better for any one to owe his place to his own exertions than to owe it to descent, to being the 'accident of an accident.' But such a House as this could not be pleasant to great noblemen. They could not like to be second in their own assembly (and yet that was their position from age to age) to a lawyer who was of yesterday,—whom everybody could remember without briefs,—who had talked for 'hire,'—who had 'hungered after six-and-eightpence.' Great peers did not gain glory from the House; on the contrary, they lost glory when they were in the House. They devised two expedients to get out of this difficulty; they invented proxies which enabled them to vote without being present,—without being offended by vigour and invective,—without being vexed by ridicule,—without leaving the rural mansion or the town palace where they were demigods. And what was more effectual still, they used their influence in the House of Commons more instead of the House of Lords. In that indirect manner a rural potentate, who half returned two county members, and wholly returned two borough members,*—who perhaps gave seats to members of the Government, who possibly seated the leader of the Opposition, became a much greater man than by sitting on his own bench, in his own House, hearing a chancellor talk. The House of Lords was a second-rate force, even when the peers were a first-rate force, because the greatest peers, those who had the greatest social importance, did not care for their own House, or like it, but gained great part of their political power by a hidden but potent influence in the competing House.

When we cease to look at the House of Lords under its dignified aspect, and come to regard it under its strictly useful aspect, we find the literary theory of the English Constitution wholly wrong, as usual. This theory says that the House of Lords is a co-ordinate estate of the realm, of equal rank with the House of Commons; that it is the aristocratic branch, just as the Commons is the popular branch; and that by the principle of our Constitution the aristocratic branch has equal authority with the popular branch. So utterly false is this doctrine that it is a remarkable peculiarity, a capital excellence of the British Constitution, that it contains a sort of Upper House, which is not of equal authority to the Lower House, yet still has some authority.

The evil of two co-equal Houses of distinct natures is obvious. Each House can stop all legislation, and yet some legislation may be necessary. At this moment we have the best instance of this which could be conceived. The Upper House of our Victorian Constitution,* representing the rich wool-growers, has disagreed with the Lower Assembly, and most business is suspended. But for a most curious stratagem the machine of government would stand still. Most constitutions have committed this blunder. The two most remarkable Republican institutions in the world commit it. In both the American and the Swiss Constitutions the Upper House has as much authority as the second; it could produce the maximum of impediment—the dead-lock, if it liked; if it does not do so, it is owing not to the goodness of the legal constitution, but to the discreetness of the members of the Chamber. In both these constitutions this dangerous division is defended by a peculiar doctrine with which I have nothing to do now. It is said that there must be in a Federal Government some institution, some authority, some body possessing a veto in which the separate States, composing the Confederation are all equal. I confess this doctrine has to me no self-evidence, and it is assumed, but not proved. The State of Delaware is *not* equal in power or influence to the State of New York, and you cannot make it so by giving it an equal veto in an Upper Chamber. The history of such an institution is indeed most natural. A little State will like, and must like, to see some token, some memorial mark of its old independence preserved in the Constitution by which that independence is extinguished. But it is one thing for an institution to be natural, and another for it to be expedient. If indeed it be that a Federal Government compels the erection of an Upper Chamber of conclusive and co-ordinate authority, it is one more in addition to the many other inherent defects of that kind of government. It may be necessary to have the blemish, but it is a blemish just as much.

There ought to be in every constitution an available authority somewhere. The sovereign power must be *come-at-able*. And the English have made it so. The House of Lords, at the passing of the Reform Act of 1832, was as unwilling to concur with the House of Commons as the Upper Chamber at Victoria to concur with the Lower Chamber. But it did concur. The Crown has the authority to create new peers; and the king of the day had promised the ministry of the day to create them.* The House of Lords did not like the precedent, and they passed the Bill. The power was not used, but its existence was as useful as its energy. Just as the knowledge that his men *can* strike makes a master yield in order that they may not strike, so the knowledge that their House could be swamped at the will of the king—at the will of the people—made the Lords yield to the people.

From the Reform Act the function of the House of Lords has been altered in English history. Before that Act it was, if not a directing Chamber, at least a Chamber of directors. The leading nobles, who had most influence in the Commons, and swayed the Commons, sat there. Aristocratic influence was so powerful in the House of Commons, that there never was any serious breach of unity. When the Houses quarrelled, it was, as in the great Aylesbury case,* about their respective privileges, and not about the national policy. The influence of the nobility was then so potent, that it was not necessary to exert it. The English Constitution, though then on this point very different from what it now is, did not even then contain the blunder of the Victorian or of the Swiss Constitution. It had not two Houses of distinct origin; it had two Houses of common origin—two Houses in which the predominant element was the same. The danger of discordance was obviated by a latent unity.

Since the Reform Act the House of Lords has become a revising and suspending House. It can alter Bills; it can reject Bills on which the House of Commons is not yet thoroughly in earnest—upon which the nation is not yet determined. Their veto is a sort of hypothetical veto. They say, We reject your Bill for this once, or these twice, or even these thrice; but if you keep on sending it up, at last we won't reject it. The House has ceased to be one of latent directors, and has become one of temporary rejectors and palpable alterers.

It is the sole claim of the Duke of Wellington to the name of a statesman that he presided over this change. He wished to guide the Lords to their true position, and he did guide them. In 1846, in the crisis of the Corn-Law struggle, and when it was a question whether the House of Lords should resist or yield, he wrote a very curious letter to the present Lord Derby:*—

'For many years, indeed from the year 1830, when I retired from office, I have endeavoured to manage the House of Lords upon the principle on which I conceive that the institution exists in the Constitution of the country, that of Conservatism. I have invariably objected to all violent and extreme measures, which is not exactly the mode of acquiring influence in a political party in England, particularly one in opposition to Government. I have invariably supported Government in Parliament upon important occasions, and have always exercised my personal influence to prevent the mischief of anything like a difference or division between the two Houses,—of which there are some remarkable instances, to which I will advert here as they will tend to show you the nature of my management, and possibly, in some degree, account for the extraordinary power which I have for so many years exercised, without any apparent claim to it.

'Upon finding the difficulties in which the late King William was involved by a promise made to create peers, the number, I believe, indefinite, I determined myself, and I prevailed upon others, the number very large, to be absent from the House in the discussion of the last stages of the Reform Bill, after the negotiations had failed for the formation of a new Administration. This course gave at the time great dissatisfaction to the party; notwithstanding that I believed it saved the existence of the House of Lords at the time, and the Constitution of the country.

'Subsequently, throughout the period from 1835 to 1841, I prevailed upon the House of Lords to depart from many principles and systems which they as well as I had adopted and voted on Irish tithes, Irish corporations, and other measures, much to the vexation and annoyance of many. But I recollect one particular measure, the union of the provinces of Upper and Lower Canada, in the early stages of which I had spoken in opposition to the measure, and had protested against it; and in the last stages of it I prevailed upon the House to agree to, and pass it, in order to avoid the injury to the public interests of a dispute between the Houses upon a question of such importance. Then I supported the measures of the Government, and protected the servant of the Government, Captain Elliot, in China.* All of which tended to weaken my influence with some of the party; others, possibly a majority, might have approved of the course which I took. It was at the same time well known that, from the commencement of Lord Melbourne's Government, I was in constant communication with it, upon all military matters, whether occurring at home or abroad, at all events. But likewise upon many others.

'All this tended, of course, to diminish my influence in the Conservative party, while it tended essentially to the ease and satisfaction of the Sovereign, and to the maintenance of good order. At length came the resignation of the Government by Sir Robert Peel, in the month of December last, and the Queen desiring Lord John Russell to form an Administration. On the 12th of December the Queen wrote to me the letter of which I enclose the copy, and the copy of my answer of the same date; of which it appears that you have never seen copies, although I communicated them immediately to Sir Robert Peel. It was impossible for me to act otherwise than is indicated in my letter to the Queen. I am the servant of the Crown and people. I have been paid and rewarded, and I consider myself retained; and that I can't do otherwise than serve as required, when I can do so without dishonour, that is to say, as long as I have health and strength to enable me to serve. But it is obvious that there is, and there must be, an end of all connection and counsel between party and me. I might with consistency, and some may think that I ought to, have declined to belong to Sir Robert Peel's Cabinet on the night of the 20th of December. But my opinion is, that if I had, Sir Robert Peel's Government would not have been framed; that we should have had —— and —— in office next morning.

'But, at all events, it is quite obvious that when that arrangement comes, which sooner or later must come, there will be an end to all influence on my part over the Conservative party, if I should be so indiscreet as to attempt to exercise any. You will see, therefore, that the stage is quite clear for you, and that you need not apprehend the consequences of differing in opinion from me when you will enter upon it; as in truth I have, by my letter to the Queen of the 12th of December, put an end to the connection between the party and me, when the party will be in opposition to her Majesty's Government.

'My opinion is, that the great object of all is that you should assume the station, and exercise the influence, which I have so long exercised in the House of Lords. The question is, how is that object to be attained? By guiding their opinion and decision, or by following it? You will see that I have endeavoured to guide their opinion, and have succeeded upon some most remarkable occasions. But it has been by a good deal of management.

'Upon the important occasion and question now before the House, I propose to endeavour to induce them to avoid to involve the country in the additional difficulties of a difference of opinion, possibly a dispute between the Houses, on a question in the decision of which it has been frequently asserted that their lordships had a personal interest; which assertion, however false as affecting each of them personally, could not be denied as affecting the proprietors of land in general. I am aware of the difficulty, but I don't despair of carrying the Bill through. You must be the best judge of the course which you ought to take, and of the course most likely to conciliate the confidence of the House of Lords. My opinion is, that you should advise the House to vote that which would tend most to public order, and would be most beneficial to the immediate interests of the country.'

This is the mode in which the House of Lords came to be what it now is, a chamber with (in most cases) a veto of delay, with (in most cases) a power of revision, but with no other rights or powers. The question we have to answer is, 'The House of Lords being such, what is the use of the Lords?'

The common notion evidently fails, that it is a bulwark against imminent revolution. As the Duke's letter in every line evinces, the wisest members, the guiding members of the House, know that the House must yield to the people if the people is determined. The two cases—that of the Reform Act and the Corn Laws—were decisive cases. The great majority of the Lords thought Reform revolution, Free-trade confiscation, and the two together ruin. If they could ever have been trusted to resist the people, they would then have resisted it. But in truth it is idle to expect a second chamber—a chamber of notables—ever to resist a popular chamber, a nation's chamber, when that chamber is vehement and the nation vehement too. There is no strength in it for that purpose. Every class chamber, every minority-chamber, so to speak, feels weak and helpless when the nation is excited. In a time of revolution there are but two powers, the sword and the people. The executive commands the sword; the great lesson which the First Napoleon taught the Parisian populace—the contribution he made to the theory of revolutions at the 18th Brumaire*—is now well known. Any strong soldier at the head of the army can use the army. But a second chamber cannot use it. It is a pacific assembly, composed of timid peers, or aged lawyers, or, as abroad, clever *littérateurs*. Such a body has no force to put down the nation, and if the nation will have it do something it must do it.

The very nature, too, as has been seen, of the Lords in the English Constitution, shows that it cannot stop revolution. The constitution contains an exceptional provision to prevent its stopping it. The executive, the appointee of the popular chamber and the nation, can make new peers, and so create a majority in the peers; it can say to the Lords, 'Use the powers of your House as we like, or you shall not use them at all. We will find others to use them; your virtue shall go out of you if it is not used as we like, and stopped when we please.' An assembly under such a threat cannot arrest, and could not be intended to arrest, a determined and insisting executive.

In fact the House of Lords, as a House, is not a bulwark that will keep out revolution, but an index that revolution is unlikely. Resting as it does upon old deference, and inveterate homage, it shows that the spasm of new forces, the outbreak of new agencies, which we call revolution, is for the time simply impossible. So long as many old leaves linger on the November trees, you know that there has been little frost and no wind: just so while the House of Lords retains much power, you may know that there is no desperate discontent in the country, no wild agency likely to cause a great demolition.

There used to be a singular idea that two chambers—a revising chamber and a suggesting chamber—were essential to a free government. The first person who threw a hard stone—an effectually hitting stone—against the theory was one very little likely to be favourable to democratic influence, or to be blind to the use of aristocracy; it was the present Lord Grey.* He had to look at the matter practically. He was the first great colonial minister of England who ever set himself to introduce representative institutions into *all* her capable colonies, and the difficulty stared him in the face that in those colonies there were hardly enough good people for one assembly, and not near enough good people for two assemblies. It happened—and most naturally happened—that a second assembly was mischievous. The second assembly was either the nominee of the Crown, which in such places naturally allied itself with better instructed minds, or was elected by people with a higher property qualification—some peculiarly well-judging people. Both these choosers chose the best men in the colony, and put them into the second assembly. But thus the popular assembly was left without those best men. The popular assembly was denuded of those guides and those leaders who would have led and guided it best. Those superior men were put aside to talk to one another, and perhaps dispute with one another; they were a concentrated instance of high but neutralised forces. They wished to do good, but they could do nothing. The Lower House, with all the best people in the colony extracted, did what it liked. The democracy was weakened rather than strengthened by the isolation of its best opponents in a weak position. As soon as experience had shown this, or seemed to show it, the theory that two chambers were essential to a good and free government vanished away.

With a perfect Lower House it is certain that an Upper House would be scarcely of any value. If we had an ideal House of Commons perfectly representing the nation, always moderate, never passionate, abounding in men of leisure, never omitting the slow and steady forms necessary for good consideration, it is certain that we should not need a higher chamber. The work would be done so well that we should not want any one to look over or revise it. And whatever is unnecessary in government is pernicious. Human life makes so much complexity necessary that an artificial addition is sure to do harm: you cannot tell where the needless bit of machinery will catch and clog the hundred needful wheels; but the chances are conclusive that it will impede them somewhere, so nice are they and so delicate. But though beside an ideal House of Commons the Lords would be unnecessary, and therefore pernicious, beside the actual House a revising and leisured legislature is extremely useful, if not quite necessary.

At present the chance majorities on minor questions in the House of Commons are subject to no effectual control. The nation never attends to any but the principal matters of policy and state. Upon these it forms that rude, rough, ruling judgment which we call public opinion; but upon other things it does not think at all, and it would be useless for it to think. It has not the materials for forming a judgment: the detail of Bills, the instrumental part of policy, the latent part of legislation, are wholly out of its way. It knows nothing about them, and could not find time or labour for the careful investigation by which alone they can be apprehended. A casual majority of the House of Commons has therefore dominant power: it can legislate as it wishes. And though the whole House of Commons upon great subjects very fairly represents public opinion, and though its judgment upon minor questions is, from some secret excellencies in its composition, remarkably sound and good; yet, like all similar assemblies, it is subject to the sudden action of selfish combinations. There are said to be two hundred 'members for the railways'* in the present Parliament. If these two hundred choose to combine on a point which the public does not care for, and which they care for because it affects their purse, they are absolute. A formidable sinister interest may always obtain the complete command of a dominant assembly by some chance and for a moment, and it is therefore of great use to have a second chamber of an opposite sort, differently composed, in which that interest in all likelihood will not rule.

The most dangerous of all sinister interests is that of the executive Government, because it is the most powerful. It is perfectly possible—it has happened, and will happen again—that the Cabinet, being very powerful in the Commons, may inflict minor measures on the nation which the nation did not like, but which it did not understand enough to forbid. If, therefore, a tribunal of revision can be found in which the executive, though powerful, is less powerful, the government will be the better; the retarding chamber will impede minor instances of parliamentary tyranny, though it will not prevent or much impede revolution.

Every large assembly is, moreover, a fluctuating body; it is not one house, so to say, but a set of houses; it is one knot of men tonight and another tomorrow night. A certain unity is doubtless preserved by the duty which the executive is supposed to undertake, and does undertake, of keeping a house; a constant element is so provided about which all sorts of variables accumulate and pass away. But even after due allowance for the full weight of this protective machinery, our House of Commons is, as all such chambers must be, subject to sudden turns and bursts of feeling, because the members who compose it change from time to time. The pernicious result is perpetual in our legislation; many acts of Parliament are medleys of different motives, because the majority which passed one set of its clauses is different from that which passed another set.

But the greatest defect of the House of Commons is that it has no leisure. The life of the House is the worst of all lives—a life of distracting routine. It has an amount of business brought before it such as no similar assembly ever has had. The British empire is a miscellaneous aggregate, and each bit of the aggregate brings its bit of business to the House of Commons. It is India one day and Jamaica the next: then again China, and then Schleswig Holstein. Our legislation touches on all subjects, because our country contains all ingredients. The mere questions which are asked of the ministers run over half human affairs; the Private Bill Acts,* the mere *privilegia* of our Government—subordinate as they ought to be—probably give the House of Commons more absolute work than the whole business, both national and private, of any other assembly which has ever sat. The whole scene is so encumbered with changing business, that it is hard to keep your head in it.

Whatever, too, may be the case hereafter, when a better system has been struck out, at present the House does all the work of legislation, all the detail, and all the clauses itself. One of the most helpless exhibitions of helpless ingenuity and wasted mind is a committee of the whole House on a Bill of many clauses which eager enemies are trying to spoil, and various friends are trying to mend. An Act of Parliament is at least as complex as a marriage settlement and it is made much as a settlement would be, if it were left to the vote and settled by the major part of persons concerned, including the unborn children. There is an advocate for every interest, and every interest clamours for every advantage. The executive Government by means of its disciplined forces, and the few invaluable members who sit and think, preserve some sort of unity. But the result is very imperfect. The best test of a machine is the work it turns out. Let any one who knows what legal documents ought to be, read first a will he has just been making and then an Act of Parliament; he will certainly say, 'I would have dismissed my attorney if he had done my business as the legislature has done the nation's business.' While the House of Commons is what it is, a good revising, regulating, and retarding House would be a benefit of great magnitude.

But is the House of Lords such a chamber? Does it do this work? This is almost an undiscussed question. The House of Lords, for thirty years at least, has been in popular discussion an accepted matter. Popular passion has not crossed the path, and no vivid imagination has been excited to clear the matter up.

The House of Lords has the greatest merit which such a chamber can have; it is *possible*. It is incredibly difficult to get a revising assembly, because it is difficult to find a class of respected revisers. A federal senate, a second House, which represents State Unity, has this advantage; it embodies a feeling at the root of society—a feeling which is older than complicated politics, which is stronger a thousand times over than common political feelings —the *local* feeling. 'My shirt,' said the Swiss state-right patriot,* 'is dearer to me than my coat.' Every State in the American Union would feel that disrespect to the Senate was disrespect to itself. Accordingly, the Senate is respected: whatever may be the merits or demerits of its action, it can act; it is real, independent, and efficient. But in common governments it is fatally difficult to make an *un*popular entity powerful in a popular government.

It is almost the same thing to say that the House of Lords is independent. It would not be powerful, it would not be possible, unless it were known to be independent. The Lords are in several respects more independent than the Commons; their judgment may not be so good a judgment, but it is emphatically their own judgment. The House of Lords, as a body, is accessible to no social bribe. And this, in our day, is no light matter. Many members of the House of Commons, who are to be influenced by no other manner of corruption, are much influenced by this its most insidious sort. The conductors of the press and the writers for it are worse—at least the more influential who come near the temptation; for 'position,' as they call it, for a certain intimacy with the aristocracy, they would do almost anything and say almost anything. But the Lords are those who give social bribes, and not those who take them. They are above corruption because they are the corruptors. They have no constituency to fear or wheedle; they have the best means of forming a disinterested and cool judgment of any class in the country. They have, too, leisure to form it. They have no occupations to distract them which are worth the name. Field sports are but playthings, though some Lords put an Englishman's seriousness into them. Few Englishmen can bury themselves in science or literature; and the aristocracy have less, perhaps, of that *impetus* than the middle classes. Society is too correct and dull to be an occupation, as in other times and ages it has been. The aristocracy live in the fear of the middle classes—of the grocer and the merchant. They dare not frame a society of enjoyment as the French aristocracy once formed it. Politics are the only occupation a peer has worth the name. He may pursue them undistractedly. The House of Lords, besides independence to revise judicially and position to revise effectually, has leisure to revise intellectually.

These are great merits; and, considering how difficult it is to get a good second chamber, and how much with our present first chamber we need a second, we may well be thankful for them. But we must not permit them to blind our eyes. Those merits of the Lords have faults close beside them which go far to make them useless. With its wealth, its place, and its leisure, the House of Lords would, on the very surface of the matter, rule us far more than it does, if it had not secret defects which hamper and weaken it.

The first of these defects is hardly to be called secret, though on the other hand, it is not well known. A severe though not unfriendly critic of our institutions* said that 'the *cure* for admiring the House of Lords was to go and look at it'—to look at it not on a great party field-day, or at a time of parade, but in the ordinary transaction of business. There are perhaps ten peers in the House, possibly only six; three is the quorum for transacting business. A few more may dawdle in or not dawdle in; those are the principal speakers, the lawyers (a few years ago when Lyndhurst, Brougham, and Campbell were in vigour,* they were by far the predominant talkers) and a few statesmen whom everyone knows. But the mass of the House is nothing. This is why orators trained in the Commons detest to speak in the Lords. Lord Chatham used to call it the 'Tapestry.' The House of Commons is a scene of life if ever there was a scene of life. Every member in the throng, every atom in the medley, has his own objects (good or bad), his own purposes (great or petty); his own notions, such as they are, of what is; his own notions, such as they are, of what ought to be. There is a motley confluence of vigorous elements, but the result is one and good. There is a 'feeling of the House,' a 'sense' of the House, and no one who knows anything of it can despise it. A very shrewd man of the world went so far as to say that 'the House of Commons has more sense than any one in it'.* But there is no such 'sense' in the House of Lords, because there is no life. The Lower Chamber is a chamber of eager politicians; the Upper (to say the least) of *not* eager ones.

This apathy is not, indeed, as great as the outside show would indicate. The committees of the Lords (as is well known) do a great deal of work, and do it very well. And, such as it is, the apathy is very natural. A House composed of rich men who can vote by proxy without coming will not come very much. But after every abatement the real indifference to their duties of most peers is a great defect, and the apparent indifference is a dangerous defect. As far as politics go there is profound truth in Lord Chesterfield's axiom,* 'that the world must judge of you by what you seem not by what you are.' The world knows what you seem; it does not know what you are. An assembly—a revising assembly especially—which does not assemble, which looks as if it does not care how it revises, is defective in a main political ingredient. It may be of use, but it will hardly convince mankind that it is so.

The next defect is even more serious; it affects not simply the apparent work of the House of Lords but the real work. For a revising legislature, it is too uniformly made up. Errors are of various kinds; but the constitution of the House of Lords only guards against a single error—that of too quick change. The Lords—leaving out a few lawyers and a few outcasts—are all landowners of more or less wealth. They all have more or less the opinions, the merits, the faults of that one class. They revise legislation, as far as they do revise it, exclusively according to the supposed interests, the predominant feelings, the inherited opinions, of that class. Since the Reform Act, this uniformity of tendency has been very evident. The Lords have felt—it would be harsh to say hostile, but still dubious, as to the new legislation. There was a spirit in it alien to their spirit, and which when they could they have tried to cast out. That spirit is what has been termed the 'modern spirit.' It is not easy to concentrate its essence in a phrase: it lives in our life, animates our actions, suggests our thoughts. We all know what it means, though it would take an essay to limit it and define it. To this the Lords object; wherever it is concerned, they are not impartial revisers, but biassed revisers.

This singleness of composition would be no fault, it would be, or might be, even a merit, if the criticism of the House of Lords, though a suspicious criticism, were yet a criticism of great understanding. The characteristic legislation of every age must have characteristic defects; it is the outcome of a character, of necessity faulty and limited. It must mistake some kind of things: it must overlook some other. If we could get hold of a complemental critic, a critic who saw what the age did not see, and who saw rightly what the age mistook, we should have a critic of inestimable value. But is the House of Lords that critic? Can it be said that its unfriendliness to the legislation of the age is founded on a perception of what the age does not see, and a rectified perception of what the age does see? The most extreme partisan, the most warm admirer of the Lords, if of fair and tempered mind, cannot say so. The evidence is too strong. On free trade, for example, no one can doubt that the Lords—in opinion, in what they wished to do, and would have done, if they had acted on their own minds—were utterly wrong. This is the clearest test of the 'modern spirit.' It is easier here to be sure it is right than elsewhere. Commerce is like war; its result is patent. Do you make money or do you not make it? There is as little appeal from figures as from battle. Now no one can doubt that England is a great deal better off because of free trade; that it has more money, and that its money is diffused more, as we should wish it diffused. In the one case in which we can unanswerably test the modern spirit, it was right, and the dubious Upper House—the House which would have rejected it, if possible—was wrong.

There is another reason. The House of Lords, being an hereditary chamber, cannot be of more than common ability. It may contain—it almost always has contained, it almost always will contain—extraordinary men. But its average born lawmakers cannot be extraordinary. Being a set of eldest sons picked out by chance and history, it cannot be very wise. It would be a standing miracle if such a chamber possessed a knowledge of its age superior to the other men of the age; if it possessed a superior and supplemental knowledge; if it descried what they did not discern, and saw truly that which they saw, indeed, but saw untruly.

The difficulty goes deeper. The task of revising, of adequately revising the legislation of this age, is not only that which a *noblesse* has no facility in doing, but one which it has a difficulty in doing. Look at the statute book for 1865—the statutes at large for the year. You will find, not pieces of literature, not nice and subtle matters, but coarse matters, crude heaps of heavy business. They deal with trade, with finance, with statute law reform, with common law reform; they deal with various sorts of business, but with business always. And there is no educated human being less likely to know business, worse placed for knowing business, than a young lord. Business is really more agreeable than pleasure; it interests the whole mind, the aggregate nature of man more continuously, and more deeply. But it does not *look* as if it did. It is difficult to convince a young man, who can have the best of pleasure, that it will. A young lord just come into £30,000 a year will not, as a rule, care much for the law of patents, for the law of 'passing tolls,' or the law of prisons. Like Hercules, he may choose virtue, but hardly Hercules could choose business. He has everything to allure him from it, and nothing to allure him to it. And even if he wish to give himself to business, he has indifferent means. Pleasure is near him, but business is far from him. Few things are more amusing than the ideas of a well-intentioned young man, who is born out of the business world, but who wishes to take to business, about business. He has hardly a notion in what it consists. It really is the adjustment of certain particular means to equally certain particular ends. But hardly any young man destitute of experience is able to separate end and means. It seems to him a kind of mystery; and it is lucky if he do not think that the forms are the main part, and that the end is but secondary. There are plenty of business men, falsely so-called, who will advise him so. The subject seems a kind of maze. 'What would you recommend me to *read*?' the nice youth asks; and it is impossible to explain to him that reading has nothing to do with it, that he has not yet the original ideas in his mind to read about; that administration is an art as painting is an art; and that no book can teach the practice of either.

Formerly this defect in the aristocracy was hidden by their other advantages. Being the only class at ease for money and cultivated in mind they were without competition; and though they might not be, as a rule, and extraordinary ability excepted, excellent in State business, they were the best that could be had. Even in old times, however, they sheltered themselves from the greater pressure of coarse work. They appointed a manager—a Peel or a Walpole, anything but an aristocrat in manner or in nature—to act for them and manage for them. But now a class is coming up trained to thought, full of money, and yet trained to business. As I write, two members of this class have been appointed to stations considerable in themselves, and sure to lead (if anything is sure in politics) to the Cabinet and power. This is the class of highly-cultivated men of business, who after a few years, are able to leave business and begin ambition. As yet these men are few in public life, because they do not know their own strength. It is like Columbus and the egg once again; a few original men will show it can be done, and then a crowd of common men will follow. These men know business partly from tradition, and this is much. There are University families—families who talk of fellowships, and who invest their children's ability in Latin verses as soon as they discover it; there used to be Indian families of the same sort, and probably will be again when the competitive system has had time to foster a new breed.* Just so there are business families to whom all that concerns money, all that concerns administration, is as familiar as the air they breathe. All Americans, it has been said, know business; it is in the air of their country. Just so certain classes know business here; and a lord can hardly know it. It is as great a difficulty to learn business in a palace as it is to learn agriculture in a park.

To one kind of business, indeed, this doctrine, does not apply. There is one kind of business in which our aristocracy have still, and are likely to retain long, a certain advantage. This is the business of diplomacy. Napoleon, who knew men well, would never, if he could help, employ men of the Revolution in missions to the old courts; he said, 'They spoke to no one, and no one spoke to them;' and so they sent home no information. The reason is obvious. The old-world diplomacy of Europe was largely carried on in drawing-rooms, and to a great extent, of necessity still is so. Nations touch at their summits. It is always the highest class which travels most, knows most of foreign nations, has the least of the territorial sectarianism, which calls itself patriotism, and is often thought to be so. Even here, indeed, in England the new trade-class is in real merit equal to the aristocracy. Their knowledge of foreign things is as great, and their contact with them often more. But, notwithstanding, the new race is not as serviceable for diplomacy as the old race. An ambassador is not simply an agent; he is also a spectacle. He is sent abroad for show as well as for substance; he is to represent the Queen among foreign courts and foreign sovereigns. An aristocracy is in its nature better suited to such work; it is trained to the theatrical part of life; it is fit for that if it is fit for anything. A shrewd judge wants 'to pass as Act that the Minister at Washington should always be a Lord.' The social prestige of an aristocracy is most valuable in a country which has no aristocracy.

But, with this exception, an aristocracy is necessarily inferior in business to the classes nearer business; and is not, therefore, a suitable class, if we had our choice of classes, out of which to frame a chamber for revising matters of business. It is indeed a singular example of how natural business is to the English race, that the House of Lords works as well as it does. The common appearance of the 'whole House' is a jest—a dangerous anomaly, which Mr Bright will sometime use;* but a great deal of substantial work is done in 'Committees,' and often very well done. The great majority of the Peers do none of their appointed work, and could do none of it; but a minority—a minority never so large and never so earnest as in this age—do it, and do it well. Still no one, who examines the matter without prejudice, can say that the work is done perfectly. In a country so rich in mind as England, far more intellectual power can be, and ought to be, applied to the revision of our laws.

And not only does the House of Lords do its work imperfectly, but often, at least, it does it timidly. Being only a section of the nation, it is afraid of the nation. Having been used for years and years, on the greatest matters to act contrary to its own judgment, it hardly knows when to act on that judgment. The depressing languor with which it damps an earnest young peer is at times ridiculous. 'When the Corn Laws are gone, and the rotten boroughs, why teaze about Clause IX in the Bill to regulate Cotton Factories?' is the latent thought of many peers. A word from the leaders, from 'the Duke,' or Lord Derby, or Lord Lyndhurst, will rouse on any matters the sleeping energies; but most lords are feeble and forlorn.

These grave defects would have been at once lessened, and in the course of years nearly effaced, if the House of Lords had not resisted the proposal of Lord Palmerston's first government to create peers for life. The expedient was almost perfect. The difficulty of reforming an old institution like the House of Lords is necessarily great; its possibility rests on continuous caste and ancient deference. And if you begin to agitate about it, to bawl at meetings about it, that deference is gone, its peculiar charm lost, its reserved sanctity gone. But, by an odd fatality, there was in the recesses of the Constitution an old prerogative which would have rendered agitation needless—which would have effected, without agitation, all that agitation could have effected. Lord Palmerston was—now that he is dead, and his memory can be clearly viewed—as firm a friend to an aristocracy, as thorough an aristocrat, as any in England; yet he proposed to use that power. If the House of Lords had still been under the rule of the Duke of Wellington, perhaps they would have acquiesced. The Duke would not indeed have reflected on all the considerations which a philosophic statesman would have set out before him; but he would have been brought right by one of his peculiarities. He disliked, above all things, to oppose the Crown. At a great crisis, at the crisis of the Corn Laws, what he considered was not what other people were thinking of, the economical issue under discussion, the welfare of the country hanging in the balance, but the Queen's ease. He thought the Crown so superior a part in the Constitution, that, even on vital occasions, he looked solely—or said he looked solely—to the momentary comfort of the present sovereign. He never was comfortable in opposing a conspicuous act of the Crown. It is very likely that, if the Duke had still been the President of the House of Lords, they would have permitted the Crown to prevail in its well-chosen scheme. But the Duke was dead, and his authority—or some of it—had fallen to a very different person. Lord Lyndhurst had many great qualities; he had a splendid intellect—as great a faculty of finding truth as any one in his generation; but he had no love of truth. With this great faculty of finding truth, he was a believer in error—in what his own party admit to be error—all his life through. He could have found the truth as a statesman just as he found it when a judge; but he never did find it. He never looked for it. He was a great partisan, and he applied a capacity of argument, and a faculty of intellectual argument rarely equalled, to support the tenets of his party. The proposal to create life-peers was proposed by the antagonistic party—was at the moment likely to injure his own party. To him this was a great opportunity. The speech he delivered on that occasion lives in the memory of those who heard it. His eyes did not at that time let him read, so he repeated by memory, and quite accurately, all the black-letter authorities bearing on the question. So great an intellectual effort has rarely been seen in an English assembly. But the result was deplorable. Not by means of his black-letter authorities, but by means of his recognised authority and his vivid impression, he induced the House of Lords to reject the proposition of the Government. Lord Lyndhurst said the Crown could not now create life-peers, and so there are no life-peers. The House of Lords rejected the inestimable, the unprecedented opportunity of being tacitly reformed. Such a chance does not come twice. The life-peers who would have been then introduced would have been among the first men in the country. Lord Macaulay was to have been among the first;* Lord Wensleydale—the most learned and not the least logical of our lawyers—to be the very first. Thirty or forty such men, added judiciously and sparingly as years went on, would have given to the House of Lords the very element which, as a criticising chamber, it needs so much. It would have given it critics. The most accomplished men in each department might then, without irrelevant considerations of family and of fortune, have been added to the Chamber of Review. The very element which was wanted to reform the House of Lords was, as it were, by a constitutional providence, offered to the House of Lords, and they refused it. By what species of effort that error can be repaired, I cannot tell; but, unless it is repaired, the intellectual capacity can never be what it would have been, will never be what it ought to be, will never be sufficient for its work.

Another reform ought to have accompanied the creation of life-peers. Proxies ought to have been abolished. Some time or other the slack attendance in the House will destroy the House of Lords. There are occasions in which appearances are realities, and this is the one of them. The House of Lords on most days looks so unlike what it ought to be, that most people will not believe it is what it ought to be. The attendance of considerate peers will, for obvious reasons, be larger when it can no longer be overpowered by the *non*-attendance, by the commissioned votes of inconsiderate peers. The abolition of proxies would have made the House of Lords a real House; the addition of life-peers would have made it a good House.

The greater of these changes would have most materially aided the House of Lords in the performance of its subsidiary functions. It always perhaps happens in a great nation, that certain bodies of sensible men posted prominently in its constitution, acquire functions, and usefully exercise functions which, at the outset, no one expected from them, and which do not identify themselves with their original design. This has happened to the House of Lords especially. The most obvious instance is the judicial function. This is a function which no theorist would assign to a second chamber in a new constitution, and which is matter of accident in ours. But I do not much rely on this. It is *not* a function of the House of Lords, but of a Committee of the House of Lords. On one occasion only, the trial of O'Connell,* the whole House, or some few in the whole House, wished to vote, and they were told they could not, or they would destroy the judicial prerogative. No one, indeed, would venture *really* to place judicial function in the chance majorities of a fluctuating assembly: it is so by a sleepy theory; it is not so in living fact. As a legal question, too, it is a matter of grave doubt whether there ought to be two supreme courts in this country—the Judicial Committee of the Privy Council, and (what is in fact though not in name) the Judicial Committee of the House of Lords. Up to a very recent time one committee might decide that a man was sane as to money, and the other committee might decide that he was insane as to land. This absurdity has been cured; but the error from which it arose has not been cured—the error of having two supreme courts, to both of which, as time goes on, the same question is sure often enough to be submitted, and each of which is sure every now and then to decide it differently. I do not reckon the judicial function of the House of Lords as one of its true subsidiary functions, first because it does not in fact exercise it, next because I wish to see it in appearance deprived of it. The supreme court of the English people ought to be a great conspicuous tribunal, ought to rule all other courts, ought to have no competitor, ought to bring our law into unity, ought not to be hidden beneath the robes of a legislative assembly.

The subsidiary functions of the House of Lords are real, and, unlike its judicial functions, are very analogous to its substantial nature. The first is the faculty of criticising the executive. An assembly in which the mass of the members have nothing to lose, where most have nothing to gain, where every one has a social position firmly fixed, where no one has a constituency, where hardly any one cares for the minister of the day, is the very assembly in which to look for, from which to expect, independent criticism. And in matter of fact we find it. The criticism of the acts of late administrations by Lord Grey has been admirable. But such criticism, to have its full value, should be many-sided. Every man of great ability puts his own mark on his own criticism; it will be full of thought and feeling, but then it is of idiosyncratic thought and feeling. We want many critics of ability and knowledge in the Upper House—not equal to Lord Grey, for they would be hard to find—but like Lord Grey. They should resemble him in impartiality; they should resemble him in clearness; they should most of all resemble him in taking the supplemental view of a subject. There is an actor's view of a subject which (I speak of mature and discussed action—of Cabinet action) is nearly sure to include everything old and near—everything ascertained and determinate. But there is also a bystander's view, which is likely to omit some one or more of these old and certain elements, but also to contain some new or distant matter which the absorbed and occupied actor could not see. There ought to be many life-peers in our secondary chamber capable of giving us this higher criticism. I am afraid we shall not soon see them, but as a first step we should learn to wish for them.

The second subsidiary action of the House of Lords is even more important. Taking the House of Commons, not after possible, but most unlikely improvements, but in matter of fact and as it stands, it is overwhelmed with work. The task of managing it falls upon the Cabinet, and that task is very hard. Every member of the Cabinet in the Commons has to 'attend the House;' to contribute by his votes, if not by his voice, to the management of the House. Even in so small a matter as the education department, Mr Lowe,* a consummate observer, spoke of the desirability of finding a chief 'not exposed to the prodigious labour of attending the House of Commons.' It is all but necessary that certain members of the Cabinet should be exempt from its toil, and untouched by its excitement. But it is also necessary that they should have the power of explaining their views to the nation; of being heard as other people are heard. There are various plans for so doing, which I may discuss a little in speaking of the House of Commons. But so much is evident: the House of Lords, for its own members, attains this object; it gives them what no competing plan does give them—*position*. The leisured members of the

Cabinet speak in the Lords with authority and power. They are not administrators with a right to speech—clerks (as is sometimes suggested) brought down to lecture a House, but not to vote in it; but they are the equals of those they speak to; they speak as they like, and reply as they choose; they address the House, not with the 'bated breath' of subordinates, but with the force and dignity of sure rank. Life-peers would enable us to use this faculty of our constitution more freely and more variously. It would give us a larger command of able leisure; it would improve the Lords as a political pulpit, for it would enlarge the list of its select preachers.

The danger of the House of Commons is, perhaps, that it will be reformed too rashly; the danger of the House of Lords certainly is, that it may never be reformed. Nobody asks that it should be so; it is quite safe against rough destruction, but it is not safe against inward decay. It may lose its veto as the Crown has lost its veto. If most of its members neglect their duties, if all its members continue to be of one class, and that not quite the best; if its doors are shut against genius that cannot found a family, and ability which has not five thousand a year, its power will be less year by year, and at last be gone, as so much kingly power is gone—no one knows how. Its danger is not assassination, but atrophy; not abolition, but decline.

6

THE HOUSE OF COMMONS

THE dignified aspect of the House of Commons is altogether secondary to its efficient use. It *is* dignified: in a government in which the most prominent parts are good because they are very stately, any prominent part, to be good at all, must be somewhat stately. The human imagination exacts keeping in government as much as in art; it will not be at all influenced by institutions which do not match with those by which it is principally influenced. The House of Commons needs to be impressive, and impressive it is: but its use resides not in its appearance, but in its reality. Its office is not to win power by awing mankind, but to use power in governing mankind.

The main function of the House of Commons is one which we know quite well, though our common constitutional speech does not recognise it. The House of Commons is an electoral chamber; it is the assembly which chooses our president. Washington and his fellow-politicians contrived an electoral college, to be composed (as was hoped) of the wisest people in the nation, which, after due deliberation, was to choose for President the wisest man in the nation. But that college is a sham; it has no independence and no life. No one knows, or cares to know, who its members are. They never discuss, and never deliberate. They were chosen to vote that Mr Lincoln be President, or that Mr Breckenridge be President; they do so vote, and they go home. But our House of Commons is a real choosing body; it elects the people it likes. And it dismisses whom it likes too. No matter that a few months since it was chosen to support Lord Aberdeen or Lord Palmerston; upon a sudden occasion it ousts the statesman to whom it at first adhered, and selects an opposite statesman whom it at first rejected. Doubtless in such cases there is tacit reference to probable public opinion; but certainly also there is much free will in the judgment of the Commons. The House only goes where it thinks in the end the nation will follow; but it takes its chance of the nation following or not following; it assumes the initiative, and acts upon its discretion or its caprice.

When the American nation has chosen its President, its virtue goes out of it, and out of the Transmissive College through which it chooses. But because the House of Commons has the power of dismissal in addition to the power of election, its relations to the Premier are incessant. They guide him, and he leads them. He is to them what they are to the nation. He only goes where he believes they will go after him. But he has to take the lead; he must choose his direction, and begin the journey. Nor must he flinch. A good horse likes to feel the rider's bit; and a great deliberative assembly likes to feel that it is under worthy guidance. A minister who succumbs to the House,—who ostentatiously seeks its pleasure,—who does not try to regulate it,—who will not boldly point out plain errors to it, seldom thrives. The great leaders of Parliament have varied much, but they have all had firmness. A great assembly is as soon spoiled by over-indulgence as a little child. The whole life of English politics is the action and reaction between Ministry and the Parliament. The appointees strive to guide, and the appointors surge under the guidance.

The elective is now the most important function of the House of Commons. It is most desirable to insist, and be tedious, on this, because our tradition ignores it. At the end of half the sessions of Parliament, you will read in the newspapers, and you will hear even from those who have looked close at the matter and should know better, 'Parliament has done nothing this session. Some things were promised in the Queen's speech, but they were only little things; and most of them have not passed.' Lord Lyndhurst used for years to recount the small outcomings of legislative achievement; and yet those were the days of the first Whig Governments, who had more to do in legislation, and did more, than any Government. The true answer to such harangues as Lord Lyndhurst's by a Minister should have been in the first person. He should have said firmly, 'Parliament has maintained ME, and that was its greatest duty; Parliament has carried on what, in the language of traditional respect, we call the Queen's Government; it has maintained what wisely or unwisely it deemed the best Executive of the English nation.'

The second function of the House of Commons is what I may call an expressive function. It is its office to express the mind of the English people on all matters which come before it. Whether it does so well or ill I shall discuss presently.

The third function of Parliament is what I may call—preserving a sort of technicality even in familiar matters for the sake of distinctness—the teaching function. A great and open council of considerable men cannot be placed in the middle of a society without altering that society. It ought to alter it for the better. It ought to teach the nation what it does not know. How far the House of Commons can so teach, and how far it does so teach, are matters for subsequent discussion.

Fourthly, the House of Commons has what may be called an informing function—a function which though in its present form quite modern is singularly analogous to a mediaeval function. In old times one office of the House of Commons was to inform the Sovereign what was wrong. It laid before the Crown the grievances and complaints of particular interests. Since the publication of the Parliamentary debates a corresponding office of Parliament is to lay these same grievances, these same complaints, before the nation, which is the present sovereign. The nation needs it quite as much as the king ever needed it. A free people is indeed mostly fair, liberty practises men in a give-and-take, which is the rough essence of justice. The English people, possibly even above other free nations, is fair. But a free nation rarely can be—and the English nation is not—quick of apprehension. It only comprehends what is familiar to it; what comes into its own experience, what squares with its own thoughts. 'I never heard such a thing in my life,' the middle-class Englishman says, and he thinks he so refutes an argument. The common disputant cannot say in reply that his experience is but limited, and that the assertion may be true, though he had never met with anything at all like it. But a great debate in Parliament *does* bring home something of this feeling. Any notion, any creed, any feeling, any grievance which can get a decent number of English members to stand up for it, is felt by almost all Englishmen to be perhaps false and pernicious opinion, but at any rate possible—an opinion within the intellectual sphere, an opinion to be reckoned with. And it is an immense achievement. Practical diplomatists say that a free government is harder to deal with than a despotic government: you may be able to get the despot to hear the other side; his ministers, men of trained intelligence, will be sure to know what makes against them; and they *may* tell him. But a free nation never hears any side save its own. The newspapers only repeat the side their purchasers like: the favourable arguments are set out, elaborated, illustrated; the adverse arguments maimed, misstated, confused. The worst judge, they say, is a deaf judge; the most dull government is a free government on matters its ruling classes will not hear. I am disposed to reckon it as the second function of Parliament in point of importance, that to some extent it makes us hear what otherwise we should not.

Lastly, there is the function of legislation, of which of course it would be preposterous to deny the great importance, and which I only deny to be *as* important as the executive management of the whole state, or the political education given by Parliament to the whole nation. There are, I allow, seasons when legislation is more important than either of these. The nation may be misfitted with its laws, and need to change them: some particular corn law may hurt all industry, and it may be worth a thousand administrative blunders to get rid of it. But generally the laws of a nation suit its life; special adaptations of them are but subordinate; the administration and conduct of that life is the matter which presses most. Nevertheless, the statute-book of every great nation yearly contains many important new laws, and the English statute-book does so above any. An immense mass, indeed, of the legislation is not, in the proper language of jurisprudence, legislation at all. A law is a general command applicable to many cases. The 'special acts' which crowd the statute-book and weary parliamentary committees are applicable to one case only. They do not lay down rules according to which railways shall be made, they enact that such a railway shall be made from this place to that place, and they have no bearing upon any other transaction. But after every deduction and abatement, the annual legislation of Parliament is a result of singular importance; were it not so, it could not be, as it often is considered, the sole result of its annual assembling.

Some persons will perhaps think that I ought to enumerate a sixth function of the House of Commons—a financial function. But I do not consider that, upon broad principle, and omitting legal technicalities, the House of Commons has any special function with regard to financial different from its functions with respect to other legislation. It is to rule in both, and to rule in both through Cabinet. Financial legislation is of necessity a yearly recurring legislation; but frequency of occurrence does not indicate a diversity of nature or compel an antagonism of treatment.

In truth, the principal peculiarity of the House of Commons in financial affairs is now-a-days not a special privilege, but an exceptional disability. On common subjects any member can propose anything, but not on money,—the minister only can propose to tax the people. This principle is commonly involved in mediaeval metaphysics as to the prerogative of the Crown, but it is as useful in the nineteenth century as in the fourteenth, and rests on as sure a principle. The House of Commons—now that it is the true sovereign, and appoints the real executive—has long ceased to be the checking, sparing, economical body it once was. It now is more apt to spend money than the minister of the day. I have heard a very experienced financier say, 'If you want to raise a certain cheer in the House of Commons make a general panegyric on economy; if you want to invite a sure defeat, propose a particular saving.' The process is simple. Every expenditure of public money has some apparent public object; those who wish to spend the money expatiate on that object; they say, 'What is £50,000 to this great country? Is this a time for cheeseparing objection? Our industry was never so productive; our resources never so immense. What is £50,000 in comparison with this great national interest?' The members who are for the expenditure always come down; perhaps a constituent or a friend who will profit by the outlay, or is keen on the object, has asked them to attend; at any rate, there is a popular vote to be given, on which the newspapers—always philanthropic, and sometimes talked over— will be sure to make encomiums. The members against the expenditure rarely come down of themselves; why should they become unpopular without reason? The object seems decent; many of its advocates are certainly sincere: a hostile vote will make enemies, and be censured by the journals. If there were not some check, the 'people's house' would soon outrun the people's money.

That check is the responsibility of the Cabinet for the national finance. If anyone could propose a tax, they might let the House spend as it would, and wash their hands of the matter; but now, for whatever expenditure is sanctioned—even when it is sanctioned against the ministry's wish—the ministry must find the money. Accordingly, they have the strongest motive to oppose extra outlay. They will have to pay the bill for it; they will have to impose taxation, which is always disagreeable, or suggest loans which, under ordinary circumstances, are shameful. The ministry is (so to speak) the breadwinner of the political family, and has to meet the cost of philanthropy and glory; just as the head of a family has to pay for the charities of his wife and the toilette of his daughters.

In truth, when a Cabinet is made the sole executive, it follows it must have the sole financial charge, for all action costs money, all policy depends on money, and it is in adjusting the relative goodness of action and policies that the executive is employed.

From a consideration of these functions, it follows that we are ruled by the House of Commons; we are indeed, so used to be so ruled, that it does not seem to be at all strange. But of all odd forms of government, the oddest really is government by a *public meeting*. Here are 658 persons, collected from all parts of England, different in nature, different in interests, different in look and language. If we think what an empire the English is, how various are its components, how incessant its concerns, how immersed in history its policy: if we think what a vast information, what a nice discretion, what a consistent will ought to mark the rulers of that empire, we shall be surprised when we see them. We see a changing body of miscellaneous persons, sometimes few, sometimes many, never the same for an hour; sometimes excited, but mostly dulled and half weary,— impatient of eloquence, catching at any joke as an alleviation. These are the persons who rule the British empire,—who rule England,— who rule Scotland,—who rule Ireland,—who rule a great deal of Asia,—who rule a great deal of Polynesia,—who rule a great deal of America, and scattered fragments everywhere.

Paley said many shrewd things,* but he never said a better thing than that it was much harder to make men see a difficulty than comprehend the explanation of it. The key to the difficulties of most discussed and unsettled questions is commonly in their undiscussed parts; they are like the background of a picture which looks obvious, easy, just what any one might have painted, but which in fact sets the figures in their right position, chastens them, and makes them what they are. Nobody will understand parliamentary government who fancies it an easy thing, a natural thing, a thing not needing explanation. You have not a perception of the first elements in this matter till you know that government by a *club* is a standing wonder.

There has been a capital illustration lately how helpless many English gentlemen are when called together on a sudden. The Government, rightly or wrongly, thought fit to entrust the quarter-sessions of each county with the duty of combating its cattle plague;* but the scene in most 'shire halls' was unsatisfactory. There was the greatest difficulty in getting, not only a right decision, but *any* decision. I saw one myself which went thus. The chairman proposed a very complex resolution, in which there was much which every one liked, and much which every one disliked, though, of course, the favourite parts of some were the objectionable parts to others. The resolution got, so to say, wedged in the meeting; everybody suggested amendments; one amendment was carried which none were satisfied with, and so the matter stood over. It is a saying in England, 'a big meeting never does anything;' and yet we are governed by the House of Commons,—by 'a big meeting.'

It may be said that the House of Commons does not rule, it only elects the rulers. But there must be something special about it to enable it to do that. Suppose the Cabinet were elected by a London club, what confusion there would be, what writing and answering! 'Will you speak to So-and-So, and ask him to vote for my man?' would be heard on every side. How the wife of A and the wife of B would plot to confound the wife of C. Whether the club elected under the dignified shadow of a queen, or without the shadow, would hardly matter at all; if the substantial choice was in them, the confusion and intrigue would be there too. I propose to begin this paper by asking, not why the House of Commons governs well? but the fundamental—almost unasked-question—how the House of Commons comes to be able to govern at all?

The House of Commons can do work which the quarter-sessions or clubs cannot do, because it is an organised body, while quarter-sessions and clubs are unorganised. Two of the greatest orators in England—Lord Brougham and Lord Bolingbroke*—spent much eloquence in attacking party government. Bolingbroke probably knew what he was doing; he was a consistent opponent of the power of the Commons; he wished to attack them in a vital part. But Lord Brougham does not know; he proposes to amend the parliamentary government by striking out the very elements which make parliamentary government possible. At present the majority of Parliament obey certain leaders; what those leaders propose they support, what those leaders reject they reject. An old Secretary of the Treasury* used to say, 'This is a bad case, an indefensible case. We must apply our *majority* to this question.' That secretary lived fifty years ago, before the Reform Bill, when majorities were very blind, and very 'applicable.' Now-a-days, the power of leaders over their followers is strictly and wisely limited: they can take their followers but a little way, and that only in certain directions. Yet still there are leaders and followers. On the Conservative side of the House there are vestiges of the despotic leadership even now. A cynical politician is said to have watched the long row of county members, so fresh and respectable-looking, and muttered, 'By Jove, they are the finest brute votes in Europe!'* But all satire apart, the principle of Parliament is obedience to leaders. Change your leader if you will, take another if you will, but obey No. 1 while you serve No. 1, and obey No. 2 when you have gone over to No. 2. The penalty of not doing so, is the penalty of impotence. It is not that you will not be able to any good, but you will not be able to do anything at all. If everybody does what he thinks right, there will be 657 amendments to every motion, and none of them will be carried or the motion either.

The moment, indeed, that we distinctly conceive that the House of Commons is mainly and above all things an elective assembly, we at once perceive that party is of its essence. There never was an election without a party. You cannot get a child into an asylum without a combination. At such places you may see 'Vote for orphan A' upon a placard, and 'Vote for orphan B (also an idiot!!!)' upon a banner, and the party of each is busy about its placard and banner. What is true at such minor and momentary elections must be much more true in a great and constant election of rulers. The House of Commons lives in a state of perpetual potential choice: at any moment it can choose a ruler and dismiss a ruler. And therefore party is inherent in it, is bone of its bone, and breath of its breath.

Secondly, though the leaders of party no longer have the vast patronage of the last century with which to bribe, they can coerce by a threat far more potent than any allurement:—they can dissolve. This is the secret which keeps parties together. Mr Cobden most justly said,* 'He had never been able to discover what was the proper moment, according to members of Parliament, for a dissolution. He had heard them say they were ready to vote for everything else, but he had never heard them say they were ready to vote for that.' Efficiency in an assembly requires a solid mass of steady votes; and these are *collected* by a deferential attachment to particular men, or by a belief in the principles those men represent, and they are *maintained* by fear of those men—by the fear that if you vote against them, you may yourself soon not have a vote at all.

Thirdly, it may seem odd to say so, just after inculcating that party organisation is the vital principle of representative government, but—that organisation is permanently efficient, because it is not composed of warm partisans. The body is eager, but the atoms are cool. If it were otherwise, parliamentary government would become the worst of governments—a sectarian government. The party in power would go all the lengths their orators proposed—all that their formulae enjoined, as far as they had ever said they would go. But the partisans of the English Parliament are not of such a temper. They are Whigs, or Radicals, or Tories, but they are much else too. They are common Englishmen, and, as Father Newman complains,* 'hard to be worked up to the dogmatic level.' They are not eager to press the tenets of their party to impossible conclusions. On the contrary, the way to lead them—the best and acknowledged way—is to affect a studied and illogical moderation. You may hear men say, 'Without committing myself to the tenet that $3 + 2$ make 5, though I am free to admit that the honourable member for Bradford has advanced very grave arguments in behalf of it, I think I may, with the permission of the Committee, assume that $2 + 3$ do not make 4, which will be a sufficient basis for the important propositions which I shall venture to submit on the present occasion.' This language is very suitable to the greater part of the House of Commons. Most men of business love a sort of twilight. They have lived all their lives in an atmosphere of probabilities and of doubt, where nothing is very clear, where there are some chances for many events, where there is much to be said for several courses, where nevertheless one course must be determinedly chosen and fixedly adhered to. They like to hear arguments suited to this intellectual haze. So far from caution or hesitation in the statement of the argument striking them as an indication of imbecility, it seems to them a sign of practicality. They got rich themselves by transactions of which they could not have stated the argumentative ground—and all they ask for is a distinct, though moderate conclusion, that they can repeat when asked; something which they feel *not* to be abstract argument, but abstract argument diluted and dissolved in real life. 'There seem to me,' an impatient young man once said, 'to be no stays in Peel's arguments.'* And that was why Sir Robert Peel was the best leader of the

Commons in our time; we like to have the rigidity taken out of an argument, and the substance left.

Nor indeed, under our system of government, are the leaders themselves of the House of Commons, for the most part, eager to carry party conclusions too far. They are in contact with reality. An Opposition, on coming into power, is often like a speculative merchant whose bills become due. Ministers have to make good their promises, and they find a difficulty in so doing. They have said the state of things is so and so, and if you give us the power we will do thus and thus. But when they come to handle the official documents, to converse with the permanent under-secretary—familiar with disagreeable facts, and though in manner most respectful, yet most imperturbable in opinion—very soon doubts intervene. Of course, something must be done: the speculative merchant cannot forget his bills; the late Opposition cannot, in office, forget those sentences which terrible admirers in the country still quote. But just as the merchant asks his debtor, 'Could you not take a bill at four months?' so the new minister says to the permanent under-secretary, 'Could you not suggest a middle course? I am of course not bound by mere sentences used in debate; I have never been accused of letting a false ambition of consistency warp my conduct; but,' &c, &c. And the end always is, that a middle course is devised which *looks* as much as possible like what was suggested in opposition, but which *is* as much as possible what patent facts—facts which seem to live in the office, so teazing and unceasing are they—prove ought to be done.

Of all modes of enforcing moderation on a party, the best is to contrive the members of that party shall be intrinsically moderate, careful, and almost shrinking men; and the next best to contrive, that the leaders of the party, who have protested most in its behalf, shall be placed in the closest contact with the actual world. Our English system contains both contrivances: it makes party government permanent and possible in the sole way in which it can be so, by making it mild.

But these expedients, though they sufficiently remove the defects which make a common club or quarter-sessions impotent, would not enable the House of Commons to govern England. A representative public meeting is subject to a defect over and above those of other public meetings. It may not be independent. The constituencies may not let it alone. But if they do not, all the checks which have been enumerated upon the evils of a party organisation would be futile. The feeling of a constituency is the feeling of a dominant party, and that feeling is elicited, stimulated, sometimes even manufactured by the local political agent. Such an opinion could not be moderate; could not be subject to effectual discussion; could not be in close contact with pressing facts; could not be framed under a chastening sense of near responsibility; could not be formed as those form their opinions who have to act upon them. Constituency government is the precise opposite of parliamentary government. It is the government of immoderate persons far from the scene of action, instead of the government of moderate persons close to the scene of action; it is the judgment of persons judging in the last resort and without a penalty, in lieu of persons judging in fear of a dissolution, and ever conscious that they are subject to an appeal.

Most persons would admit these conditions of parliamentary government when they read them, but two at least of the most prominent ideas in the public mind are inconsistent with them. The scheme to which the arguments of our demagogues distinctly tend, and the scheme to which the predilections of some most eminent philosophers cleave, are both so. They would not only make parliamentary government work ill, but they would prevent its working at all; they would not render it bad for they would make it impossible.

The first of these is the ultra-democratic theory. This theory demands that every man of twenty-one years of age (if not every woman, too) should have an equal vote in electing Parliament. Suppose that last year there were twelve million adult males in England. Upon this theory each man is to have one twelve-millionth share in electing a Parliament; the rich and wise are not to have, by explicit law, more votes than the poor and stupid; nor are any latent contrivances to give them an influence equivalent to more votes. The machinery for carrying out such a plan is very easy. At each census the country ought to be divided into 658 electoral districts, in each of which the number of adult males should be the same; and these districts ought to be the only constituencies, and elect the whole Parliament. But if the above prerequisites are needful for parliamentary government, that Parliament would not work.

Such a Parliament could not be composed of moderate men. The electoral districts would be, some of them, in purely agricultural places, and in these the parson and the squire would have almost unlimited power. They would be able to drive or send to the poll an entire labouring population. These districts would return an unmixed squirearchy. The scattered small towns, which now send so many members to Parliament, would be lost in the clownish mass; their votes would send to Parliament no distinct members. The agricultural part of England would choose its representatives from quarter-sessions exclusively. On the other hand, a large part of the constituencies would be town districts; and these would send up persons representing the beliefs or the unbeliefs of the lowest classes in their towns. They would, perhaps, be divided between the genuine representatives of the artizans,—not possibly of the best of the artizans, who are a select and intellectual class, but of the common order of workpeople,—and the merely pretended members for that class, whom I may call the members for the public-houses. In all the big towns in which there is electioneering these houses are the centres of illicit corruption and illicit management. There are pretty good records of what that corruption and management are, but there is no need to describe them here. Everybody will understand what sort of things I mean, and the kind of unprincipled members that are returned by them. Our new Parliament, therefore, would be made up of two sorts of representatives from the town lowest class, and one sort of representatives from the agricultural lowest class. The genuine representatives of the country would be men of one marked sort, and the genuine representatives for the county men of another marked sort, but very opposite: one would have the prejudices of town artizans, and the other the prejudices of county magistrates. Each class would speak a language of its own; each would be unintelligible to the other; and the only thriving class would be the immoral representatives, who were chosen by corrupt machination, and who would probably get a good profit on the capital they laid out in that corruption. If it be true that a parliamentary government is possible only when the overwhelming majority of the representatives are men essentially moderate, of no marked varieties, free from class prejudices, this ultra-democratic Parliament could not maintain that government, for its members would be remarkable for two sorts of moral violence and one sort of immoral.

I do not for a moment rank the scheme of Mr Hare* with the scheme of the ultra-democrats. One can hardly help having a feeling of romance about it. The world seems growing young when grave old lawyers and mature philosophers propose a scheme promising so much. It is from these classes that young men suffer commonly the chilling demonstration that their fine plans are opposed to rooted obstacles, that they are repetitions of other plans which failed long ago, and that we must be content with the very moderate results of tried machinery. But Mr Hare and Mr Mill offer as the effect of their new scheme results as large and improvements as interesting as a young enthusiast ever promised to himself in his happiest mood.

I do not give any weight to the supposed impracticability of Mr Hare's scheme because it is new. Of course it cannot be put in practice till it is old. A great change of this sort happily cannot be sudden; a free people cannot be confused by new institutions which they do not understand, for they will not adopt them till they understand them. But if Mr Hare's plan would accomplish what its friends say, or half what they say, it would be worth working for, if it were not adopted till the year 1966. We ought incessantly to popularise the principle by writing; and what is better than writing, small preliminary bits of experiment. There is so much that is wearisome and detestable in all other election machineries, that I well understand, and wish I could share, the sense of relief with which the believers in this scheme throw aside all their trammels, and look to an almost ideal future, when this captivating plan is carried.

Mr Hare's scheme cannot be satisfactorily discussed in the elaborate form in which he presents it. No common person readily apprehends all the details in which, with loving care, he has embodied it. He was so anxious to prove what could be done, that he has confused most people as to what it is. I have heard a man say, 'He never could remember it two days running.' But the difficulty which I feel is fundamental, and wholly independent of detail.

There are two modes in which constituencies may be made. First, the law may make them, as in England and almost everywhere: the law may say such and such qualifications shall give a vote for constituency X; those who have that qualification shall *be* constituency X. These are what we may call compulsory constituencies, and we know all about them. Or, secondly, the law may leave the electors themselves to make them. The law may say all the adult males of a country shall vote, or those males who can read and write, or those who have £50 a year, or any persons any way defined, and then leave those voters to group themselves as they like. Suppose there were

658,000 voters to elect the House of Commons; it is possible for the legislature to say, 'We do not care how you combine. On a given day let each set of persons give notice in what group they mean to vote; if every voter gives notice, and every one looks to make the most of his vote, each group will have just 1,000. But the law shall not make this necessary—it shall take the 658 most numerous groups, no matter whether they have 2,000, 1,000, or 900, or 800 votes,—the most numerous groups, whatever their number may be; and these shall be the constituencies of the nation.' These are voluntary constituencies, if I may so call them; the simplest kind of voluntary constituencies. Mr Hare proposes a far more complex kind; but to show the merits and demerits of the voluntary principle the simplest form is much the best.

The temptation to that principle is very plain. Under the compulsory form of constituency the votes of the minorities are thrown away. In the city of London, now, there are many Tories, but all the members are Whigs; every London Tory, therefore, is by law and principle misrepresented: his city sends to Parliament not the member whom he wished to have, but the member he wished *not* to have. But upon the voluntary system the London Tories, who are far more than 1,000 in number, may combine; they may make a constituency, and return a member. In many existing constituencies the disfranchisement of minorities is hopeless and chronic. I have myself had a vote for an agricultural county for twenty years, and I am a Liberal. But two Tories have always been returned, and all my life will be returned. As matters now stand, my vote is of no use. But if I could combine with 1,000 other Liberals in that and other Conservative counties, we might choose a Liberal member.

Again, this plan gets rid of all our difficulties as to the size of constituencies. It is said to be unreasonable that Liverpool should return only the same number of members as King's Lynn or Lyme Regis; but upon the voluntary plan, Liverpool could come down to King's Lynn. The Liberal minority in King's Lynn could communicate with the Liberal minority in Liverpool, and make up 1,000; and so everywhere. The numbers of popular places would gain what is called their legitimate advantage; they would, when constituencies are voluntarily made, be able to make, and be willing to make, the greatest number of constituencies.

Again, the admirers of a great man could make a worthy constituency for him. As it is, Mr Mill was returned by the electors of Westminster; and they have never, since they had members, done themselves so great an honour. But what did the electors of Westminster know of Mr Mill? What fraction of his mind could be imagined by any percentage of their minds? A great deal of his genius most of them would not like. They meant to do homage to mental ability, but it was the worship of an unknown god—if ever there was such a thing in this world. But upon the voluntary plan, one thousand out of the many thousand students of Mr Mill's books could have made an appreciating constituency for him.

I could reckon other advantages, but I have to object to the scheme, not to recommend it. What are the counterweights which overpower these merits? I reply that the voluntary composition of constituencies appears to me inconsistent with the necessary prerequisites of parliamentary government as they have been just laid down.

Under the voluntary system, the crisis of politics is not the election of the member, but the making the constituency. President-making is already a trade in America; and constituency-making would, under the voluntary plan, be a trade here. Every party would have a numerical problem to solve. The leaders would say, 'We have 350,000 votes, so we must take care to have 350 members;' and the only way to obtain them is to organise. A man who wanted to compose part of a liberal constituency must not himself hunt for 1,000 other Liberals; if he did, after writing 10,000 letters, he would probably find he was making part of a constituency of 100, all whose votes would be thrown away, the constituency being too small to be reckoned. Such a Liberal must write to the great Registration Association in Parliament Street; he must communicate with its able managers, and they would soon use his vote for him. They would say, 'Sir, you are late; Mr Gladstone, sir, is full. He got his 1,000 last year. Most of the gentlemen you read of in the papers are full. As soon as a gentleman makes a nice speech, we get a heap of letters to say, "Make us into that gentleman's constituency." But we cannot do that. Here is our list. If you do not want to throw your vote away, you must be guided by us: here are three very satisfactory gentlemen (and one is an Honourable): you may vote for either of these, and we will write your name down; but if you go voting wildly, you'll be thrown out altogether.'

The evident result of this organisation would be the return of party men mainly. The member-makers would look, not for independence, but for subservience—and they could hardly be blamed for so doing. They are agents for the Liberal party; and, as such, they should be guided by what they take to be the wishes of their principal. The mass of the Liberal party wishes measure A, measure B, measure C. The managers of the registration—the skilled manipulators—are busy men. They would say, 'Sir, here is our card; if you want to get into parliament on our side, you must go for that card; it was drawn up by Mr Lloyd; he used to be engaged on railways, but since they passed this new voting plan, we get him to attend to us; it is a sound card; stick to that and you will be right.' Upon this (in theory) voluntary plan, you would get together a set of members bound hard and fast with party bands and fetters, infinitely tighter than any members now.

Whoever hopes anything from desultory popular action if matched against systematised popular action, should consider the way in which the American President is chosen. The plan was that the citizens at large should vote for the statesman they liked best. But no one does anything of the sort. They vote for the ticket made by the 'caucus,' and the caucus is a sort of representative meeting which sits voting and voting till they have cut out all the known men against whom much is to be said, and agreed on some unknown man against whom there is nothing known, and therefore nothing to be alleged. Caucuses, or their equivalent, would be far worse here in constituency-making than there in President-making, because on great occasions the American nation can fix on some one great man whom it knows, but the English nation could not fix on 658 great men and choose them. It does not know so many, and if it did, would go wrong in the difficulties of the manipulation.

But though a common voter could only be ranged in an effectual constituency, and a common candidate only reach a constituency by obeying the orders of the political election-contrivers on his side, certain voters and certain members would be quite independent of both. There are organisations in this country which would soon make a set of constituencies for themselves. Every chapel would be an office for vote-transferring before the plan had been known three months. The Church would be much slower in learning it, and much less handy in using it; but would learn. At present the Dissenters are a most energetic and valuable component of the Liberal party; but under the voluntary plan they would not be a component—they would be a separate, independent element. We now propose to group boroughs; but then they would combine chapels. There would be a member for the Baptist congregation of Tavistock, cum Totnes, cum, &c &c.

The full force of this cannot be appreciated except by referring to the former proof that the mass of a Parliament ought to be men of moderate sentiments, or they will elect an immoderate ministry, and enact violent laws. But upon the plan suggested, the House would be made up of party politicians selected by a party committee, chained to that committee and pledged to party violence, and of characteristic, and therefore immoderate representatives, for every 'ism' in all England. Instead of a deliberative assembly of moderate and judicious men, we should have a various compound of all sorts of violence.

I may seem to be drawing a caricature, but I have not reached the worst. Bad as these members would be, if they were left to themselves—if, in a free Parliament, they were confronted with the perils of government, close responsibility might improve them and make them tolerable. But they would not be left to themselves. A voluntary constituency will nearly always be a despotic constituency. Even in the best case, where a set of earnest men choose a member to expound their earnestness, they will look after him to see that he does expound it. The members will be like the minister of a dissenting congregation. That congregation is collected by a unity of sentiment in doctrine A, and the preacher is to preach doctrine A; if he does not, he is dismissed. At present the member is free because the constituency is not in earnest: no constituency has an acute, accurate doctrinal creed in politics. The law made the constituencies by geographical divisions; and they are not bound together by close unity of belief. They have vague preferences for particular doctrines; and that is all. But a voluntary constituency would be a church with tenets; it would make its representative the messenger of its mandates, and the delegate of its determinations. As in the case of a dissenting congregation, one great minister sometimes rules it, while ninety-nine ministers in the hundred are ruled by it, so here one noted man would rule his electors, but the electors would rule all the others.

Thus, the members for a good voluntary constituency would be hopelessly enslaved, because of its goodness; but the members for a bad voluntary constituency would be yet more enslaved because of its badness. The makers of these constituencies would keep the despotism in their own hands. In America there is a division of politicians into wire-pullers and blowers; under the voluntary system the member of Parliament would only be the momentary mouthpiece—the impotent blower; while the constituency-maker would be the latent wire-puller—the constant autocrat. He would write to gentlemen in Parliament, and say, 'You were elected upon "the Liberal ticket;" if you deviate from that ticket you cannot be chosen again.' And there would be no appeal for a common-minded man. He is no more likely to make a constituency for himself than a mole is likely to make a planet.

It may indeed be said that against a septennial Parliament such machinations would be powerless; that a member elected for seven years might defy the remonstrances of an earnest constituency, or the imprecations of the latent manipulators. But after the voluntary composition of constituencies, there would soon be but short-lived Parliaments. Earnest constituencies would exact frequent elections; they would not like to part with their virtue for a long period; it would anger them to see it used contrary to their wishes, amid circumstances which at the election no one thought of. A seven years' Parliament is often chosen in one political period, lasts through a second, and is dissolved in a third. A constituency collected by law and on compulsion endures this change because it has no collective earnestness; it does not mind seeing the power it gave used in a manner that it could not have foreseen. But a self-formed constituency of eager opinions, a missionary constituency, so to speak, would object; it would think it its bounden duty to object; and the crafty manipulators, though they said nothing, in silence would object still more. The two together would enjoin annual elections, and would rule their members unflinchingly.

The voluntary plan, therefore, when tried in this easy form, is inconsistent with the extrinsic independence as well as with the inherent moderation of a Parliament—two of the conditions which, as we have seen, are essential to the bare possibility of Parliamentary government. The same objections, as is inevitable, adhere to that principle under its more complicated forms. It is in vain to pile detail on detail when the objection is one of first principle. If the above reasoning be sound, compulsory constituencies are necessary, voluntary constituencies destructive; the optional transferability of votes is not a salutary aid, but a ruinous innovation.

I have dwelt upon the proposal of Mr Hare and upon the ultra-democratic proposal, not only because of the high intellectual interest of the former and the possible practical interest of the latter, but because they tend to bring into relief two at least of the necessary conditions of parliamentary government. But besides these necessary qualities which are needful before a parliamentary government can work at all, there are some additional prerequisites before it can work well. That a House of Commons may work well it must perform, as we saw, five functions well: it must elect a ministry well, legislate well, teach the nation well, express the nation's will well, bring matters to the nation's attention well.

The discussion has a difficulty of its own. What is meant by 'well?' Who is to judge? Is it to be some panel of philosophers, some fancied posterity, or some other outside authority. I answer, no philosophy, no posterity, no external authority, but the English nation here and now.

Free government is self-government. A government of the people by the people. The best government of this sort is that which the people think best. An imposed government, a government like that of the English in India, may very possibly be better; it may represent the views of a higher race than the governed race, but it is not therefore a free government. A free government is that which the people subject to it voluntarily choose. In a casual collection of loose people the only possible free government is a democratic government. Where no one knows or cares for, or, respects any one else all must rank equal; no one's opinion can be more potent than that of another. But, as has been explained, a deferential nation has a structure of its own. Certain persons are by common consent agreed to be wiser than others, and their opinion is, by consent, to rank for much more than its numerical value. We may in these happy nations weigh votes as well as count them, though in less favoured countries we can count only. But in free nations, the votes so weighed or so counted must decide. A perfect free government is one which decides perfectly according to those votes; an imperfect, one which so decides imperfectly; a bad, one which does not so decide at all. Public opinion is the test of this polity; the best opinion which, with its existing habits of deference, the nation will accept: if the free government goes by that opinion, it is a good government of its species; if it contravenes that opinion, it is a bad one.

Tried by this rule the House of Commons does its appointing business well. It chooses rulers as we wish rulers to be chosen. If it did not, in a speaking and writing age we should soon know. I have heard a great Liberal statesman say, 'The time was coming when we must advertise for a grievance.' What a good grievance it would be were the ministry appointed and retained by the Parliament a ministry detested by the nation. An anti-present government league would be instantly created, and it would be more instantly powerful and more instantly successful than the Anti-Corn Law League.

It has, indeed, been objected that the choosing business of Parliament is done ill, because it does not choose strong governments. And it is certain that when public opinion does not definitely decide upon a marked policy, and when in consequence parties in the Parliament are nearly even, individual cupidity and changeability may make Parliament change its appointees too often: may induce them never enough to trust any of them; may make it keep all of them under a suspended sentence of coming dismissal. But the experience of Lord Palmerston's second Government proves, I think, that these fears are exaggerated. When the choice of a nation is really fixed on a statesman, Parliament will fix upon him too. The parties in the Parliament of 1859 were as nearly divided as any probable Parliament; a great many Liberals did not much like Lord Palmerston, and they would have gladly co-operated in an attempt to dethrone him. But the same influences acted on Parliament within which acted on the nation without. The moderate men of both parties were satisfied that Lord Palmerston's was the best Government, and they therefore preserved it though it was hated by the immoderate on both sides. We have then found by a critical instance that a government supported by what I may call 'the common element,'—by the like-minded men of unlike parties,—will be retained in power, though parties are even, and though, as Treasury counting reckons, the majority is imperceptible. If happily, by its intelligence and attractiveness, a cabinet can gain a hold upon the great middle part of Parliament, it will continue to exist notwithstanding the hatching of small plots and the machinations of mean factions.

On the whole, I think it indisputable that the selecting task of Parliament is performed as well as public opinion wishes it to be performed; and if we want to improve that standard, we must first improve the English nation, which imposes that standard. Of the substantial part of its legislative task the same, too, may I think be said. The manner of our legislation is indeed detestable, and the machinery for settling that manner odious. A committee of the whole House, dealing, or attempting to deal, with the elaborate clauses of a long Bill, is a wretched specimen of severe but misplaced labour. It is sure to wedge some clause into the Act, such as that which the judge said 'seemed to have fallen by itself, *perhaps*, from heaven, into the mind of the legislature,' so little had it to do with anything on either side or around it. At such times government by a public meeting displays its inherent defects, and is little restrained by its necessary checks. But the essence of our legislature may be separated from its accidents. Subject to two considerable defects I think Parliament passes laws as the nation wish to have them passed.

Thirty years ago this was not so. The nation had outgrown its institutions, and was cramped by them. It was a man in the clothes of a boy; every limb wanted more room, and every garment to be fresh made. 'D—mn me,' said Lord Eldon* in the dialect of his age, 'if I had to begin life again I would begin as an agitator.' The shrewd old man saw that the best life was that of a miscellaneous objector to the old world, though he loved that world, believed in it, could imagine no other. But he would not say so now. There is no worse trade than agitation at this time. A man can hardly get an audience if he wishes to complain of anything. Now-a-days, not only does the mind and policy of Parliament (subject to the exceptions before named) possess the common sort of moderation essential to the possibility of parliamentary government, but also that exact gradation, that precise species of moderation, most agreeable to the nation at large. Not only does the nation endure a parliamentary government, which it would not do if Parliament were immoderate, but it likes parliamentary government. A sense of satisfaction permeates the country because most of the country feels it has got the precise thing that suits it.

The exceptions are two. First. That Parliament leans too much to the opinions of the landed interest. The Cattle Plague Act is a conspicuous instance of this defect. The details of that Bill may be good or bad, and its policy wise or foolish. But the manner in which it was hurried through the House savoured of despotism. The cotton trade or the wine trade could not, in their maximum of peril, have obtained such aid in such a manner. The House of Commons would hear of no pause and would heed no arguments. The greatest number of them feared for their incomes. The land of England returns many members annually for the counties; these members the constitution gave them. But what is curious is that the landed interest gives no seats to other classes, but takes plenty of seats *from* other classes. Half the boroughs in England are represented by considerable landowners and when rent is in question, as in the cattle case, they think more of themselves than of those who sent them. In number the landed gentry in the House far surpass any other class. They have, too, a more intimate connection with one another; they were educated at the same schools; know one another's family name from boyhood; form a society; are the same kind of men; marry the same kind of women. The merchants and manufacturers in Parliament are a motley race—one educated here, another there, a third not educated at all; some are of the second generation of traders, who consider self-made men intruders upon an hereditary place; others are self-made, and regard the men of inherited wealth, which they did not make and do not augment, as beings of neither mind nor place, inferior to themselves because they have no brains, and inferior to lords because they have no rank. Traders have no bond of union, no habits of intercourse; their wives, if they care for society, want to see not the wives of other such men, but 'better people,' as they say—the wives of men certainly with land, and, if Heaven help, with titles. Men who study the structure of Parliament, not in abstract books, but in the concrete London world, wonder not that the landed interest is very powerful, but that it is not despotic. I believe it would be despotic if it were clever, or rather if its representatives were so, but it has a fixed device to make them stupid. The counties not only elect landowners, which is natural and perhaps wise, but also elect only landowners *of their own county*, which is absurd. There is no free trade in agricultural mind; each county prohibits the import of able men from other counties. That is why eloquent sceptics— Bolingbroke and Disraeli*—have been so apt to lead the unsceptical Tories. They will have people with a great piece of land in a particular spot, and of course these people generally cannot speak, and often cannot think. And so eloquent men who laugh at the party come to lead the party. The landed interest has much more influence than it should have; but it wastes that influence so much that the excess is, except on singular occurrences (like the cattle plague), of secondary moment.

It is almost another side of the same matter to say that the structure of Parliament gives too little weight to the growing districts of the country and too much to the stationary. In old times the South of England was not only the pleasantest but the greatest part of England. Devonshire was a great maritime county when the foundations of our representation were fixed; Somersetshire and Wiltshire great manufacturing counties. The harsher climate of the northern counties was associated with a ruder, a sterner, and a sparser people. The immense preponderance which our Parliament gave before 1832, and, though pruned and mitigated, still gives to England south of the Trent, then corresponded to a real preponderance in wealth and mind. How opposite the present contrast is we all know. And the case gets worse every day. The nature of modern trade is to give to those who have much and take from those who have little. Manufacture goes where manufacture is, because there, and there alone, it finds attendant and auxiliary manufacture. Every railway takes trade from the little town to the big town, because it enables the customer to buy in the big town. Year by year the North (as we may roughly call the new industrial world) gets more important, and the South (as we may call the pleasant remnant of old times) gets less important. It is a grave objection to our existing parliamentary constitution that it gives much power to regions of past greatness, and refuses equal power to regions of present greatness.

I think (though it is not a popular notion) that by far the greater part of the cry for parliamentary reform is due to this inequality. The great capitalists, Mr Bright and his friends, believe they are sincere in asking for more power for the working man,* but, in fact, they very naturally and very properly want more power for themselves. They cannot endure—they ought not to endure—that a rich, able manufacturer should be a less man than a small, stupid squire. The notions of political equality which Mr Bright puts forward are as old as political speculation, and have been refuted by the first efforts of that speculation. But for all that they are likely to last as long as political society, because they are based upon indelible principles in human nature. Edmund Burke called the first East Indians, 'Jacobins to a man,'* because they did not feel their 'present importance equal to their real wealth.' So long as there is an uneasy class, a class which has not its just power, it will rashly clutch and blindly believe the notion that all men should have the same power.

I do not consider the exclusion of the working classes from effectual representation a defect in *this* aspect of our parliamentary representation. The working classes contribute almost nothing to our corporate public opinion, and therefore, the fact of their want of influence in Parliament does not impair the coincidence of Parliament with public opinion. They are left out in the representation, and also in the thing represented.

Nor do I think the number of persons of aristocratic descent in Parliament impairs the accordance of Parliament with public opinion. No doubt the direct descendants and collateral relatives of noble families supply members to Parliament in far greater proportion than is warranted by the number of such families in comparison with the whole nation. But I do not believe that these families have the least corporate character, or any common opinions, different from others of the landed gentry. They have the opinions of the proper-tied rank in which they were born. The English aristocracy have never been a caste apart, and are not a caste apart now. They would keep up nothing that other landed gentlemen would not. And if any landed gentlemen are to be sent to the House of Commons, it is desirable that many should be men of some rank. As long as we keep up a double set of institutions,—one dignified and intended to impress the many, the other efficient and intended to govern the many,—we should take care that the two match nicely, and hide where the one begins and where the other ends. This is in part effected by conceding some subordinate power to the august part of our polity, but it is equally aided by keeping an aristocratic element in the useful part of our polity. In truth, the deferential instinct secures both. Aristocracy is a power in the 'constituencies.' A man who is an honourable or a baronet, or better yet, perhaps, a real earl, though Irish, is coveted by half the electing bodies; and, *ceteris pari-bus*,* a manufacturer's son has no chance with him. The reality of the deferential feeling in the community is tested by the actual election of the class deferred to, where there is a large free choice betwixt it and others.

Subject therefore to the two minor, but still not inconsiderable, defects I have named, Parliament conforms itself accurately enough, both as a chooser of executives and as a legislature, to the formed opinion of the country. Similarly, and subject to the same exceptions, it expresses the nation's opinion in words well, when it happens that words, not laws, are wanted. On foreign matters, where we cannot legislate, whatever the English nation thinks, or thinks it thinks, as to the critical events of the world, whether in Denmark, in Italy, or America, and no matter whether it thinks wisely or unwisely, that same something, wise or unwise, will be thoroughly well said in Parliament. The lyrical function of Parliament, if I may use such a phrase, is well done; it pours out in characteristic words the characteristic heart of the nation. And it can do little more useful. Now that free government is in Europe so rare and in America so distant, the opinion, even the incomplete, erroneous, rapid opinion of the free English people is invaluable. It may be very wrong, but it is sure to be unique; and if it is right, it is sure to contain matter of great magnitude, for it is only a first-class matter in distant things which a free people ever sees or learns. The English people must miss a thousand minutiae that continental bureaucracies know even too well; but if they see a cardinal truth which those bureaucracies miss, that cardinal truth may greatly help the world.

But if in these ways, and subject to these exceptions, Parliament by its policy and its speech well embodies and expresses public opinion, I own I think it must be conceded that it is not equally successful in elevating public opinion. The teaching task of Parliament is the task it does worst. Probably at this moment it is natural to exaggerate this defect. The greatest teacher of all in Parliament, the headmaster of the nation, the great elevator of the country—so far as Parliament elevates it—must be the Prime Minister; he has an influence, an authority, a facility in giving a great tone to discussion, or a mean tone, which no other man has. Now Lord Palmerston for many years steadily applied his mind to giving, not indeed a mean tone, but a light tone, to the proceedings of Parliament. One of his greatest admirers has since his death told a story of which he scarcely sees, or seems to see, the full effect. When Lord Palmerston was first made leader of the House, his jaunty manner was not at all popular, and some predicted failure. 'No,' said an old member, 'he will soon educate us *down* to his level; the House will soon prefer this Ha! Ha!

style to the wit of Canning and the gravity of Peel.' I am afraid that we must own that the prophecy was accomplished. No prime minister, so popular and so influential, has ever left in the public memory so little noble teaching. Twenty years hence, when men inquire as to the then fading memory of Palmerston, we shall be able to point to no great truth which he taught, no great distinct policy he embodied, no noble words which once fascinated his age, and which, in after years, men would not willingly let die. But we shall be able to say 'he had a genial manner, a firm, sound sense; he had a kind of cant of insincerity, but we always knew what he meant; he had the brain of a ruler in the clothes of a man of fashion.' Posterity will hardly understand the words of the facetious reminiscent, but we now feel their effect. The House of Commons, since it caught its tone from such a statesman, has taught the nation worse, and elevated it less, than usual.

I think, however, that a correct observer would decide that in general, and on principle, the House of Commons does not teach the public as much as it might teach it, or as the public would wish to learn. I do not wish very abstract, very philosophical, very hard matters to be stated in Parliament. The teaching there given must be popular, and to be popular it must be concrete, embodied, short. The problem is to know the highest truth which the people will bear, and to inculcate and preach that. Certainly Lord Palmerston did not preach it. He a little degraded us by preaching a doctrine just below our own standard;—a doctrine not enough below us to repel us much, but yet enough below to harm us by augmenting a worldliness which needed no addition, and by diminishing a love of principle and philosophy which did not want deduction.

In comparison with the debates of any other assembly, it is true the debates by the English Parliament are most instructive. The debates in the American Congress have little teaching efficacy; it is the characteristic vice of Presidential Government to deprive them of that efficacy; in that government a debate in the legislature has little effect, for it cannot turn out the executive, and the executive can veto all it decides. The French Chambers are suitable appendages to an Empire which desires the power of despotism without its shame; they prevent the enemies of the Empire being quite correct when they say there is no free speech: a few permitted objectors fill the air with eloquence, which every one knows to be often true, and always vain. The debates in an English Parliament fill a space in the world which, in these auxiliary chambers, is not possible. But I think any one who compares the discussions on great questions in the higher part of the press, with the discussions in Parliament, will feel that there is (of course amid much exaggeration and vagueness) a greater vigour and a higher meaning in the writing than in the speech; a vigour which the public appreciate—a meaning that they like to hear.

The *Saturday Review* said, some years since, that the ability of Parliament was a 'protected ability;' that there was at the door a differential duty of at least £2,000 a year. Accordingly the House of Commons, representing only mind coupled with property, is not equal in mind to a legislature chosen for mind only, and whether accompanied by wealth or not. But I do not for a moment wish to see a representation of pure mind; it would be contrary to the main thesis of this essay. I maintain that Parliament ought to embody the public opinion of the English nation; and, certainly, that opinion is much more fixed by its property than by its mind. The 'too clever by half' people, who live in 'Bohemia,' ought to have no more influence in Parliament than they have in England, and they can scarcely have less. Only, after every great abatement and deduction, I think the country would bear a little more mind; and that there is a profusion of opulent dullness in Parliament which might a little—though only a little—be pruned away.

The only function of Parliament which remains to be considered is the informing function, as I just now called it: the function which belongs to it, or to members of it, to bring before the nation the ideas, grievances, and wishes of special classes. This must not be confounded with what I have called its teaching function. In life, no doubt, the two run one into another. But so do many things which it is very important in definition to separate. The fact of two things being often found together is rather a reason for, than an objection to, separating them in idea. Sometimes they are *not* found together, and then we may be puzzled if we have not trained ourselves to separate them. The teaching function brings true ideas before the nation: and is the function of its highest minds. The expressive function brings only special ideas, and is the function of but special minds. Each class has its ideas, wants, and notions; and certain brains are ingrained with them. Such sectarian conceptions are not those by which a determining nation should regulate its action, nor are orators, mainly animated by such conceptions, safe guides in policy. But those orators should be heard; those conceptions should be kept in sight. The great maxim of modern thought is not only the toleration of everything, but the examination of everything. It is by examining very bare, very dull, very unpromising things, that modern science has come to be what it is. There is a story of a great chemist who said he owed half his fame to his habit of examining, after his experiments, what was going to be thrown away: everybody knew the result of the experiment itself, but in the refuse matter there were many little facts and unknown changes, which suggested the discoveries of a famous life, to a person capable of looking for them. So with the special notions of neglected classes. They may contain elements of truth which though small, are the very elements which we now require, because we already know all the rest.

This doctrine was well known to our ancestors. They laboured to give a *character* to the various constituencies, or to many of them. They wished that the shipping trade, the wool trade, the linen trade, should each have their spokesman: that the unsectional Parliament should know what each section in the nation thought before it gave the national decision. This is the true reason for admitting the working classes to a share in the representation, at least as far as the composition of Parliament is to be improved by that admission. A great many ideas, a great many feelings have gathered among the town artizans—a peculiar intellectual life has sprung up among them. They believe that they have interests which are misconceived or neglected; that they know something which others do not know; that the thoughts of Parliament are not as their thoughts. They ought to be allowed to try to convince Parliament; their notions ought to be stated as those of other classes are stated; their advocates should be heard as other people's advocates are heard. Before the Reform Bill, there was a recognised machinery for that purpose. The member for Westminster, and other members, were elected by universal suffrage (or what was in substance such); those members, did in their day, state what were the grievances and ideas—or were thought to be the grievances and ideas—of the working classes. It was the single, unbending franchise introduced in 1832 that has caused this difficulty, as it has others.

Until such a change is made the House of Commons will be

defective, just as, the House of Lords was defective. It will not *look* right. As long as the Lords do not come to their own House, we may prove on paper that it is a good revising chamber, but it will be difficult to make the literary argument felt. Just so, as long as a great class, congregated in political localities, and known to have political thoughts and wishes, is without notorious and palpable advocates in Parliament, we may prove on paper that our representation is adequate, but the world will not believe it. There is a saying of the eighteenth century, that in politics 'gross appearances are great realities.' It is in vain to demonstrate that the working classes have no grievances; that the middle classes have done all possible for them, and so on with a crowd of arguments which I need not repeat, for the newspapers keep them in type, and we can say them by heart. But so long as the 'gross appearance' is that there are no evident, incessant representatives to speak the wants of artizans, the 'great reality' will be a diffused dissatisfaction. Thirty years ago it was vain to prove that Gatton and Old Sarum were valuable seats, and sent good members.* Everybody said, 'Why, there are no people there.' Just so everybody must say now, 'Our representative system must be imperfect, for an immense class has no members to speak for it.' The only answer to the cry against constituencies *without* inhabitants was to transfer their power to constituencies *with* inhabitants. Just so, the way to stop the complaint that artizans have no members is to give them members,—to create a body of representatives, chosen by arti- zans, believing, as Mr Carlyle* would say, 'that artizanism is the one thing needful.'

7

ON CHANGES OF MINISTRY*

THERE is one error as to the English Constitution which crops-up periodically. Circumstances which often, though irregularly, occur naturally suggest that error, and as surely as they happen it revives. The relation of Parliament, and especially of the House of Commons, to the Executive Government is the specific peculiarity of our constitution, and an event which frequently happens much puzzles some people as to it.

That event is a change of ministry. All our administrators go out together. The whole executive government changes—at least, all the heads of it change in a body, and at every such change some speculators are sure to exclaim that such a habit is foolish. They say, 'No doubt Mr Gladstone and Lord Russell may have been wrong about Reform;* no doubt Mr Gladstone may have been cross in the House of Commons; but why should either or both of these events change all the heads of all our practical departments? What could be more absurd than what happened in 1858?* Lord Palmerston was for once in his life over-buoyant; he gave rude answers to stupid inquiries; he brought into the Cabinet a nobleman concerned in an ugly trial about a woman; he, or his Foreign Secretary, did not answer a French despatch by a despatch, but told our ambassador to reply orally. And because of these trifles, or at any rate, these isolated *un*-administrative mistakes, all our administration had fresh heads. The Poor Law Board had a new chief, the Home Department a new chief, the Public Works a new chief. Surely this was absurd.' Now, is this objection good or bad? Speaking generally, is it wise so to change all our rulers?

The practice produces three great evils. First, it brings in on a sudden new persons and untried persons to preside over our policy. A little while ago Lord Cranborne* had no more idea that he would now be Indian Secretary than that he would be a bill broker. He had never given any attention to Indian affairs; he can get them up, because he is an able educated man who can get up anything. But they are not 'part and parcel' of his mind; not his subjects of familiar reflection, nor things of which he thinks by predilection, of which he cannot help thinking. But because Lord Russell and Mr Gladstone did not please the House of Commons about Reform, there he is. A perfectly inexperienced man, so far as Indian affairs go, rules all our Indian empire. And if all our heads of offices change together, so very frequently it must be. If twenty offices are vacant at once, there are almost never twenty tried, competent, clever men ready to take them. The difficulty of making up a government is very much like the difficulty of putting together a Chinese puzzle: the spaces do not suit what you have to put into them. And the difficulty of matching a ministry is more than that of fitting a puzzle, because the ministers to be put in can object, though the bits of a puzzle cannot. One objector can throw out the combination. In 1847 Lord Grey would not join Lord John Russell's projected government if Lord Palmerston was to be Foreign Secretary; Lord Palmerston *would* be Foreign Secretary, and so the government was not formed. The cases in which a single refusal prevents a government are rare, and there must be many concurrent circumstances to make it effectual. But the cases in which refusals impair or spoil a government are very common. It almost never happens that the ministry-maker can put into his offices exactly whom he would like; a number of place-men are always too proud, too eager, or too obstinate to go just where they should.

Again, this system not only makes new ministers ignorant, but keeps present ministers indifferent. A man cannot feel the same interest that he might in his work if he knows that by events over which he has no control,—by errors in which he had no share,—by metamorphoses of opinion which belong to a different sequence of phenomena, he may have to leave that work in the middle and may very likely never return to it. The new man put into a fresh office ought to have the best motive to learn his task thoroughly, but, in fact, in England he has not at all the best motive. The last wave of party and politics brought him there, the next may take him away. Young and eager men take, even at this disadvantage, a keen interest in office work, but most men, especially old men, hardly do so. Many a battered minister may be seen to think much more of the vicissitudes which make him and unmake him, than of any office matter.

Lastly, a sudden change of ministers may easily cause a mischievous change of policy. In many matters of business, perhaps in most, a continuity of mediocrity is better than a hotch-potch of excellences.

For example, now that progress in the scientific arts is revolutionising the instruments of war, rapid changes in our head-preparers for land and sea war are most costly and most hurtful. A single competent selector of new inventions would probably in the course of years, after some experience, arrive at something tolerable; it is in the nature of steady, regular, experimenting ability to diminish, if not vanquish such difficulties. But a quick succession of chiefs has no similar facility. They do not learn from each others' experience;— you might well expect the new head boy at a public school to learn from the experience of the last head boy. The most valuable result of many years is a nicely balanced mind instinctively heedful of various errors; but such a mind is the incommunicable gift of individual experience, and an outgoing minister can no more leave it to his successor than an elder brother can pass it on to a younger. Thus a desultory and incalculable policy may follow from a rapid change of ministers.

These are formidable arguments, but four things may, I think, be said in reply to, or mitigation of them. A little examination will show that this change of ministers is essential to a Parliamentary government;—that something like it will happen in all elective governments, and that worse happens under presidential government;—that it is not necessarily prejudicial to a good administration, but that, on the contrary, something like it is a prerequisite of good administration;—that the evident evils of English administration are not the results of Parliamentary government, but of grave deficiencies in other parts of our political and social state;—that, in a word, they result not from what we have, but from what we have *not*.

As to the first point, those who wish to remove the choice of ministers from Parliament have not adequately considered what a Parliament is. A Parliament is nothing less than a big meeting of more or less idle people. In proportion as you give it power it will inquire into everything, settle everything, meddle in anything. In an ordinary despotism, the powers of a despot are limited by his bodily capacity, and by the calls of pleasure; he is but one man;—there are but twelve hours in his day, and he not disposed to employ more than a small part in dull business;—he keeps the rest for the court, or the harem, or for society. He is at the top of the world, and all the pleasures of the world are set before him. Mostly there is only a very small part of political business which he cares to understand, and much of it (with the shrewd sensual sense belonging to the race) he knows that he will never understand. But a Parliament is composed of a great number of men by no means at the top of the world. When you establish a predominant Parliament, you give over the rule of the country to a despot who has unlimited time,—who has unlimited vanity,—who has, or believes he has, unlimited comprehension, whose pleasure is in action, whose life is work. There is no limit to the curiosity of Parliament. Sir Robert Peel once suggested that a list should be taken down of the questions asked of him in a single evening; they touched more or less on fifty subjects, and there were a thousand other subjects which by parity of reason might have been added too. As soon as bore A ends, bore B begins. Some inquire from genuine love of knowledge, or from a real wish to improve what they ask about,—others ask to see their name in the papers,—others to show a watchful constituency that they are alert,—others to get on and to get a place in the government,—others from an accumulation of little motives they could not themselves analyse, or because it is their habit to ask things. And a proper reply must be given. It was said that 'Darby Griffith destroyed Lord Palmerston's first Government,'* and undoubtedly the cheerful impertinence with which in the conceit of victory that minister answered grave men much hurt his Parliamentary power. There is one thing which no one will permit to be treated lightly,—himself. And so there is one too which a sovereign assembly will never permit to be lessened or ridiculed,—its own power. The minister of the day will have to give an account in Parliament of all branches of administration, to say why they act when they do, and why they do not when they don't.

Nor is chance inquiry all a public department has most to fear. Fifty members of Parliament may be zealous for a particular policy affecting the department, and fifty others for another policy, and between them they may divide its action, spoil its favourite aims, and prevent its consistently working out either of their own aims. The process is very simple. Every department at times looks as if it was in a scrape; some apparent blunder, perhaps some real blunder, catches the public eye. At once the antagonist Parliamentary sections, which want to act on the department, seize the opportunity. They make speeches, they move for documents, they amass statistics. They declare 'that in no other country is such a policy possible as that which the department is pursuing; that it is medieval; that it costs money; that it wastes life; that America does the contrary; that Prussia does the contrary.' The newspapers follow according to their nature. These bits of administrative scandal amuse the public. Articles on them are very easy to write, easy to read, easy to talk about. They please the vanity of mankind. We think as we read, 'Thank God, *I* am not as that man; *I* did not send green coffee to the Crimea;* *I* did not send patent cartridge to the common guns, and common cartridge to the breech-loaders. *I* make money; that miserable public functionary only wastes money.' As for the defence of the department, no one cares for it or reads it. Naturally at first hearing it does not sound true. The opposition have the unrestricted selection of the point of attack, and they seldom choose a case in which the department, upon the surface of the matter, seems to be right. The case of first impression will always be that something shameful has happened; that such and such men did die; that this and that gun would not go off; that this or that ship will not sail. All the pretty reading is unfavourable, and all the praise is very dull.

Nothing is more helpless than such a department in Parliament if it has no authorised official defender. The wasps of the House fasten on it; here they perceive is something easy to sting, and safe, for it cannot sting in return. The small grain of foundation for complaint germinates, till it becomes a whole crop. At once the minister of the day is appealed to; he is at the head of the administration, and he must put the errors right, if such there are. The opposition leader says, 'I put it to the right honourable gentleman, the First Lord of the Treasury. He is a man of business. I do not agree with him in his choice of ends, but he is an almost perfect master of methods and means. What he wishes to do he does do. Now I appeal to him whether such gratuitous errors, such fatuous incapacity, are to be permitted in the public service. Perhaps the right honourable gentleman will grant me his attention while I show from the very documents of the department,' &c, &c. What is the minister to do? He never heard of this matter; he does not care about the matter. Several of the supporters of the Government are interested in the opposition to the department; a grave man, supposed to be wise, mutters, 'This is *too* bad.' The Secretary of the Treasury tells him, 'The House is uneasy. A good many men are shaky. A. B. said yesterday he had been dragged through the dirt four nights following.

Indeed I am disposed to think myself that the department has been somewhat lax. Perhaps an inquiry,' &c, &c. And upon that the Prime Minister rises and says, 'That Her Majesty's Government having given very serious and grave consideration to this most important subject, are not prepared to say that in so complicated a matter the department has been perfectly exempt from error. He does not indeed concur in all the statements which have been made; it is obvious that several of the charges advanced are inconsistent with one another. If A had really died from eating green coffee on the Tuesday, it is plain he could not have suffered from insufficient attendance on the following Thursday. However, on so complex a subject, and one so foreign to common experience, he will not give a judgment. And if the honourable member would be satisfied with him having the matter inquired into by a committee of that House, he will be prepared to accede to the suggestion.'

Possibly the outlying department, distrusting the ministry, crams a friend. But it is happy indeed if it chances on a judicious friend. The persons most ready to take up that sort of business are benevolent amateurs, very well intentioned, very grave, very respectable, but also rather dull. Their words are good, but about the joints their arguments are weak. They speak very well, but while they are speaking, the decorum is so great that everybody goes away. Such a man is no match for a couple of House of Commons gladiators. They pull what he says to shreds. They show or say that he is wrong about his facts. Then he rises in a fuss and must explain: but in his hurry he mistakes, and cannot find the right paper, and becomes first hot, then confused, next inaudible, and so sits down. Probably he leaves the House with the notion that the defence of the department has broken down, and so the *Times* announces to all the world as soon as it awakes.

Some thinkers have naturally suggested that the heads of departments should as such have the right of speech in the House. But the system when it has been tried has not answered. M. Guizot tells us* from his own experience that such a system is not effectual. A great popular assembly has a corporate character; it has its own privileges, prejudices, and notions. And one of these notions is that its own members—the persons it sees every day—whose qualities it knows, whose minds it can test, are those whom it can most trust. A clerk speaking from without would be an unfamiliar object. He would be an outsider. He would speak under suspicion; he would speak without dignity. Very often he would speak as a victim. All the bores of the House would be upon him. He would be put upon examination. He would have to answer interrogatories. He would be put through the figures and cross-questioned in detail. The whole effect of what he said would be lost in *quaestiunculae** and hidden in a controversial detritus.

Again, such a person would rarely speak with great ability. He would speak as a scribe. His habits must have been formed in the quiet of an office; he is used to red tape, placidity, and the respect of subordinates. Such a person will hardly ever be able to stand the hurly-burly of a public assembly. He will lose his head,—he will say what he should not. He will get hot and red; he will feel he is a sort of culprit. After being used to the flattering deference of deferential subordinates, he will be pestered by fuss and confounded by invective. He will hate the House as naturally as the House does not like him. He will be an incompetent speaker addressing a hostile audience.

And what is more, an outside administrator addressing Parliament, can move Parliament only by the goodness of his arguments. He has no votes to back them up with. He is sure to be at chronic war with some active minority of assailants or others. The natural mode in which a department is improved on great points and new points is by external suggestion; the worst foes of a department are the plausible errors which the most visible facts suggest, and which only half invisible facts confute. Both the good ideas and the bad ideas are sure to find advocates first in the press and then in Parliament. Against these a permanent clerk would have to contend by argument alone. The Minister, the head of the parliamentary Government, will not care for him. The Minister will say in some undress soliloquy, 'These permanent "fellows" must look after themselves. I cannot be bothered. I have only a majority of nine, and a very shaky majority, too. I cannot afford to make enemies for those whom I did not appoint. They did nothing for me, and I can do nothing for them.' And if the permanent clerk come to ask his help he will say in decorous language, 'I am sure that if the department can evince to the satisfaction of Parliament that its past management has been such as the public interests require, no one will be more gratified than myself. I am not aware if it will be in my power to attend in my place on Monday; but if I can be so fortunate, I shall listen to your official statement with my very best attention.' And so the permanent public servant will be teazed by the wits, oppressed by the bores, and massacred by the innovators of Parliament.

The incessant tyranny of Parliament over the public offices is prevented and can only be prevented by the appointment of a parliamentary head, connected by close ties with the present ministry and the ruling party in Parliament. The parliamentary head is a protecting machine. He and the friends he brings stand between the department and the busybodies and crotchet-makers of the House and the country. So long as at any moment the policy of an office could be altered by chance votes in their House of Parliament, there is no security for any consistency. Our guns and our ships are not, perhaps, very good now. But they would be much worse if any thirty or forty advocates for this gun or that gun could make a motion in Parliament, beat the department, and get their ships or their guns adopted. The 'Black Breech Ordnance Company' and the 'Adamantine Ship Company' would soon find representatives in Parliament, if forty or fifty members would get the national custom for their rubbish. But this result is now prevented by the parliamentary head of the department. As soon as the opposition begins the attack, he looks up his means of defence. He studies the subject, compiles his arguments, and builds little piles of statistics, which he hopes will have some effect. He has his reputation at stake, and he wishes to show that he is worth his present place, and fit for future promotion. He is well-known, perhaps liked, by the House—at any rate the House attends to him; he is one of the regular speakers whom they hear and heed. He is sure to be able to get himself heard, and he is sure to make the best defence he can. And after he has settled his speech, he loiters up to the Secretary of the Treasury, and says quietly, 'They have got a motion against me on Tuesday, you know. I hope you will have your men here. A lot of fellows have crotchets, and though they do not agree a bit with one another, they are all against the department; they will all vote for the inquiry.' And the Secretary answers, 'Tuesday, you say; no (looking at a paper), I do not think it will come on Tuesday. There is Higgins on Education. He is good for a long time. But anyhow it shall be all right.' And then he glides about and speaks a word here and a word there, in consequence of which, when the anti-official motion is made, a considerable array of steady, grave faces sits behind the Treasury Bench—nay, possibly a rising man who sits in outlying independence below the gangway rises to defend the transaction; the department wins by thirty-three, and the management of that business pursues its steady way.

This contrast is no fancy picture. The experiment of conducting the administration of a public department by an independent unsheltered authority has often been tried, and always failed. Parliament always poked at it, till it made it impossible. The most remarkable is that of the Poor Law. The administration of that law is not now very good, but it is not too much to say that almost the whole of its goodness has been preserved by its having an official and party protector in the House of Commons. Without that contrivance we should have drifted back into the errors of the old Poor Law, and superadded to them the present meanness and incompetence in our large towns. All would have been given up to local management. Parliament would have interfered with the central board till it made it impotent, and the local authorities would have been despotic. The first administration of the new Poor Law was by 'Commissioners'— the three kings of Somerset House, as they were called.* The system was certainly not tried in untrustworthy hands. At the crisis Mr Chadwick,* one of the most active and best administrators in England, was the secretary and the motive power: the principal Commissioner was Sir George Lewis,* perhaps the best selective administrator of our time. But the House of Commons would not let the Commission alone. For a long time it was defended because the Whigs had made the Commission, and felt bound as a party to protect it. The new law started upon a certain intellectual impetus, and till that was spent its administration was supported in a rickety existence by an abnormal strength. But afterwards the Commissioners were left to their intrinsic weaknesses. There were members for all the localities, but there were none for them. There were members for every crotchet and corrupt interest, but there were none for them. The rural guardians would have liked to eke out wages by rates; the city guardians hated control, and hated to spend money. The Commission had to be dissolved, and a parliamentary head was added; the result is not perfect, but it is an amazing improvement on what would have happened in the old system. The new system has not worked well because the central authority has too little power; but under the previous system the central authority was getting to have, and by this time would have had, no power at all. And if Sir George Lewis and Mr Chadwick could not maintain an outlying department in the face of Parliament, how unlikely that an inferior compound of discretion and activity will ever maintain it!

These reasonings show why a changing Parliamentary head, a head changing as the ministry changes, is a necessity of good Parliamentary government, and there is happily a natural provision that there will be such heads. Party organisation ensures it. In America, where on account of the fixedly recurring presidential election, and the perpetual minor elections, party organisation is much more effectually organised than anywhere else, the effect on the offices is tremendous. Every office is filled anew at every presidential change, at least every change which brings in a new party. Not only the greatest posts, as in England, but the minor posts change their occupants. The scale of the financial operations of the Federal government is now so increased that most likely in that department, at least, there must in future remain a permanent element of great efficiency; a revenue of £90,000,000 sterling cannot be collected and expended with a trifling and changing staff. But till now the Americans have tried to get on not only with changing heads to a bureaucracy, as the English, but without any stable bureaucracy at all. They have facilities for trying it which no one else has. All Americans can administer, and the number of them really fit to be in succession lawyers, financiers, or military managers is wonderful; they need not be as afraid of a change of all their officials as European countries must, for the incoming substitutes are sure to be much better there than here; and they do not fear, as we English fear, that the outgoing officials will be left destitute in middle life, with no hope for the future and no recompense for the past, for in America (whatever may be the cause of it) opportunities are numberless, and a man who is ruined by being 'off the rails' in England soon there gets on another line. The Americans will probably to some extent modify their past system of total administrative cataclysms, but their very existence in the only competing form of free government should prepare us for and make us patient with the mild transitions of Parliamentary government.

These arguments will, I think, seem conclusive, to almost every one; but, at this moment, many people will meet them thus: they will say, 'You prove what we do not deny, that this system of periodical change is a necessary ingredient in Parliamentary government, but you have not proved what we do deny, that this change is a good thing. Parliamentary government may have that effect, among others, for anything we care: we maintain merely that it is a defect.' In answer, I think it may be shown not, indeed, that this precise change is necessary to a permanently perfect administration, but that some analogous change, some change of the same species, is so.

At this moment, in England, there is a sort of leaning towards bureaucracy—at least, among writers and talkers. There is a seizure of partiality to it. The English people do not easily change their rooted notions, but they have a vast many unrooted notions. Any great European event is sure for a moment to excite a sort of twinge of conversion to something or other. Just now, the triumph of the Prussians*—the bureaucratic people, as is believed, *par excellence*—has excited a kind of admiration for bureaucracy, which a few years since we should have thought impossible. I do not presume to criticise the Prussian bureaucracy of my own knowledge; it certainly is not a pleasant institution for foreigners to come across, though agreeableness to travellers is but of very second-rate importance. But it is quite certain that the Prussian bureaucracy, though we, for a moment, half admire it at a distance, does not permanently please the most intelligent and liberal Prussians at home. What are two among the principal aims of the *Fortschritt Partei*—the party of progress—as Mr Grant Duff, the most accurate and philosophical of our describers, delineates them?*

First, 'a liberal system, conscientiously carried out in all the details of the administration, with a view to avoiding the scandals now of frequent occurrence, when an obstinate or bigoted official sets at defiance the liberal initiations of the government, trusting to backstairs influence.'

Second, 'an easy method of bringing to justice guilty officials, who are at present, as in France, in all conflicts with simple citizens, like men armed *cap-à-pie** fighting with undefenceless.' A system against which intelligent native liberals bring even with colour of reason such grave objections, is a dangerous model for foreign imitation.

The defects of bureaucracy are, indeed, well known. It is a form of government which has been tried often enough in the world and it is easy to show what, human nature being what it in the long run is, the defects of a bureaucracy must in the long run be.

It is an inevitable defect, that bureaucrats will care more for routine than for results; or, as Burke put it,* 'that they will think the substance of business not to be much more important than the forms of it.' Their whole education and all the habit of their lives make them do so. They are brought young into the particular part of the public service to which they are attached; they are occupied for years in learning its forms—afterwards, for years too, in applying these forms to trifling matters. They are, to use the phrase of an old writer, 'but the tailors of business; they cut the clothes, but they do not find the body.' Men so trained must come to think the routine of business not a means but an end—to imagine the elaborate machinery of which they form a part, and from which they derive their dignity, to be a grand and achieved result, not a working and changeable instrument. But in a miscellaneous world, there is now one evil and now another. The very means which best helped you yesterday, may very likely be those which most impede you tomorrow—you may want to do a different thing tomorrow, and all your accumulation of means for yesterday's work is but an obstacle to the new work. The Prussian military system is the theme of popular wonder now, yet it sixty years pointed the moral against the form. We have all heard the saying that 'Frederic the Great lost the battle of Jena.'* It was the system he had established—a good system for his wants and his times, which, blindly adhered to, and continued into a different age,—put to strive with different competitors,—brought his country to ruin. The 'dead and formal' Prussian system was then contrasted with the 'living' French system—the sudden outcome of the new explosive democracy. The system which now exists is the product of the reaction; and the history of its predecessor is a warning what its future history may be too. It is not more celebrated for its day than Frederic's for his, and principle teaches that a bureaucracy, elated by sudden success, and marvelling at its own merit, is the most improving and shallow of governments.

Not only does a bureaucracy thus tend to under-government, in point of quality; it tends to over-government, in point of quantity. The trained official hates the rude, untrained public. He thinks that they are stupid, ignorant, reckless—that they cannot tell their own interest—that they should have the leave of the office before they do anything. Protection is the natural inborn creed of every official body; free trade is an extrinsic idea, alien to its notions, and hardly to be assimilated with life; and it is easy to see how an accomplished critic, used to a free and active life, could thus describe the official.

'Every imaginable and real social interest,' says Mr Laing,* 'religion, education, law, police, every branch of public or private business, personal liberty to move from place to place, even from parish to parish within the same jurisdiction. Liberty to engage in any branch of trade or industry, on a small or large scale, all the objects, in short, in which body, mind, and capital can be employed in civilised society, were gradually laid hold of for the employment and support of functionaries, were centralised in *bureau*, were superintended, licensed, inspected, reported upon, and interfered with by a host of officials scattered over the land, and maintained at the public expense, yet with no conceivable utility in their duties. They are not, however, gentlemen at large, enjoying salary without service. They are under a semi-military discipline. In Bavaria, for instance, the superior civil functionary can place his inferior functionary under house-arrest, for neglect of duty, or other offence against civil functionary discipline. In Wurtemberg, the functionary cannot marry without leave from his superior. Voltaire says somewhere,* that, "the art of government is to make two-thirds of a nation pay all it possibly can pay for the benefit of the other third." This is realised in Germany by the functionary system. The functionaries are not there for the benefit of the people, but the people for the benefit of the functionaries. All this machinery of functionarism, with its numerous ranks and gradations in every district, filled with a staff of clerks and expectants in every department looking for employment, appointments, or promotions, was intended to be a new support of the throne in the new social state of the Continent; a third class, in connection with the people by their various official duties of interference in all public or private affairs, yet attached by their interests to the kingly power. The *Beamptenstand*, or functionary class, was to be the equivalent to the class of nobility, gentry, capitalists, and men of larger landed property than the peasant-proprietors, and was to make up in numbers for the want of individual weight and influence. In France, at the expulsion of Louis Philippe, the civil functionaries were stated to amount to 807,030 individuals. This civil army was more than double of the military. In Germany, this class is necessarily more numerous in proportion to the population, the landwehr system imposing many more restrictions than the conscription on the free action of the people, and requiring more officials to manage it, and the semi-feudal jurisdictions and forms of law requiring much more writing and intricate forms of procedure before the courts than the Code Napoleon.'

A bureaucracy is sure to think that its duty is to augment official power, official business, or official members, rather than to leave free the energies of mankind; it overdoes the quantity of government, as well as impairs its quality.

The truth is, that a skilled bureaucracy—a bureaucracy trained from early life to its special avocation, is, though it boasts of an appearance of science, quite inconsistent with the true principles of the art of business. That art has not yet been condensed into precepts, but a great many experiments have been made and a vast floating vapour of knowledge floats through society. One of the most sure principles is, that success depends on a due mixture of special and nonspecial minds—of minds which attend to the means, and of minds which attend to the end. The success of the great joint-stock banks of London*—the most remarkable achievement of recent business—has been an example of the use of this mixture. These banks are managed by a board of persons mostly *not* trained to the business, supplemented by, and annexed to, a body of specially trained officers, who have been bred to banking all their lives. These mixed banks have quite beaten the old banks, composed exclusively of pure bankers; it is found that the board of directors has greater and more flexible knowledge—more insight into the wants of a commercial community—knows when to lend and when not to lend, better than the old bankers, who had never looked at life, except out of the bank windows. Just so the most successful railways in Europe have been conducted—not by engineers or by traffic managers—but by capitalists; by men of a certain business culture, if of no other. These capitalists buy and use the services of skilled managers, as the unlearned attorney buys and uses the services of a skilled barrister, and manage far better than any of the different sorts of special men under them. They combine these different specialities—make it clear where the realm of one ends and that of the other begins, add to it a wide knowledge of large affairs, which no special man can have, and which is only gained by diversified action. But this utility of leading minds used to generalise, and acting upon various materials, is entirely dependent upon their position. They must not be at the bottom—they must not even be half way up—they must be at the top. A merchant's clerk would be a child at a bank counter; but the merchant himself could, very likely, give good, clear, and useful advice in a bank court. The merchant clerk would be equally at sea in a railway office, but the merchant himself could give good advice, very likely, at a board of directors. The summits (if I may so say) of the various kinds of business are, like the tops of mountains, much more alike than the parts below—the bare principles are much the same; it is only the rich variegated details of the lower strata that so contrast with one another. But it needs travelling to know that the summits *are* the same. Those who live on one mountain believe that *their* mountain is wholly unlike all others.

The application of this principle to Parliamentary government is very plain; it shows at once that the intrusion from without upon an office of an exterior head of the office, is not an evil; but that, on the contrary, it is essential to the perfection of that office. If it is left to itself, the office will become technical, self-absorbed, self-multiplying. It will be likely to overlook the end in the means; it will fail from narrowness of mind; it will be eager in seeming to do; it will be idle in real doing. An extrinsic chief is the fit corrector of such errors. He can say to the permanent chief, skilled in the forms and pompous with the memories of his office, 'Will you, sir, explain to me how this regulation conduces to the end in view? According to the natural view of things, the applicant should state the whole of his wishes to one clerk on one paper; you make him say it to five clerks on five papers.' Or, again, 'Does it not appear to you, sir, that the reason of this formality is extinct? When we were building wood ships, it was quite right to have such precautions against fire; but now that we are building iron ships,' &c, &c. If a junior clerk asked these questions, he would be 'pooh-poohed!' It is only the head of an office that can get them answered. It is he, and he only, that brings the rubbish of office to the burning-glass of sense.

The immense importance of such a fresh mind is greatest in a country where business changes most. A dead, inactive, agricultural country may be governed by an unalterable bureau for years and years, and no harm come of it. If a wise man arranged the bureau rightly in the beginning, it may run rightly a long time. But, if the country be a progressive, eager, changing one, soon the bureau will either cramp improvement, or be destroyed itself.

This conception of the use of a Parliamentary head shows how wrong is the obvious notion which regards him as the principal administrator of his office. The late Sir George Lewis* used to be fond of explaining this subject. He had every means of knowing. He was bred in the permanent civil service. He was a very successful Chancellor of the Exchequer, a very successful Home Secretary, and he died Minister for War. He used to say, 'It is not the business of a Cabinet Minister to work his department. His business is to see that it is properly worked. If he does much, he is probably doing harm. The permanent staff of the office do what he chooses to do much better, or if they cannot, they ought to be removed. He is only a bird of passage, and cannot compete with those who are in the office all their lives round.' Sir George Lewis was a perfect Parliamentary head of an office, so far as that head is to be a keen critic and rational corrector of it.

Sir George Lewis was not perfect: he was not even an average good head in another respect. The use of a fresh mind applied to the official mind is not only a corrective use: it is also an animating use. A public department is very apt to be dead to what is wanting for a great occasion till the occasion is past. The vague public mind will appreciate some signal duty before the precise, occupied administration perceives it. The Duke of Newcastle was of this use at least in the Crimean war.* He roused up his department, though when roused it could not act. A perfect parliamentary minister would be one who should add the animating capacity of the Duke of Newcastle to the accumulated sense, the detective instinct, and the *laissez faire* habit of Sir George Lewis.

As soon as we take the true view of Parliamentary office we shall perceive that, fairly, frequent change in the official is an advantage, not a mistake. If his function is to bring a representative of outside sense and outside animation in contact with the inside world, he ought often to be changed. No man is a perfect representative of outside sense. 'There is some one,' says the true French saying, 'who is more able than Talleyrand, more able than Napoleon. *C'est tout le monde*.' That many-sided sense finds no microcosm in any single individual. Still less are the critical function and the animating function of a Parliamentary minister likely to be perfectly exercised by one and the same man. Impelling power and restraining wisdom are as opposite as any two things, and are rarely found together. And even if the natural mind of the Parliamentary minister was perfect, long contact with the office would destroy his use. Inevitably he would accept the ways of office, think its thoughts, live its life. The 'dyer's hand would be subdued to what it works in.'* If the function of a Parliamentary minister is to be an outsider to his office, we must not choose one who, by habit, thought, and life, is acclimatised to its ways.

There is every reason to expect that a Parliamentary statesman will be a man of quite sufficient intelligence, quite enough various knowledge, quite enough miscellaneous experience, to represent effectually general sense in opposition to bureaucratic sense. Most Cabinet ministers in charge of considerable departments are men of superior ability. I have heard an eminent living statesman of long experience say that in his time he only knew one instance to the contrary. And there is the best protection that it shall be so. A considerable Cabinet minister has to defend his Department in the face of mankind; and though distant observers and sharp writers may depreciate it, this is a very difficult thing. A fool, who has publicly to explain great affairs, who has publicly to answer detective questions, who has publicly to argue against able and quick opponents, must soon be shown to be a fool. The very nature of Parliamentary government answers for the discovery of substantial incompetence.

At any rate, none of the competing forms of government have nearly so effectual a procedure for putting a good untechnical minister to correct and impel the routine ones. There are but four important forms of government in the present state of the world,—the Parliamentary, the Presidential, the Hereditary, and the Dictatorial, or Revolutionary. Of these I have shown that, as now worked in America, the Presidential form of government is incompatible with a skilled bureaucracy. If the whole official class change when a new party goes out or comes in, a good official system is impossible. Even if more officials should be permanent in America than now, still, vast numbers will always be changed. The whole issue is based on a single election—on the choice of President; by that internecine conflict all else is won or lost. The managers of the contest have that greatest possible facility in using what I may call patronage-bribery. Everybody knows that, as a fact, the President can give what places he likes to what persons, and when his friends tell A. B., 'If we win C. D. shall be turned out of Utica Post-office, and you, A. B., shall have it,'

A. B. believes it, and is justified in doing so. But no individual member of Parliament can promise place effectually. *He* may not be able to give the places. His party may come in, but he will be powerless. In the United States party intensity is aggravated, by concentrating and overwhelming importance on a single contest, and the efficiency of promised offices as a means of corruption is augmented, because the victor can give what he likes to whom he likes.

Nor is this the only defect of a Presidential government in reference to the choice of officers. The President has the principal anomaly of a Parliamentary government without having its corrective. At each change of party the President distributes (as here) the principal offices to his principal supporters. But he has an opportunity for singular favouritism. The minister lurks in the office; he need do nothing in public; he need not show for years whether he is a fool or wise. The nation can tell what a Parliamentary member is by the open test of Parliament; but no one, save from actual contact, or by rare position, can tell anything certain of a Presidential minister.

The case of a minister under an hereditary form of government is yet worse. The hereditary king may be weak; may be under the government of women; may appoint a minister from childish motives, may remove one from absurd whims. There is no security that an hereditary king will be competent to choose a good chief minister, and thousands of such kings have chosen millions of bad ministers.

By the Dictatorial, or Revolutionary, sort of government, I mean that very important sort in which the sovereign—the absolute sovereign—is selected by insurrection. In theory, one would have certainly hoped that by this time such a crude elective machinery would have been reduced to a secondary part. But, in fact, the greatest nation (or, perhaps, after the exploits of Bismarck, I should say one of the two greatest nations of the Continent) vacillates between the Revolutionary and the Parliamentary, and now is governed under the revolutionary form. France elects its ruler in the streets of Paris. Flatterers may suggest that the democratic empire will become hereditary, but close observers know that it cannot. The idea of the government is that the Emperor represents the people in capacity, in judgment, in instinct. But no family through generations can have sufficient, or half sufficient, mind to do so. The representative despot must be chosen by fighting, as Napoleon I and Napoleon III were chosen. And such a government is likely, whatever be its other defects, to have a far better and abler administration than any other government. The head of the government must be a man of the most consummate ability. He cannot keep his place, he can hardly keep his life, unless he' is. He is sure to be active, because he knows that his power, and perhaps his head, may be lost if he be negligent. The whole frame of his State is strained to keep down revolution. The most difficult of all political problems is to be solved—the people are to be at once thoroughly restrained and thoroughly pleased. The executive must be like a steel shirt of the middle ages—extremely hard and extremely flexible. It must give way to attractive novelties which do not hurt; it must resist such as are dangerous; it must maintain old things which are good and fitting; it must alter such as cramp and give pain. The dictator dare not appoint a bad minister if he would. I admit that such a despot is a better selector of administrators than a parliament; that he will know how to mix fresh minds and used minds better; that he is under a stronger motive to combine them well; that here is to be seen the best of all choosers with the keenest motives to choose. But I need not prove in England that the revolutionary selection of rulers obtains administrative efficiency at a price altogether transcending its value; that it shocks credit by its catastrophes; that for intervals it does not protect property or life; that it maintains an undergrowth of fear through all prosperity; that it may take years to find the true capable despot; that the interregna of the incapable are full of all evil; that the fit despot may die as soon as found; that the good administration and all else hang by the thread of his life.

But if, with the exception of this terrible, revolutionary government, a Parliamentary government upon principle surpasses all its competitors in administrative efficiency, why is it that our English Government, which is beyond comparison the best of Parliamentary governments, is not celebrated through the world for administrative efficiency? It is noted for many things, why is it not noted for that? Why, according to popular belief, is it rather characterised by the very contrary?

One great reason of the diffused impression is, that the English Government attempts so much. Our military system is that which is most attacked. Objectors say we spend much more on our army than the great military monarchies, and yet with an inferior result. But, then, what we attempt, is incalculably more difficult. The continental monarchies have only to defend compact European territories by the many soldiers whom they force to fight; the English try to defend without any compulsion—only by such soldiers as they persuade to serve—territories far surpassing all Europe in magnitude, and situated all over the habitable globe. Our Horse Guards and War Office may not be at all perfect—I believe they are not; but if they had sufficient recruits selected by force of law—if they had, as in Prussia, the absolute command of each man's time for a few years, and the right to call him out afterwards when they liked, we should be much surprised at the sudden ease and quickness with which they did things. I have no doubt too that any accomplished soldier of the Continent would reject as possible what we after a fashion effect. He would not attempt to defend a vast scattered empire, with many islands, a long frontier line in every continent, and a very tempting bit of plunder at the centre, by mere volunteer recruits who mostly come from the worst class of the people,—whom the Great Duke* called the 'scum of the earth,'—who come in uncertain numbers year by year,—who by some political accident may not come in adequate numbers, or at all, in the year we need them most. Our War Office attempts what foreign War Offices (perhaps rightly) would not try at; their officers have means of incalculable force denied to ours, though ours is set to harder tasks.

Again, the English navy undertakes to defend a line of coast and a set of dependencies far surpassing those of any continental power. And the extent of our operations is a singular difficulty just now. It requires us to keep a large stock of ships and arms. But on the other hand, there are most important reasons why we should not keep much. The naval art and the military art are both in a state of transition; the last discovery of today is out of date and superseded by an antagonistic discovery tomorrow. Any large accumulation of vessels or guns is sure to contain much that will be useless, unfitting, antediluvian, when it comes to be tried. There are two cries against the Admiralty which go on side by side: one says, 'We have not ships enough, no "relief" ships, no *navy*, to tell the truth;' the other cry says, 'We have all the wrong ships, all the wrong guns, and nothing but the wrong; in their foolish constructive mania the Admiralty have been building when they ought to have been waiting; they have heaped a curious museum of exploded inventions, but they have given us nothing serviceable.' The two cries for opposite policies go on together, and blacken our Executive together, though each is a defence of the Executive against the other.

Again, the Home Department in England struggles with difficulties of which abroad they have long got rid. We love independent 'local authorities,' little centres of outlying authority. When the metropolitan executive most wishes to act, it cannot act effectually because these lesser bodies hesitate, deliberate, or even disobey. But local independence has no necessary connection with Parliamentary government. The degree of local freedom desirable in a country varies according to many circumstances, and a Parliamentary government may consist with any degree of it. We certainly ought not to debit Parliamentary government as a general and applicable polity with the particular vices of the guardians of the poor in England, though it is so debited every day.

Again, as our administration has in England this peculiar difficulty, so on the other hand foreign competing administrations have a peculiar advantage. Abroad a man under Government is a superior being; he is higher than the rest of the world; he is envied by almost all of it. This gives the Government the easy pick of the *élite* of the nation. All clever people are eager to be under Government, and are hardly to be satisfied elsewhere. But in England there is no such superiority, and the English have no such feeling. We do not respect a stamp-office clerk, or an exciseman's assistant. A pursy grocer considers he is much above either. Our Government cannot buy for minor clerks the best ability of the nation in the cheap currency of pure honour, and no government is rich enough to buy very much of it in money. Our mercantile opportunities allure away the most ambitious minds. The foreign *bureaux* are filled with a selection from the ablest men of the nation, but only a very few of the best men approach the English offices.

But these are neither the only nor even the principal reasons why our public administration is not so good, as, according to principle and to the unimpeded effects of Parliamentary government, it should be. There are two great causes at work, which in their consequence run out into many details, but which in their fundamental nature may be briefly described. The first of these causes is our ignorance. No polity can get out of a nation more than there is in the nation. A free government is essentially a government by persuasion;

and as are the people to be persuaded, and as are the persuaders, so will that government be. On many parts of our administration the effect of our extreme ignorance is at once plain. The foreign policy of England has for many years been, according to the judgment now in vogue, inconsequent, fruitless, casual; aiming at no distinct pre-imagined end, based on no steadily preconceived principle. I have not room to discuss with how much or how little abatement this decisive censure should be accepted. However, I entirely concede that our recent foreign policy has been open to very grave and serious blame. But would it not have been a miracle if the English people, directing their own policy, and being what they are, had directed a good policy? Are they not, above all nations, divided from the rest of the world, insular both in situation and in mind, both for good and for evil? Are they not out of the current of common European causes and affairs? Are they not a race contemptuous of others? Are they not a race with no special education or culture as to this modern world, and too often despising such culture? Who could expect such a people to comprehend the new and strange events of foreign places? So far from wondering that the English Parliament has been inefficient in foreign policy, I think it is wonderful, and another sign of the rude, vague imagination that is at the bottom of our people, that we have done so well as we have.

Again, the very conception of the English Constitution, as distinguished from a purely Parliamentary constitution is, that it contains 'dignified' parts—parts, that is, retained, not for their intrinsic use, but from their imaginative attraction upon an uncultured and rude population. All such elements tend to diminish simple efficiency. They are like the additional and solely-ornamental wheels introduced into the clocks of the middle ages, which tell the then age of the moon or the supreme constellation;—which make little men or birds come out and in theatrically. All such ornamental work is a source of friction and error; it prevents the time being marked on accurately; each new wheel is a new source of imperfection. So if authority is given to a person, not on account of his working fitness, but on account of his imaginative efficiency, he will commonly impair good administration. He may do something better than good work of detail, but will spoil good work of detail. The English aristocracy is often of this sort. It has an influence over the people of vast value still, and of infinite value formerly. But no man would select the cadets of an aristocratic house as desirable administrators. They have peculiar disadvantages in the acquisition of business knowledge, business training, and business habits, and they have no peculiar advantages.

Our middle class, too, is very unfit to give us the administrators we ought to have. I cannot now discuss whether all that is said against our education is well grounded; it is called by an excellent judge 'pretentious, insufficient, and unsound.'* But I will say that it does not fit men to be men of business as it ought to fit them. Till lately the very simple attainments and habits necessary for a banker's clerk had a scarcity-value. The sort of education which fits a man for the higher posts of practical life is still very rare; there is not even a good agreement as to what it is. Our public officers cannot be as good as the corresponding officers of some foreign nations till our business education is as good as theirs.

But strong as is our ignorance in deteriorating our administration, another cause is stronger still. There are but two foreign administrations probably better than ours, and both these have had something which we have not had. Theirs in both cases were arranged by a man of genius, after careful forethought, and upon a special design. Napoleon built upon a clear stage which the French Revolution bequeathed him. The originality once ascribed to his edifice was indeed untrue; Tocqueville and Lavergne have shown that he did but run up a conspicuous structure in imitation of a latent one before concealed by the medieval complexities of the old *régime*.* But what we are concerned with now, is not Napoleon's originality, but his work. He undoubtedly settled the administration of France upon an effective, consistent, and enduring system; the succeeding governments have but worked the mechanism inherited from him. Frederic the Great did the same in the new monarchy of Prussia. Both the French system and the Prussian are new machines, made in civilised times to do their appropriate work.

The English offices have never, since they were made, been arranged with any reference to one another; or rather they were never made, but grew as each could. The sort of free-trade which prevailed in public institutions in the English middle ages is very curious. Our three courts of law—the Queen's Bench, the Common Pleas, and the Exchequer—for the sake of the fees extended an originally contracted sphere into the entire sphere of litigation. *Boni* *judicis est ampliare jurisdictionem*, went the old saying; or, in English, 'It is the mark of a good judge to augment the fees of his court,' his own income, and the income of his subordinates. The central administration, the Treasury, never asked any account of the moneys the courts thus received; so long as it was not asked to pay anything, it was satisfied. Only last year one of the many remnants of this system cropped-up, to the wonder of the public. A clerk in the Patent Office stole some fees, naturally the men of the nineteenth century thought our principal finance minister, the Chancellor of the Exchequer, would be, as in France, responsible for it. But the English law was different somehow. The Patent Office was under the Lord Chancellor, and the Court of Chancery is one of the multitude of our institutions which owe their existence to fee competition,— and so it was the Lord Chancellor's business to look after the fees, which of course, as an occupied judge, he could not. A certain Act of Parliament did indeed require that the fees of the Patent Office should be paid into the 'Exchequer;' and, again, the 'Chancellor of Exchequer,' was thought to be responsible in the matter, but only by those who did not know. According to our system the Chancellor of the Exchequer is the enemy of the Exchequer; a whole series of enactments try to protect it from him. Until a few months ago there was a very lucrative sinecure called the 'Comptrollership of the Exchequer,'*—designed to guard the Exchequer against its Chancellor, and the last holder, Lord Monteagle, used to say he was the pivot of the English Constitution. I have not room to explain what he meant, and it is not needful; what is to the purpose is that, by an inherited series of historical complexities, a defaulting clerk in an office of no litigation, was not under the natural authority, the finance minister, but under a far-away judge who had never heard of him.

The whole office of the Lord Chancellor is a heap of anomalies. He is a judge, and it is contrary to obvious principle that any part of administration should be entrusted to a judge; it is of very grave moment that the administration of justice should be kept clear of sinister temptations. Yet the Lord Chancellor, our chief judge, sits in the Cabinet, and makes party speeches in the Lords. Lord Lyndhurst was a principal Tory politician, and yet he presided in the O'Connell case.* Lord Westbury was in chronic wrangle with the bishops, but he gave judgment upon 'Essays and Reviews.'* In truth, the Lord Chancellor became a Cabinet Minister because, being near the person of the sovereign, he was high in court precedence, and not upon a political theory, wrong or right.

A friend once told me that an intelligent Italian asked him about the principal English officers, and that he was very puzzled to explain their duties, and especially to explain the relation of their duties to their titles. I do not remember all the cases, but I can recollect that the Italian could not comprehend why the First 'Lord of the Treasury' had as a rule nothing to do with the Treasury, or why the 'Woods and Forests' looked after the sewerage of towns. This conversation was years before the cattle plague, but I should like to have heard the reasons why the Privy Council office had charge of that malady. Of course one could give a historical reason, but I mean an administrative reason—a reason which would show, not how it came to have the duty, but why in future it should keep it.

But the unsystematic and casual arrangement of our public offices is not more striking than their difference of arrangement for the one purpose they have in common. They all, being under the ultimate direction of a Parliamentary official, ought to have the best means of bringing the whole of the higher concerns of the office before that official. When the fresh mind rules, the fresh mind requires to be informed. And most business being rather alike, the machinery for bringing it before the extrinsic chief ought, for the most part, to be similar; at any rate, where it is different, it ought to be different upon reason, and where it is similar, similar upon reason. Yet there are almost no two offices which are exactly alike in the defined relationship of the permanent official to the Parliamentary chief. Let us see. The *army and navy* are the most similar in nature, yet there is in the army a permanent office, called the Horse Guards, to which there is nothing else like. In the navy, there is a curious anomaly—a Board of Admiralty, also changing with every government, which is to instruct the First Lord in what he does not know. The relations between the First Lord and the Board have not always been easily intelligible, and those between the War Office and the Horse Guards are in extreme confusion. Even now a Parliamentary paper relating to them has just been presented to the House of Commons, which says that the fundamental and ruling document cannot be traced beyond the possession of Sir George Lewis, who was Secretary for War three years since; and the confused details are endless, as they must be in a chronic contention of offices. At the *Board of Trade* there is only the hypothesis of a Board; it has long ceased to exist. Even the President and Vice-President do not regularly meet for the transaction of affairs. The patent of the latter is only to transact business in the absence of the President, and if the two are not intimate, and the President chooses to act himself, the Vice-President sees no papers and does nothing. At the *Treasury* the shadow of a Board exists, but its members have no power, and are the very officials whom Canning said existed to make a House, to keep a House, and to cheer the ministers. The *India Office* has a fixed 'Council;' but the *Colonial Office*, which rules over our other dependencies and colonies, has not, and never had, the vestige of a council. *Any* of these various Constitutions may be right, but all of them can scarcely be right.

In truth the real constitution of a permanent office to be ruled by a permanent chief has been discussed only once in England, that case was a peculiar and anomalous one, and the decision then taken was dubious. A new India Office when the East Company was abolished, had to be made.* The late Mr James Wilson,* a consummate judge of administrative affairs, then maintained that no council ought to be appointed *eo nomine*,* but that the true Council of a Cabinet minister was a certain number of highly paid, much occupied, responsible secretaries, whom the minister could consult, either separately or together, as, and when, he chose. Such secretaries, Mr Wilson maintained, must be able, for no minister will sacrifice his own convenience, and endanger his own reputation by appointing a fool to a post so near himself, and where he can do so much harm. A member of a Board may easily be incompetent; if some other members and the chairman are able, the addition of one or two stupid men will not be felt; they will receive their salaries and do nothing. But a permanent under-secretary, charged with a real control over much important business, must be able, or his superior will be blamed, and there will be 'a scrape in Parliament.'

I cannot here discuss, nor am I competent to discuss, the best mode of composing public offices, and of adjusting them to a Parliamentary head. There ought be on record skilled evidence on the subject before a person without specific experience can to any purpose think about it. But I may observe that the plan which Mr Wilson suggested is that followed in the most successful part of our administration, the 'Ways and Means' part. When the Chancellor of the Exchequer prepares a Budget, he requires from the responsible heads of the revenue department their estimates of the public revenue upon the preliminary hypothesis that no change is made, but that last year's taxes will continue; if, afterwards, he thinks of making an alteration, he requires a report on that too. If he has to renew Exchequer bills, or operate anyhow in the City, he takes the opinion, oral or written, of the ablest and most responsible person at the National Debt Office, and the ablest and most responsible at the Treasury. Mr Gladstone, by far the greatest Chancellor of the Exchequer of this generation, one of the very greatest of any generation, has often gone out of his way to express his obligation to these responsible skilled advisers. The more a man knows himself, the more habituated he is to action in general, the more sure he is to take and to value responsible counsel emanating from ability and suggested by experience. That this principle brings good fruit is certain. We have by unequivocal admission—the best budget in the world. Why should not the rest of our administration be as good if we did but apply the same method to it?

8

ITS SUPPOSED CHECKS AND BALANCES

IN a former essay I devoted an elaborate discussion to the comparison of the royal and the unroyal form of Parliamentary Government. I showed that at the formation of a ministry, and during the continuance of a ministry, a really sagacious monarch might be of rare use. I ascertained that it was a mistake to fancy that at such times a constitutional monarch had no *rôle* and no duties. But I proved likewise that the temper, the disposition, and the faculties then needful to fit a constitutional monarch for usefulness were very rare, at least as rare as the faculties of a great absolute monarch, and that a common man in that place is apt to do at least as much harm as good—perhaps more harm. But in that essay I could not discuss fully the functions of a king at the conclusion of an administration, for then the most peculiar parts of the English government—the power to dissolve the House of Commons, the power to create new peers—come into play, and until the nature of the House of Lords and the nature of the House of Commons had been explained, I had no premises for an argument as to the characteristic action of the king upon them. We have since considered the functions of the two houses, and also the effects of changes of ministry on our administrative system; we are now, therefore, in a position to discuss the functions of a king at the end of an administration.

I may seem over formal in this matter, but I am very formal on purpose. It appears to me that the functions of our executive in dissolving the Commons and augmenting the Peers are among the most important, and the least appreciated, parts of our whole government, and that hundreds of errors have been made in copying the English constitution from not comprehending them.

Hobbes told us long ago,* and everybody now understands that there must be a supreme authority, a conclusive power in every state on every point somewhere. The idea of government involves it—when that idea is properly understood. But there are two classes of government. In one the supreme determining power is upon all points the same; in the other, that ultimate power is different upon different points—now resides in one part of the constitution, and now in another. The Americans thought that they were imitating the English in making their constitution upon the last principle—in having one ultimate authority for one sort of matter, and another for another sort. But in truth, the English constitution is the type of the opposite species; it has only one authority for all sorts of matters. To gain a living conception of the difference let us see what the Americans did.

First, they altogether retained what, in part, they could not help, the sovereignty of the separate states. A fundamental article of the Federal constitution* says powers not 'delegated' to the central government are 'reserved to the states respectively.' And the whole recent history of the Union—perhaps all its history—has been more determined by that enactment than by any other single cause. The sovereignty of the principal matters of state has rested not with the highest government, but with the subordinate governments. The Federal government could not touch slavery—the 'domestic institution' which divided the Union into two halves, unlike one another in morals, politics, and social condition, and at last set them to fight. This determining political fact was not in the jurisdiction of the highest government in the country, where you might expect its highest wisdom, nor in the central government, where you might look for impartiality; but in local governments, where petty interests were sure to be considered, and where only inferior abilities were likely to be employed. The capital fact was observed for the minor jurisdictions. Again there has been only one matter comparable to slavery in the United States, and that has been vitally affected by the State governments also. Their ultra-democracy is not a result of Federal legislation, but of State legislation. The Federal constitution deputed one of the main items of its structure to the subordinate governments. One of its clauses provides that the suffrage for the Federal House of Representatives shall be, in each State, the same as for the most numerous branch of the legislature of that State; and as each State fixes the suffrage for its own legislatures, the States altogether fix the suffrage for the Federal Lower Chamber. By another clause of the Federal constitution the States fix the electoral qualification for voting at a Presidential election. The primary element in a free government—the determination how many people shall have a share in it—in America depends not on the government but on certain subordinate local, and sometimes, as in the South now, hostile bodies.

Doubtless the framers of the constitution had not much choice in the matter. The wisest of them were anxious to get as much power for the central government, and to leave as little to the local governments as they could. But a cry was got up that this wisdom would create a tyranny and impair freedom, and with that help, local jealousy triumphed easily. All Federal government is, in truth, a case in which what I have called the dignified elements of government do not coincide with the serviceable elements. At the beginning of every league the separate States are the old governments which attract and keep the love and loyalty of the people; the Federal government is a useful thing, but new and unattractive. It must concede much to the State governments, for it is indebted to them for motive power: they are the governments which the people voluntarily obey. When the State governments are not thus loved, they vanish as the little Italian and the little German potentates vanished; no federation is needed; a single central government rules all.

But the division of the sovereign authority in the American constitution is far more complex than this. The part of that authority left to the Federal government is itself divided and subdivided. The greatest instance is the most obvious. The Congress rules the law, but the President rules the administration. One means of unity the constitution does give; the President can veto laws he does not like. But when two-thirds of both houses are unanimous (as has lately happened), they can overrule the President and make the laws without him: so here there are three separate repositories of the legislative power in different cases: first, Congress and the President when they agree; next, the President when he effectually exerts his power; then the requisite two-thirds of Congress when they overrule the President. And the President need not be over-active in carrying out a law he does not approve of. He may indeed be impeached for gross neglect; but between criminal non-feasance and zealous activity there are infinite degrees. Mr Johnson* does not carry out the Freedmen's Bureau Bill as Mr Lincoln, who approved of it, would have carried it out. The American constitution has a special contrivance for varying the supreme legislative authority in different cases, and dividing the administrative authority from it in all cases.

But the administrative power itself is not left thus simple and undivided. One most important part of administration is international policy, and the supreme authority here is not in the President, still less in the House of Representatives, but in the Senate. The President can only make treaties, 'provided two-thirds of Senators present' concur. The sovereignty therefore for the greatest international questions is in a different part of the State altogether from any common administrative or legislative question. It is put in a place by itself.

Again, the Congress declares war, but they would find it very difficult, according to the recent construction of their laws, to compel the President to make a peace. The authors of the constitution doubtless tended that Congress should be able to control the American executive as our Parliament controls ours. They placed the granting of supplies in the House of Representatives exclusively. But they forgot to look after 'paper money;' and now it has been held that the President has power to emit such money without consulting Congress at all. The first part of the late war was so carried on by Mr Lincoln; he relied not on the grants of Congress, but on the prerogative of emission. It sounds a joke, but it is true nevertheless, that this power to issue greenbacks is decided to belong to the President as commander-in-chief of the army; it is part of what was called the 'war power.' In truth, money was wanted in the late war, and the administration got it in the readiest way; and the nation, glad not to be more taxed, wholly approved of it. But the fact remains that the President has now, by precedent and decision, a mighty power to continue a war without the consent of Congress, and perhaps against its wish. Against the united will of the American *people* a President would of course be impotent; such is the genius of the place and nation that he would never think of it. But when the nation was (as of late) divided into two parties, one cleaving to the President the other to the Congress, the now unquestionable power of the President to issue paper money may give him the power to continue the war though Parliament (as we should speak) may enjoin the war to cease.

And lastly, the whole region of the very highest questions is withdrawn from the ordinary authorities of the State, and reserved for special authorities. The 'constitution' cannot be altered by any authorities within the constitution, but only by authorities without it. Every alteration of it, however urgent or trifling, must be sanctioned by a complicated proportion of States or legislatures. The consequence is that the most obvious evils cannot be quickly remedied;

that the most absurd fictions must be framed to evade the plain sense of mischievous clauses; that a clumsy working and curious technicality mark the politics of a rough and ready people, The practical arguments and the legal disquisitions in America are often like those of trustees carrying out a misdrawn will—the sense of what they mean is good, but it can never be worked out fully or defended simply, so hampered is it by the old words of an odd testament.

These instances (and others might be added) prove, as history proves too, what was the principal thought of the American constitution-makers. They shrank from placing sovereign power anywhere. They feared that it would generate tyranny; George III had been a tyrant to them; and come what might, they would not make a George III. Accredited theories said that the English Constitution divided the sovereign authority, and in imitation the Americans split up theirs.

The result is seen now. At the critical moment of their history there is no ready, deciding power. The South, after a great rebellion, lies at the feet of its conquerors; its conquerors have to settle what to do with it. They must decide the conditions upon which the Secessionists shall again become fellow citizens, shall again vote, again be represented, again perhaps govern. The most difficult of problems is how to change late foes into free friends. The safety of their great public debt, and with that debt their future credit and their whole power in future wars, may depend on their not giving too much power to those who must see in the debt the cost of their own subjugation, and who must have an inclination towards the repudiation of it, now that their own debt,—the cost of their defence—has been repudiated. A race, too, formerly enslaved, is now at the mercy of men who hate and despise it, and those who set it free are bound to give it a fair chance for new life. The slave was formerly protected by his chains; he was an article of value; but now he belongs to himself, no one but himself has an interest in his life; and he is at the mercy of the 'mean whites,' whose labour he depreciates, and who regard him with a loathing hatred. The greatest moral duty ever set before a government, and the most fearful political problem ever set before a government, are now set before the American. But there is no decision, and no possibility of a decision. The President wants one course, and has power to prevent any other; the

Congress wants another course, and has power to prevent any other. The splitting of sovereignty into many parts amounts to there being no sovereign.

The Americans of 1787 thought they were copying the English Constitution, but they were contriving a contrast to it. Just as the American is the type of *composite* governments, in which the supreme power is divided between many bodies and functionaries, the English is the type of *simple* constitutions, in which the ultimate power upon all questions is in the hands of the same persons.

The ultimate authority in the English Constitution is a newly-elected House of Commons. No matter whether the question upon which it decides be administrative or legislative; no matter whether it concerns high matters of the essential constitution or small matters of daily detail; no matter whether it be a question of making a war or continuing a war; no matter whether it be the imposing a tax or the issuing a paper currency; no matter whether it be a question relating to India, or Ireland, or London,—a new House of Commons can despotically and finally resolve.

The House of Commons may, as was explained, assent in minor matters to the revision of the House of Lords, and submit in matters about which it cares little to the suspensive veto of the House of Lords; but when sure of the popular assent, and when freshly elected, it is absolute,—it can rule as it likes and decide as it likes. And it can take the best security that it does not decide in vain. It can ensure that its decrees shall be executed, for it, and it alone, appoints the executive; it can inflict the most severe of all penalties on neglect, for it can remove the executive. It can choose, to effect its wishes, those who wish the same; and so its will is sure to be done. A stipulated majority of both Houses of the American Congress can overrule by stated enactment their executive; but the popular branch of our legislature can make and unmake ours.

The English constitution, in a word, is framed on the principle of choosing a single sovereign authority, and making it good: the American, upon the principle of having many sovereign authorities, and hoping that their multitude may atone for their inferiority. The Americans now extol their institutions, and so defraud themselves of their due praise. But if they had not a genius for politics; if they had not a moderation in action singularly curious where superficial speech is so violent; if they had not a regard for law, such as no great people have yet evinced, and infinitely surpassing ours,—the multiplicity of authorities in the American Constitution would long ago have brought it to a bad end. Sensible shareholders, I have heard a shrewd attorney say, can work *any* deed of settlement; and so the men of Massachusetts could, I believe, work *any* constitution.[1] But political philosophy must analyse political history; it must distinguish what is due to the excellence of the people, and what to the excellence of the laws; it must carefully calculate the exact effect of each part of the constitution, though thus it may destroy many an idol of the multitude, and detect the secret of utility where but few imagined it to lie.

How important singleness and unity are in political action no one, I imagine, can doubt. We may distinguish and define its parts; but policy is a unit and a whole. It acts by laws—by administrators; it requires now one, now the other; unless it can easily move both it will be impeded soon; unless it has an absolute command of both its work will be imperfect. The interlaced character of human affairs requires a single determining energy; a distinct force for each artificial compartment will make but a motley patchwork, if it live long enough to make anything. The excellence of the British Constitution is, that it has achieved this unity; that in it the sovereign power is single, possible, and good.

The success is primarily due to the peculiar provision of the English Constitution, which places the choice of the executive in the 'people's house;' but it could not have been thoroughly achieved except for two parts, which I venture to call the 'safety-valve' of the constitution, and the 'regulator.'

The safety-valve is the peculiar provision of the constitution, of which I spoke at great length in my essay on the House of Lords. The head of the executive can overcome the resistance of the second chamber by choosing new members of that chamber; if he do not find a majority, he can make a majority. This is a safety-valve of the truest kind. It enables the popular will—the will of which the executive is the exponent, the will of which it is the appointee—to carry out within the constitution desires and conceptions which one

---

[1] Of course I am not speaking here of the South and South-East, as they now are. How any free government is to exist in societies where so many bad elements are so much perturbed, I cannot imagine.

branch of the constitution dislikes and resists. It lets forth a dangerous accumulation of inhibited power, which might sweep this constitution before it, as like accumulations have often swept away like constitutions.

The regulator, as I venture to call it, of our single sovereignty is the power of dissolving the otherwise sovereign chamber confided to the chief executive. The defects of the popular branch of a legislature as a sovereign have been expounded at length in a previous essay. Briefly, they may be summed up in three accusations.

First. Caprice is the commonest and most formidable vice of a choosing chamber. Wherever in our colonies parliamentary government is unsuccessful, or is alleged to be unsuccessful, this is the vice which first impairs it. The assembly cannot be induced to maintain any administration; it shifts its selection now from one minister to another minister, and in consequence there is not government at all.

Secondly. The very remedy for such caprice entails another evil. The only mode by which a cohesive majority and a lasting administration can be upheld in a Parliamentary government, is party organisation; but that organisation itself tends to aggravate party violence and party animosity. It is, in substance, subjecting the whole nation to the rule of a section of the nation, selected because of its speciality. Parliamentary government is, in its essence, a sectarian government, and is possible only when sects are cohesive.

Thirdly. A Parliament, like every other sort of sovereign, has peculiar feelings, peculiar prejudices, peculiar interests; and it may pursue these in opposition to the desires, and even in opposition to the well-being of the nation. It has its selfishness as well as its caprice and its parties.

The mode in which the regulating wheel of our constitution produces its effect is plain. It does not impair the authority of Parliament as a species, but it impairs the power of the individual Parliament. It enables a particular person outside parliament to say, 'You members of Parliament are not doing your duty. You are gratifying caprice at the cost of the nation. You are indulging party spirit at the cost of the nation. You are helping yourselves at the cost of the nation. I will see whether the nation approves what you are doing or not; I will appeal from Parliament No. 1 to Parliament No. 2.'

By far the best way to appreciate this peculiar provision of our constitution is to trace it in action,—to see, as we saw before of the other powers of English royalty, how far it is dependent on the existence of an hereditary king, and how far it can be exercised by a premier whom Parliament elects. When we examine the nature of the particular person required to exercise the power, a vivid idea of that power is itself brought home to us.

First. As to the caprice of parliament in the choice of a premier, who is the best person to check it? clearly the premier himself. He is the person most interested in maintaining his administration, and therefore the most likely person to use efficiently and dextrously the power by which it is maintained. The intervention of an extrinsic king occasions a difficulty. A capricious Parliament may always hope that his caprice may coincide with theirs. In the days when George III assailed his governments, the premier was habitually deprived of his due authority. Intrigues were encouraged because it was always dubious whether the king-hated minister would be permitted to appeal from the intriguers, and always a chance that the conspiring monarch might appoint one of the conspirators to be premier in his room. The caprice of Parliament is better checked when the faculty of dissolution is intrusted to its appointee, than when it is set apart in an outlying and alien authority.

But, on the contrary, the party zeal and the self-seeking of Parliament are best checked by an authority which has no connection with Parliament or dependence upon it—supposing that such authority is morally and intellectually equal to the performance of the intrusted function. The Prime Minister obviously being the nominee of a party majority is likely to share its feeling, and is sure to be obliged to *say* that he shares it. The actual contact with affairs is indeed likely to purify him from many prejudices, to tame him of many fanaticisms, to beat out of him many errors. The present Conservative Government contains more than one member who regards his party as intellectually benighted; who either never speaks their peculiar dialect, or who speaks it condescendingly, and with an 'aside;' who respects their accumulated prejudices as the 'potential energies' on which he subsists, but who despises them while he lives by them. Years ago Mr Disraeli called Sir Robert Peel's Ministry—the last Conservative Ministry that had real power—'an organised hypocrisy,'* so much did the ideas of its 'head' differ from the sensations of its 'tail.' Probably he now comprehends—if he did not always— that the air of Downing Street brings certain ideas to those who live there, and that the hard, compact prejudices of opposition are soon melted and mitigated in the great gulf stream of affairs. Lord Palmerston, too, was a typical example of a leader lulling rather than arousing, assuaging rather than acerbating the minds of his followers. But though the composing effect of close difficulties will commonly make a premier cease to be an immoderate partisan, yet a partisan to some extent he must be, and a violent one he may be; and in that case he is not a good person to check the party. When the leading sect (so to speak) in Parliament is doing what the nation do not like, an instant appeal ought to be registered, and Parliament ought to be dissolved. But a zealot of a premier will not appeal; he will follow his formulae; he will believe he is doing good service when, perhaps, he is but pushing to unpopular consequences the narrow maxims of an inchoate theory. At such a minute a constitutional king—such as Leopold the First was, and as Prince Albert might have been—is invaluable; he can and will appeal to the nation; he can and will prevent Parliament from hurting the nation.

Again, too, on the selfishness of Parliament an extrinsic check is clearly more efficient than an intrinsic. A premier who is made by Parliament may share the bad impulses of those who chose him; or, at any rate, he may have made 'capital' out of them—he may have seemed to share them. The self-interests, the jobbing propensities of the assembly are sure indeed to be of very secondary interest to him. What he will care most for is the permanence, is the interest—whether corrupt or uncorrupt—of his own ministry. He will be disinclined to anything coarsely unpopular. In the order of nature, a new assembly must come before long, and he will be indisposed to shock the feelings of the electors from whom that assembly must emanate. But though the interest of the minister is inconsistent with appalling jobbery, he will be inclined to mitigated jobbery. He will temporise; he will try to give a seemly dress to unseemly matters; to do as much harm as will content the assembly, and yet not so much harm as will offend the nation. He will not shrink from becoming a *particeps criminis*;* he will but endeavour to dilute the crime. The intervention of an extrinsic, impartial, and capable authority—if such can be found—will undoubtedly restrain the covetousness as well as the factiousness of a choosing assembly.

But can such a head be found? In one case I think it has been found. Our colonial governors are precisely *Dei ex machinâ*.* They are always intelligent, for they have to live by a difficult trade; they are nearly sure to be impartial, for they come from the ends of the earth; they are sure not to participate in the selfish desires of any colonial class or body, for long before those desires can have attained fruition they will have passed to the other side of the world; be busy with other faces and other minds, be almost out of hearing what happens in a region they have half forgotten. A colonial governor is a super-parliamentary authority, animated, by a wisdom which is probably in quantity considerable and is different from that of the local Parliament, even if not above it. But even in this case the advantage of this extrinsic authority is purchased at a heavy price—a price which must not be made light of, because it is often worth paying. A colonial governor is a ruler who has no permanent interest in the colony he governs; who perhaps had to look for it in the map when he was sent thither; who takes years before he really understands its parties and its controversies; who, though without prejudice himself, is apt to be a slave to the prejudices of local people near him; who inevitably, and almost laudably, governs not in the interest of the colony, which he may mistake, but in his own interest, which he sees and is sure of. The first desire of a colonial governor is not to get into a 'scrape,' not to do anything which may give trouble to his superiors—the Colonial Office—at home, which may cause an untimely and dubious recall, which may hurt his after career. He is sure to leave upon the colony the feeling that they have a ruler who only half knows them, and does not so much as half care for them. We hardly appreciate this common feeling in our colonies, because *we* appoint their *sovereign*; but we should understand it in an instant if, by a political metamorphosis, the choice were turned the opposite way—if *they* appointed our *sovereign*. We should then say at once, 'How is it possible a man from New Zealand can understand England? how is it possible that a man longing to get back to the antipodes can care for England? how can we trust one who lives by the fluctuating favour of a distant authority? how can we heartily obey one who is but a foreigner with the accident of an identical language?'

I dwell on the evils which impair the advantage of colonial governorship because that is the most favoured case of super-parliamentary royalty, and because from looking at it we can bring freshly home to our minds what the real difficulties of that institution are.

We are so familiar with it that we do not understand it. We are like people who have known a man all their lives, and yet are quite surprised when he displays some obvious characteristic which casual observers have detected at a glance. I have known a man who did not know what colour his sister's eyes were, though he had seen her every day for twenty years; or rather, he did not know *because* he had so seen her: so true is the philosophical maxim that we neglect the constant element in our thoughts, though it is probably the most important, and attend almost only to the varying elements—the differentiating elements (as men now speak)—though they are apt to be less potent. But when we perceive by the roundabout example of a colonial governor how difficult the task of a constitutional king is in the exercise of the function of dissolving parliament, we at once see how unlikely it is that an hereditary monarch will be possessed of the requisite faculties.

An hereditary king is but an ordinary person, upon an average, at best; he is nearly sure to be badly educated for business; he is very little likely to have a taste for business; he is solicited from youth by every temptation to pleasure; he probably passed the whole of his youth in the vicious situation of the heir-apparent, who can do nothing because he has no appointed work, and who will be considered almost to outstep his function if he undertake optional work. For the most part, a constitutional king is a *damaged* common man; not forced to business by necessity as a despot often is, but yet spoiled for business by most of the temptations which spoil a despot. History, too, seems to show that hereditary royal families gather from the repeated influence of their corrupting situation some dark taint in the blood, some transmitted and growing poison, which hurts their judgments, darkens all their sorrow, and is a cloud on half their pleasure. It has been said, not truly, but with a possible approximation to truth, 'That in 1802 every hereditary monarch was insane.'* Is it likely that this sort of monarchs will be able to catch the exact moment when, in opposition to the wishes of a triumphant ministry, they ought to dissolve Parliament? To do so with efficiency they must be able to perceive that the Parliament is wrong, and that the nation knows it is wrong. Now to know that Parliament is wrong, a man must be, if not a great statesman, yet a considerable statesman—a statesman of some sort. He must have great natural vigour, for no less will comprehend the hard principles of national policy. He must have incessant industry, for no less will keep him abreast with the involved detail to which those principles relate, and the miscellaneous occasions to which they must be applied. A man made common by nature, and made worse by life, is not likely to have either; he is nearly sure not to be *both* clever and industrious. And a monarch in the recesses of a palace, listening to a charmed flattery, unbiassed by the miscellaneous world, who has always been hedged in by rank, is likely to be but a poor judge of public opinion. He may have an inborn tact for finding it out; but his life will never teach it him, and will probably enfeeble it in him.

But there is a still worse case, a case which the life of George III—which is a sort of museum of the defects of a constitutional king—suggests at once. The Parliament may be wiser than the people, and yet the king may be of the same mind with the people. During the last years of the American war, the Premier, Lord North, upon whom the first responsibility rested, was averse to continuing it, and knew it could not succeed. Parliament was much of the same mind; if Lord North had been able to come down to Parliament with a peace in his hand, Parliament would probably have rejoiced, and the nation under the guidance of Parliament, though saddened by its losses, probably would have been satisfied. The opinion of that day was more like the American opinion of the present day than like our present opinion. It was much slower in its formation than our opinion now, and obeyed much more easily sudden impulses from the central administration. If Lord North had been able to throw the undivided energy and the undistracted authority of the Executive Government into the excellent work of making a peace and carrying a peace, years of bloodshed might have been spared, and an entail of enmity cut off that has yet to run out. But there was a power behind the Prime Minister; George III was madly eager to continue the war, and the nation—not seeing how hopeless the strife was, not comprehending the last antipathy which their obstinacy was creating—ignorant, dull, and helpless, was ready to go on too. Even if Lord North had wished to make peace, and had persuaded Parliament accordingly, all his work would have been useless; a superior power could and would have appealed from a wise and pacific Parliament to a sullen and warlike nation. The check which finds for the special vices of our Parliament was misused to curb its wisdom.

The more we study the nature of Cabinet Government, the more we shall shrink from exposing at a vital instant its delicate machinery to a blow from a casual, incompetent, and perhaps semi-insane outsider. The preponderant probability is that on a great occasion the Premier and Parliament will really be wiser than the king. The Premier is sure to be able, and is sure to be most anxious to decide well; if he fail to decide, he loses his place, though through all blunders the king keeps his; the judgment of the man, naturally very discerning, is sharpened by a heavy penalty, from which the judgment of the man by nature much less intelligent is exempt. Parliament, too, is for the most part a sound, careful, and practical body of men. Principle shows that the power of dismissing a Government with which Parliament is satisfied, and of dissolving that Parliament upon an appeal to the people, is not a power which a common hereditary monarch will in the long run be able beneficially to exercise.

Accordingly this power has almost, if not quite, dropped out of the reality of our constitution. Nothing, perhaps, would more surprise the English people than if the Queen by a *coup d'état* and on a sudden destroyed a ministry firm in the allegiance and secure of a majority in Parliament. That power indisputably, in theory, belongs to her; but it has passed so far away from the minds of man, that it would terrify them, if she used it, like a volcanic eruption from Primrose Hill. The last analogy to it is not one to be coveted as a precedent. In 1835 William IV dismissed an administration* which, though disorganised by the loss of its leader in the Commons, was an existing Government, had a premier in the Lords ready to go on, and a leader in the Commons willing to begin. The King fancied that public opinion was leaving the Whigs and going over to the Tories, and he thought he should accelerate the transition by ejecting the former. But the event showed that he misjudged. His *perception* indeed was right; the English people were wavering in their allegiance to the Whigs, who had no leader that touched the popular heart, none in whom Liberalism could personify itself and become a passion—who besides were a body long used to opposition, and therefore making blunders in office—who were borne to power by a popular impulse which they only half comprehended, and perhaps less than half shared. But the King's *policy* was wrong; he impeded the re-action instead of aiding it. He forced on a premature Tory Government, which was as unsuccessful as all wise people perceived that it must be. The popular distaste to the Whigs was as yet but incipient, inefficient; and the intervention of the Crown was advantageous to them, because it looked inconsistent with the liberties of the people. And in so far as William IV was right in detecting an incipient change of opinion, he did but detect an erroneous change. What was desirable was the prolongation of Liberal rule. The commencing dissatisfaction did but relate to the personal demerits of the Whig leaders, and other temporary adjuncts of free principles, and not to those principles intrinsically. So that the last precedent for a royal onslaught on a ministry ended thus:—in opposing the right principles, in aiding the wrong principles, in hurting the party it was meant to help. After such a warning, it is likely that our monarchs will pursue the policy which a long course of quiet precedent at present directs—they will leave a Ministry trusted by Parliament to the judgment of Parliament.

Indeed, the dangers arising from a party spirit in Parliament exceeding that of the nation, and of a selfishness in Parliament contradicting the true interest of the nation, are not great dangers in a country where the mind of the nation is steadily political, and where its control over its representatives is constant. A steady opposition to a formed public opinion is hardly possible in our House of Commons, so incessant is the national attention to politics, and so keen the fear in the mind of each member that he may lose his valued seat. These dangers belong to early and scattered communities, where there are no interesting political questions, where the distances are great, where no vigilant opinion passes judgment on parliamentary excesses, where few care to have seats in the chamber, and where many of those few are from their characters and their antecedents better not there than there. The one great vice of parliamentary government in an adult political nation, is the caprice of Parliament in the choice of a ministry. A nation can hardly control it here; and it is not good that, except within wide limits, it should control it. The Parliamentary judgment of the merits or demerits of an administration very generally depends on matters which the Parliament, being close at hand, distinctly sees, and which the distant nation does not see. But where personality enters, capriciousness begins. It is easy to imagine a House of Commons which is discontented with all statesmen, which is contented with none, which is made up of little parties, which votes in small knots, which will adhere steadily to no leader, which gives every leader a chance and a hope. Such

Parliaments require the imminent check of possible dissolution; but that check is (as has been shown) better in the premier than in the sovereign; and by the late practice of our constitution, its use is yearly ebbing from the sovereign and yearly centring in the premier. The Queen can hardly now refuse a defeated minister the chance of a dissolution, any more than she can dissolve in the time of an undefeated one, and without his consent.

We shall find the case much the same with the safety-valve, as I have called it, of our constitution. A good, capable, hereditary monarch would exercise it better than a premier, but a premier could manage it well enough; and a monarch capable of doing better will be born only once in a century, whereas monarchs likely to do worse will be born every day.

There are two modes in which the power of our executive to create Peers—to nominate, that is, additional members of our upper and revising chamber—now acts: one constant, habitual, noticed by the popular mind as it goes on; and the other possible and terrific, scarcely ever really exercised, but always by its reserved magic maintaining a great and a restraining influence. The Crown creates Peers, a few year by year, and thus modifies continually the characteristic feeling of the House of Lords. I have heard people say, who ought to know, that the *English* peerage (the only one upon which unhappily the power of new creation now acts) is now more Whig than Tory. Thirty years ago the majority was indisputably the other way. Owing to very curious circumstances English parties have not alternated in power as a good deal of speculation predicts they would, and a good deal of current language assumes they have. The Whig party were in office some seventy years (with very small breaks), from the death of Queen Anne to the coalition between Lord North and Mr Fox; then the Tories (with only such breaks) were in power for nearly fifty years, till 1832; and since, the Whig party has always, with very trifling intervals, been predominant. Consequently, each continuously-governing party has had the means of modifying the upper house to suit its views. The profuse Tory creations of half a century had made the House of Lords bigotedly Tory before the first Reform Act, but it is wonderfully mitigated now. The Irish Peers and the Scotch Peers—being nominated by an almost unaltered constituency, and representing the feelings of the majority of that constituency only (no minority having any voice)—present an unchangeable Tory element. But the element in which change is permitted has been changed. Whether the English Peerage be or be not predominantly now Tory, it is certainly not Tory after the fashion of the Toryism of 1832. The Whig additions have indeed sprung from a class commonly rather adjoining upon Toryism than much inclining to Radicalism. It is not from men of large wealth that a very great impetus to organic change should be expected. The additions to the Peers have matched nicely enough with the old Peers, and therefore they have effected more easily a greater and more permeating modification. The addition of a contrasting mass would have excited the old leaven, but the delicate infusion of ingredients similar in genus, though different in species, has modified the new compound without irritating the old original.

This ordinary and common use of the peer-creating power is always in the hands of the premier, and depends for its characteristic use on being there. He, as the head of the predominant party, is the proper person to modify gradually the permanent chamber which, perhaps, was at starting hostile to him; and, at any rate, can be best harmonised with the public opinion he represents by the additions he makes. Hardly any contrived constitution possesses a machinery for modifying its secondary house so delicate, so flexible, and so constant. If the power of creating life peers had been added, the mitigating influence of the responsible executive upon the House of Lords would have been as good as such a thing can be.

The catastrophic creation of Peers for the purpose of swamping the upper house is utterly different. If an able and impartial exterior king is at hand, this power is best in that king. It is a power only to be used on great occasions, when the object is immense, and the party strife unmitigated. This is the conclusive, the swaying power of the moment, and of course, therefore, it had better be in the hands of a power both capable and impartial, than of a premier who must in some degree be a partisan. The value of a discreet, calm, wise monarch, if such should happen at the acute crisis of a nation's destiny, is priceless. He may prevent years of tumult, save bloodshed and civil war, lay up a store of grateful fame to himself, prevent the accumulated intestine hatred of each party to its opposite. But the question comes back, Will there be such a monarch just then? What is the chance of having him just then? What will be the use of the monarch whom the accidents of inheritance, such as we know them to be, must upon an average bring us just then?

The answer to these questions is not satisfactory, if we take it from the little experience we have had in this rare matter. There have been but two cases at all approaching to a catastrophic creation of Peers—to a creation which would suddenly change the majority of the Lords in English history. One was in Queen Anne's time.* The majority of peers in Queen Anne's time were Whig, and by profuse and quick creations Harley's Ministry changed it to a Tory majority. So great was the popular effect, that in the next reign one of the most contested ministerial proposals was a proposal to take the power of indefinite peer creation from the Crown, and to make the number of Lords fixed, as that of the Commons is fixed. But the sovereign had little to do with the matter. Queen Anne was one of the smallest people ever set in a great place. Swift bitterly and justly said* 'she had not a store of amity by her for more than one friend at a time,' and just then her affection was concentrated on a waiting-maid. Her waiting-maid told her to make peers, and she made them. But of large thought and comprehensive statesmanship she was as destitute as Mrs Masham.* She supported a bad ministry by the most extreme of measures, and she did it on caprice. The next case, the case of William IV, is far less perfectly known to us. We are to know it now—Lord Grey promises the correspondence* of that king with his father during his ministry, in which all the facts must be accurately set forth. But according to our present information, the King was in the natural state of an imbecile man at a crisis. His mind went hither and thither; he listened first to his minister, then to the queen, then perhaps to a secretary. He thought, Can the Duke do anything? Will Peel do nothing? Must Grey do everything? The vital question in every mind was, Will the King create Peers? but the King did not know. He vacillated. The extreme power of the constitution in his hands was like a gun in the hands of a startled woman, who is so frightened that she can neither let it off nor put it down. First he refused to create Peers, and caused a crisis when the greatest people in the land told others not to pay taxes, when the Birmingham unions were exciting people to madness, when the stoppage of the Bank of England was talked of as a political expedient, when 'RUN FOR GOLD' was placarded all over London. Then the King (according to Lord Brougham, at least) signed a written engagement with the Whigs that he would create as many Peers as they wished. 'I wonder you could press him,' Lord Grey said to Lord Brougham, 'when you saw the abject state he was in.' A bystander observed that he had never seen so large a matter on so small a bit of paper. In fact, you may place power in weak hands at a revolution, but you cannot keep it in weak hands. It runs out of them into strong ones. An ordinary hereditary sovereign—a William IV, or a George IV—is unable to exercise the peer-creating power when most wanted. A half-insane king, like George III, would be worse. He might use it by accountable impulse when not required; and refuse to use it out of sullen madness when required.

The existence of a fancied check on the premier is in truth an evil, because it prevents the enforcement of a real check. It would be easy to provide by law that an extraordinary number of Peers—say more than ten annually—should not be created except on a vote of some large majority, suppose three-fourths of the lower house. This would ensure that the premier should not use the reserve force of the constitution as if it were an ordinary force; that he should not use it except when the whole nation fixedly wished it; that it should be kept for a revolution, not expended on administration; and it would ensure that he should then have it to use. Queen Anne's case and William IV's case prove that neither object is certainly attained by entrusting this critical and extreme force to the chance idiosyncrasies and habitual mediocrity of an hereditary sovereign.

It may be asked why I argue at such length a question in appearance so removed from practice, and in one point of view so irrelevant to my subject. No one proposes to remove Queen Victoria; if any one is in a safe place on earth, she is in a safe place. In these very essays it has been shown that the mass of our people would obey no one else, that the reverence she excites is the potential energy—as science now speaks—out of which all minor forces are made, and from which lesser functions take their efficiency. But looking not to the present hour, and this single country, but to the world at large and coming times, no question can be more practical.

What grows upon the world is a certain matter-of-factness. The test of each century, more than of the century before, is the test of results. New countries are arising all over the world where there are no fixed sources of reverence; which have to make them; which have to create institutions which must generate loyalty by conspicuous utility. This matter-of-factness is the growth even in Europe of the two greatest and newest intellectual agencies of our time. One of these is business. We see so much of the material fruits of commerce, that we forget its mental fruits. It begets a mind desirous of things, careless of ideas, not acquainted with the niceties of words. In all labour there should be profit, is its motto. It is not only true that we have 'left swords for ledgers,' but war itself is made as much by the ledger as by the sword. The soldier—that is, the great soldier—of today is not a romantic animal, dashing at forlorn hopes, animated by frantic sentiment, full of fancies as to a ladye-love or a sovereign; but a quiet, grave man, busied in charts, exact in sums, master of the art of tactics, occupied in trivial detail; thinking, as the Duke of Wellington was said to do, *most* of the shoes of his soldiers; despising all manner of *éclat* and eloquence; perhaps, like Count Moltke,* 'silent in seven languages.' We have reached a 'climate' of opinion where figures rule, where our very supporter of Divine right, as we deemed him, our Count Bismarck,* amputates kings right and left, applies the test of results to each, and lets none live who are not to do something. There has in truth been a great change during the last five hundred years, in the predominant occupations of the ruling part of mankind; formerly they passed their time either in exciting action or inanimate repose. A feudal baron had nothing between war and the chase—keenly animating things both—and what was called 'inglorious ease.' Modern life is scanty in excitements, but incessant in quiet action. Its perpetual commerce is creating a 'stock-taking habit'; the habit of asking each man, thing, and institution, 'Well, what have you done since I saw you last?'

Our physical science, which is becoming the dominant culture of thousands, and which is beginning to permeate our common literature to an extent which few watch enough, quite tends the same way. The two peculiarities are its homeliness and its inquisitiveness: its value for the most 'stupid' facts, as one used to call them, and its incessant wish for verification—to be sure, by tiresome seeing and hearing, that they are facts. The old excitement of thought has half died out, or rather it is diffused in quiet pleasure over a life, instead of being concentrated in intense and eager spasms. An old philosopher—a Descartes, suppose—fancied that out of primitive truths, which he could by ardent excogitation know, he might by pure deduction evolve the entire universe. Intense self-examination, and intense reason would, he thought, make out everything. The soul 'itself by itself,' could tell all it wanted if it would be true to its sublime isolation. The greatest enjoyment possible to man was that which this philosophy promises its votaries—the pleasure of being always right, and always reasoning—without ever being bound to look at anything. But our most ambitious schemes of philosophy now start quite differently. Mr Darwin begins:—*

'When on board H.M.S. *Beagle*, as naturalist, I was much struck with certain facts in the distribution of the organic beings inhabiting South America, and in the geological relations of the present to the past inhabitants of that continent. These facts, as will be seen in the latter chapters of this volume, seemed to throw some light on the origin of species—that mystery of mysteries, as it has been called by one of our greatest philosophers. On my return home, it occurred to me, in 1837, that something might perhaps be made out on this question by patiently accumulating and reflecting on all sorts of facts which could possibly have any bearing on it. After five years' work I allowed myself to speculate on the subject, and drew up some short notes; these I enlarged in 1844 into a sketch of the conclusions, which then seemed to me probable: from that period to the present day I have steadily pursued the same object. I hope that I may be excused for entering on these personal details, as I give them to show that I have not been hasty in coming to a decision.'

If he hopes finally to solve his great problem, it is by careful experiments in pigeon fancying, and other sorts of artificial variety making. His hero is not a self-inclosed, excited philosopher, but 'that most skilful breeder, Sir John Sebright,* who used to say, with respect to pigeons, that he would produce any given feathers in three years, but it would take him six years to obtain a head and a beak.' I am not saying that the new thought is better than the old; it is no business of mine to say anything about that; I only wish to bring home to the mind, as nothing but instances can bring it home, how matter-of-fact, how petty, as it would at first sight look, even our most ambitious science has become.

In the new communities which our emigrating habit now constantly creates, this prosaic turn of mind is intensified. In the American mind and in the colonial mind there is, as contrasted with the old English mind, a *literalness*, a tendency to say, 'The facts are so-and-so, whatever may be thought or fancied about them.' We used before the civil war to say that the Americans worshipped the almighty dollar; we now know that they can scatter money almost recklessly when they will. But what we meant was half right—they worship visible value; obvious, undeniable, intrusive result. And in Australia and New Zealand the same turn comes uppermost. It grows from the struggle with the wilderness. Physical difficulty is the enemy of early communities, and an incessant conflict with it for generations leaves a mark of reality on the mind—a painful mark almost to us, used to impalpable fears and the half-fanciful dangers of an old and complicated society. The 'new Englands' of all latitudes are bare-minded (if I may so say) as compared with the 'old.'

When, therefore, the new communities of the colonised world have to choose a government, they must choose one in which *all* the institutions are of an obvious evident utility. We catch the Americans smiling at our Queen with her secret mystery, and our Prince of Wales with his happy inaction. It is impossible, in fact, to convince their prosaic minds that constitutional royalty is a rational government, that it is suited to a new age and an unbroken country, that those who start afresh can start with it. The princelings who run about the world with excellent intentions, but an entire ignorance of business, are to them a locomotive advertisement that this sort of government is European in its limitations and mediaeval in its origin; that though it has yet a great part to play in the old states, it has no place or part in new states. The *réalisme impitoyable** which good critics find in a most characteristic part of the literature of the nineteenth century, is to be found also in its politics. An ostentatious utility must characterise its creations.

The deepest interest, therefore, attaches to the problem of this essay. If hereditary royalty had been essential to parliamentary government, we might well have despaired of that government. But accurate investigation shows that this royalty is not essential; that, upon an average, it is not even in a high degree useful; that though a king with high courage and fine discretion,—a king with a genius for the place,—is useful, and at rare moments priceless, yet that a common king, a king such as birth brings, is of no use at difficult crises, while in the common course of things his aid is neither likely nor required—he will do nothing, and he need do nothing. But we happily find that a new country need not fall back into the fatal division of powers incidental to a presidential government; it may, if other conditions serve, obtain the ready, well-placed, identical sort of sovereignty which belongs to the English Constitution, under the unroyal form of Parliamentary Government.

9

ITS HISTORY, AND THE EFFECTS OF THAT HISTORY—
CONCLUSION

A VOLUME might seem wanted to say anything worth saying on the History of the English Constitution, and a great and new volume might still be written on it, if a competent writer took it in hand. The subject has never been treated by any one combining the lights of the newest research and the lights of the most matured philosophy. Since the masterly book of Hallam* was written, both political thought and historical knowledge have gained much, and we might have a treatise applying our strengthened calculus to our augmented facts. I do not pretend that I could write such a book, but there are a few salient particulars which may be fitly brought together, both because of their past interest and of their present importance.

There is a certain common polity, or germ of polity, which we find in all the rude nations that have attained civilisation. These nations seem to begin in what I may call a consultative and tentative absolutism. The king of early days, in vigorous nations, was not absolute as despots now are; there was then no standing army to repress rebellion, no organised *espionage* to spy out discontent, no skilled bureaucracy to smooth the ruts of obedient life. The early king was indeed consecrated by a religious sanction; he was essentially a man apart, a man above others, divinely anointed, or even God-begotten. But in nations capable of freedom this religious domination was never despotic. There was indeed no legal limit: the very words could not be translated into the dialect of those times. The notion of law as we have it—of a rule imposed by human authority, capable of being altered by that authority when it likes, and in fact, so altered habitually—could not be conveyed to early nations, who regarded law half as an invincible prescription, and half as a Divine revelation. Law 'came out of the king's mouth;' he gave it as Solomon gave judgment,—embedded in the particular case, and upon the authority of Heaven as well as his own. A Divine limit to the Divine revealer was impossible, and there was no other source of law. But though there was no legal limit, there was a practical limit to subjection in (what may be called) the pagan part of human nature,—the inseparable obstinacy of freemen. They *never* would do exactly what they were told.

To early royalty, as Homer describes it in Greece and as we may well imagine it elsewhere, there were always two adjuncts: one, the 'old men,' the men of weight, the council, the βουλή, of which the king asked advice, from the debates in which the king tried to learn what he could do and what he ought to do. Besides this there was the ἀγορά, the purely listening assembly as some have called it, but the *tentative* assembly as I think it might best be called. The king came down to his assembled people in form to announce his will, but in reality, speaking in very modern words, to 'feel his way.' He was sacred, no doubt; and popular, very likely; still he was half like a popular premier speaking to a high-spirited chamber: there were limits to his authority and power; limits which he would discover by trying whether eager cheers received his mandate, or only hollow murmurs and a thinking silence.

This polity is a good one for its era and its place, but there is a fatal defect in it. The reverential associations upon which the government is built are transmitted according to one law, and the capacity needful to work the government is transmitted according to another law. The popular homage clings to the line of god-descended kings; it is transmitted by inheritance. But very soon that line comes to a child or an idiot, or one by some defect or other incapable. Then we find everywhere the truth of the old saying, that liberty thrives under weak princes; then the listening assembly begins not only to murmur, but to speak; then the grave council begins not so much to suggest as to inculcate, not so much to advise as to enjoin.

Mr Grote has told at length how out of these appendages of the original kingdom the free States of Greece derived their origin, and how they gradually grew—the oligarchical States expanding the council, and the democratical expanding the assembly. The history has as many varieties in detail as there were Greek cities, but the essence is the same everywhere. The political characteristic of the early Greeks, and of the early Romans, too, is that out of the *tentacula* of a monarchy they developed the organs of a republic.

English history has been in substance the same, though its form is different, and its growth far slower and longer. The scale was larger, and the elements more various. A Greek city soon got rid of its kings, for the political sacredness of the monarch would not bear the daily inspection and constant criticism of an eager and talking multitude. Everywhere in Greece the slave population—the most ignorant, and therefore the most unsusceptible of intellectual influences—was struck out of the account. But England began as a kingdom of considerable size, inhabited by distinct races, none of them fit for prosaic criticism, and all subject to the superstition of royalty. In early England, too, royalty was much more than a superstition. A very strong executive was needed to keep down a divided, an armed, and an impatient country; and therefore the problem of political development was delicate. A formed free government in a homogeneous nation may have a strong executive; but during the transition state, while the republic is in course of development and the monarchy in course of decay, the executive is of necessity weak. The polity is divided, and its action feeble and failing. The different English people have progressed, too, at different rates. The change in the state of the higher classes since the Middle Ages is enormous, and it is all improvement; but the lower have varied little, and many argue that in some important respects they have got worse, even if in others they have got better. The development of the English Constitution was of necessity slow, because a quick one would have exhausted the executive and killed the State, and because the most numerous classes, who changed very little, were not prepared for any catastrophic change in our institutions.

In its outline the process of development has been simple. The exact nature of all Anglo-Norman institutions is perhaps dubious: at least, in nearly all cases there have been many controversies. Political zeal, whether Whig, or Tory, has wanted to find a model in the past; and the whole state of society being confused, the precedents altering with the caprice of men and the chance of events, ingenious advocacy has had a happy field. But all that I need speak of is quite plain. There was a great 'council' of the realm, to which the king summoned the most considerable persons in England, the persons he most wanted to advise him, and the persons whose tempers he was most anxious to ascertain. Exactly who came to it at first is obscure and unimportant. I need not distinguish between the 'magnum concilium in Parliament' and the 'magnum concilium out of Parliament'. Gradually the principal assemblies summoned by the English sovereign took the precise and definite form of Lords and Commons, as in their outside we now see them. But their real nature was very different. The Parliament of today is a ruling body; the mediaeval Parliament was, if I may say so, an *expressive* body. Its function was to tell the executive—the king—what the nation wished he should do; to some extent, to guide him by new wisdom, and, to a very great extent, to guide him by new facts. These facts were their own feelings, which were the feelings of the people, because they were part and parcel of the people. From thence the king learned or had the means to learn, what the nation would endure, and what it would not endure;—what he might do, and what he might not do. If he much mistook this, there was a rebellion.

There are, as is well known, three great periods in the English Constitution. The first of these is the ante-Tudor period. The English Parliament then seemed to be gaining extraordinary strength and power. The title to the crown was uncertain; some monarchs were imbecile. Many ambitious men wanted to 'take the people into partnership.' Certain precedents of that time were cited with grave authority centuries after, when the time of freedom had really arrived. But the causes of this rapid growth soon produced an even more sudden decline. Confusion fostered it, and confusion destroyed it. The structure of society then was feudal; the towns were only an adjunct and a make-weight. The principal popular force was an aristocratic force, acting with the co-operation of the gentry and yeomanry, and resting on the loyal fealty of sworn retainers. The head of this force, on whom its efficiency depended, was the high nobility. But the high nobility killed itself out. The great barons who adhered to the 'Red Rose' or the 'White Rose,' or who fluctuated from one to the other, became poorer, fewer, and less potent every year. When the great struggle ended at Bosworth, a large part of the greatest combatants were gone. The restless, aspiring, rich barons, who made the civil war, were broken by it. Henry VII attained a kingdom in which there was a Parliament to advise, but scarcely a Parliament to control.

The consultative government of the ante-Tudor period had little resemblance to some of the modern governments which French philosophers call by that name. The French Empire, I believe, calls itself so. But its assemblies are symmetrical 'shams.' They are elected by a universal suffrage, by the ballot, and in districts once marked out with an eye to equality, and still retaining a look of equality. But our English parliaments were *un*symmetrical realities. They were elected anyhow; the sheriff had a considerable license in sending writs to boroughs, that is, he could in part pick his constituencies; and in each borough there was a rush and scramble for the franchise, so that the strongest local party got it, whether few or many. But in England at that time there was a great and distinct desire to know the opinion of the nation, because there was a real and close necessity. The nation was wanted to do something—to assist the sovereign in some war, to pay some old debt, to contribute its force and aid in the critical conjuncture of the time. It would not have suited the ante-Tudor kings to have had a fictitious assembly; they would have lost their sole *feeler*, their only instrument for discovering national opinion. Nor could they have manufactured such an assembly if they wished. The instrument in that behalf is the centralised executive, and there was then no *préfet* by whom the opinion of a rural locality could be made to order, and adjusted to suit the wishes of the capital. Looking at the mode of election, a theorist would say that these parliaments were but 'chance' collections of influential Englishmen. There would be many corrections and limitations to add to that statement if it were wanted to make it accurate, but the statement itself hits exactly the principal excellence of those parliaments. If not 'chance' collections of Englishmen, they were 'undesigned' collections; no administrations made them or could make them. They were *bonâ-fide* counsellors, whose opinion might be wise or unwise, but was anyhow of paramount importance, because their co-operation was wanted for what was in hand.

Legislation as a positive power was very secondary in those old parliaments. I believe no statute at all, as far as we know, was passed in the reign of Richard I, and all the ante-Tudor acts together would look meagre enough to a modern Parliamentary agent* who had to live by them. But the negative action of parliament upon the law was essential to its whole idea, and ran through every part of its use. That the king could not change what was then the almost sacred *datum* of the common law, without seeing whether his nation liked it or not, was an essential part of the 'tentative' system. The king had to feel his way in this exceptional, singular act, as those ages deemed original legislation, as well as in lesser acts. The legislation was his at last; he enacted after consulting his Lords and Commons; his was the sacred mouth which gave holy firmness to the enactment; but he only dared alter the rule regulating the common life of his people after consulting those people; he would not have been obeyed if he had, by a rude age which did not fear civil war as we fear it now. Many most important enactments of that period (and the fact is most characteristic) are declaratory acts. They do not profess to enjoin by inherent authority what the law shall in future be, but to state and mark what the law is; they are declarations of immemorial custom, not precepts of new duties. Even in the 'Great Charter'* the notion of new enactments was secondary; it was a great mixture of old and new; it was a sort of compact defining what was doubtful in floating custom, and was re-enacted over and over again, as boundaries are perambulated once a year, and rights and claims tending to desuetude thereby made patent and clear of new obstructors. In truth, such great 'charters' were rather treaties between different orders and factions, confirming ancient rights, or what claimed to be such, than laws in our ordinary sense. They were the 'deeds of arrangement' of medieval society affirmed and re-affirmed from time to time, and the principal controversy was, of course, between the king and nation—the king trying to see how far the nation would let him go, and the nation murmuring and recalcitrating, and seeing how many acts of administration they could prevent, and how many of its claims they could resist.

Sir James Mackintosh says that Magna Charta 'converted the right of taxation into the shield of liberty,'* but it did nothing of the sort. The liberty existed before, and the right to be taxed was an efflorescence and instance of it, not a substratum or a cause. The necessity of consulting the great council of the realm before taxation, the principle that the declaration of grievances by the Parliament was to precede the grant of supplies to the sovereign, are but conspicuous instances of the primitive doctrine of the ante-Tudor period, and the king must consult the great council of the realm before he did anything, since he always wanted help. The right of self-taxation was justly inserted in the 'great treaty;' but it would have been a dead letter, save for the armed force and aristocratic organisation which compelled the king to make a treaty; it was a result, not a basis—an example, not a cause.

The civil wars of many years killed out the old councils (if I might so say); that is, destroyed three parts of the greater noblesse, who were its most potent members; tired the smaller noblesse and the gentry and overthrew the aristocratic organisation on which all previous effectual resistance to the sovereign had been based.

The second period of the British Constitution begins with the accession of the House of Tudor, and goes down to 1688; it is in substance the history of the growth, development, and gradually acquired supremacy of the new great council. I have no room and no occasion to narrate again the familiar steps by which the slavish Parliament of Henry VIII grew into the murmuring Parliament of Queen Elizabeth, the mutinous Parliament of James I, and the rebellious Parliament of Charles I. The steps were many, but the energy was one—the growth of the English middle-class, using that word in its most inclusive sense, and its animation under the influence of Protestantism. No one, I think, can doubt that Lord Macaulay is right in saying* that political causes would not alone have then provoked such a resistance to the sovereign, unless propelled by religious theory. Of course, the English people went to and fro from Catholicism to Protestantism, and from Protestantism to Catholicism (not to mention that the Protestantism was of several shades and sects), just as the first Tudor kings and queens wished. But that was in the pre-Puritan era. The mass of Englishmen were in an undecided state, just as Hooper tells us his father was*—'Not believing in Protestantism, yet not disinclined to it.' Gradually, however, a strong Evangelic spirit (as we should now speak) and a still stronger anti-Papal spirit entered into the middle sort of Englishmen, and added to that force, fibre, and substance, which they have never wanted, an ideal warmth and fervour which they have almost always wanted. Hence the saying that Cromwell founded the English Constitution. Of course, in seeming, Cromwell's work died with him; his dynasty was rejected, his republic cast aside; but the spirit which culminated in him never sank again; never ceased to be a potent, though often a latent and volcanic, force in the country. Charles II said that he would never go again on his travels* for anything or anybody; and he well knew that though the men whom he met at Worcester might be dead, still the spirit which warmed them was alive and young in others.

But the Cromwellian republic and the strict Puritan creed were utterly hateful to most Englishmen. They were, if I may venture on saying so, like the 'Rouge' element in France and elsewhere—the sole revolutionary force in the entire State, and were hated as such.

That force could do little of itself; indeed, its bare appearance tended to frighten and alienate the moderate and dull as well as the refined and reasoning classes. Alone it was impotent against the solid clay of the English apathetic nature. But give this fiery element a body of decent-looking earth; give it an excuse for breaking out on an occasion, when the decent, the cultivated, and the aristocratic classes could join with it, and they could conquer by means of it, and it could be disguised in their covering.

Such an excuse was found in 1688. James II, by incredible and pertinacious folly, irritated not only the classes which had fought *against* his father, but also those who had fought *for* his father. He offended the Anglican classes as well as the Puritan classes; all the Whig nobles and half the Tory nobles, as well as the dissenting bourgeois. The rule of Parliament was established by the concurrence of the usual supporters of royalty with the usual opponents of it. But the result was long weak. Our revolution has been called the minimum of a revolution, because in law, at least, it only changed the dynasty, but exactly on that account it was the greatest shock to the common multitude, who see the dynasty but see nothing else. The support of the main aristocracy held together the bulk of the deferential classes, but it held them together imperfectly, uneasily, and unwillingly. Huge masses of crude prejudice swayed hither and thither for many years. If an able Stuart had with credible sincerity professed Protestantism, probably he might have overturned the House of Hanover. So strong was inbred reverence for hereditary right, that until the accession of George III the English Government was always subject to the unceasing attrition of a competitive sovereign.

This was the result of what I insist on tediously, but what is most necessary to insist on, for it is a cardinal particular in the whole topic. Many of the English people—the higher and more educated portion—had come to comprehend the nature of constitutional government, but the mass did not comprehend it. They looked to the sovereign as the government, and to the sovereign only. These were carried forward by the magic of the aristocracy, and principally by the influence of the great Whig families with their adjuncts. Without that aid reason or liberty would never have held them.

Though the rule of Parliament was definitely established in 1688, yet the mode of exercising that rule has since changed. At first

Parliament did not know how to exercise it; the organisation of parties and the appointment of cabinets by parties grew up in the manner Macaulay has described so well. Up to the latest period the sovereign was supposed, to a mischievous extent, to interfere in the choice of the persons to be Ministers. When George III finally became insane, in 1810, every one believed that George IV, on assuming power as Prince Regent, would turn out Mr Perceval's government* and empower Lord Grey or Lord Grenville, the Whig leaders, to form another. The Tory ministry was carrying on a successful war—a war of existence—against Napoleon; but in the people's mind, the necessity at such an occasion for an unchanged government, did not outweigh the fancy that George IV was a Whig. And a Whig, it is true, he had been before the French Revolution, when he lived an indescribable life in St James's Street with Mr Fox.* But Lord Grey and Lord Grenville were rigid men, and had no immoral sort of influence. What liberalism of opinion the Regent ever had was frightened out of him (as of other people) by the Reign of Terror. He felt, according to the saying of another monarch, that 'he lived by being a royalist.'* It soon appeared that he was most anxious to retain Mr Perceval, and that he was most eager to quarrel with the Whig Lords. As we all know, he kept the ministry whom he found in office; but that it should have been thought he could then change them, is a significant example how exceedingly modern our notions of the despotic action of Parliament in fact are.

By the steps of the struggle thus rudely mentioned (and by others which I have no room to speak of, nor need I), the change which in the Greek cities was effected both in appearance and in fact, has been effected in England, though in reality only, and not in outside. Here, too, the appendages of a monarchy have been converted into the essence of a republic; only here, because of a more numerous heterogeneous political population, it is needful to keep the ancient show while we secretly interpolate the new reality.

This long and curious history has left its trace on almost every part of our present political condition; its effects lie at the root of many of our most important controversies; and because these effects are not rightly perceived, many of these controversies are misconceived.

One of the most curious peculiarities of the English People is its dislike of the executive government. We are not in this respect '*un vrai peuple moderne*,'* like the Americans. The Americans conceive of their executive as one of their appointed agents; when it intervenes in common life, it does so, they consider, in virtue of the mandate of the sovereign people, there is no invasion or dereliction of freedom in that people interfering with itself. The French, the Swiss, and all nations who breathe the full atmosphere of the nineteenth century, think so too. The material necessities of this age require a strong executive; a nation destitute of it cannot be clean, or healthy, or vigorous like a nation possessing it. By definition, a nation calling itself free should have no jealousy of the executive, for freedom means that the nation, the political part of the nation, wields the executive. But our history has reversed the English feeling: our freedom is the result of centuries of resistance, more or less legal, or more or less illegal, more or less audacious, or more or less timid, to the executive Government. We have, accordingly, inherited the traditions of conflict, and preserve them in the fullness of victory. We look on State action, not as our own action, but as alien action; as an imposed tyranny from without, not as the consummated result of our own organised wishes. I remember at the Census of 1851* hearing a very sensible old lady say that 'the liberties of England were at an end;' if Government might be thus inquisitorial, if they might ask who slept in your house, or what your age was, what, she argued, might they ask and what might they not do.

The natural impulse of the English people is to resist authority. The introduction of effectual policemen was not liked. I know people, old people I admit, who to this day consider them an infringement of freedom, and an imitation of the *gendarmes* of France. If the original policemen had been started with the present helmets, the result might have been dubious; there might have been a cry of military tyranny, and the inbred insubordination of the English people might have prevailed over the very modern love of *perfect* peace and order. The old notion that the Government is an extrinsic agency still rules our imaginations, though it is no longer true, and though in calm and intellectual moments we well know it is not. Nor is it merely our history which produces this effect; we might get over that, but the results of that history co-operate. Our double Government so acts: when we want to point the antipathy to the executive, we refer to the jealousy of the Crown, so deeply imbedded in the very substance of constitutional authority; so many people are loath to admit the Queen, in spite of law and fact, to be the people's appointee and agent, that it is a good rhetorical emphasis to speak of her prerogative as something *non*-popular and to be distrusted. By the very nature of our Government our executive cannot be liked and trusted as the Swiss or the American is liked and trusted.

Out of the same history and the same results proceed our tolerance of those 'local authorities' which so puzzle many foreigners. In the struggle with the Crown these local centres served as props and fulcrums. In the early parliaments it was the local bodies who sent members to parliament, the counties, and the boroughs; and in that way, and because of their *free* life, the parliament was free too. If active, real bodies had not sent the representatives, they would have been powerless. This is very much the reason why our old rights of suffrage were so various; the Government let whatever people happened to be the strongest in each town choose the members. They applied to the electing bodies the test of 'natural selection;' whatever set of people were locally strong enough to elect, did so. Afterwards, in the civil war, many of the corporations, like that of London, were important bases of resistance. The case of London is typical and remarkable. Probably, if there is any body more than another, which an educated Englishman now-a-days regards with little favour, it is the Corporation of London. He connects it with hereditary abuses perfectly preserved, with large revenues imperfectly accounted for, with a system which stops the principal city government at an old archway, with the perpetuation of a hundred detestable parishes, with the maintenance of a horde of luxurious and useless bodies. For the want of all which makes Paris nice and splendid we justly reproach the Corporation of London; for the existence of much of what makes London mean and squalid we justly reproach it too. Yet the Corporation of London was for centuries a bulwark of English liberty. The conscious support of the near and organised capital gave the Long Parliament* a vigour and vitality which they could have found nowhere else. Their leading patriots took refuge in the City, and the nearest approach to an English 'sitting in permanence' is the committee at Guildhall, where all members 'that came were to have voices.' Down to George III's time* the City was a useful centre of popular judgment. Here, as elsewhere, we have built into our polity pieces of the scaffolding by which it was erected.

De Tocqueville indeed used to maintain that in this matter the

English were not merely historically excusable, but likewise politically judicious. He founded what may be called the *culte* of corporations.* And it was natural that in France, where there is scarcely any power of self-organisation in the people, where the *préfet* must be asked upon every subject, and take the initiative in every movement, a solitary thinker should be repelled from the exaggerations of which he knew the evil, to the contrary exaggeration of which he did not. But in a country like England, where business is in the air, where we can organise a vigilance committee on every abuse and an executive committee for every remedy—as a matter of political instruction, which was De Tocqueville's point—we need not care how much power is delegated to outlying bodies, and how much is kept for the central body. We have had the instruction municipalities could give us: we have been through all that. Now we are quite grown up, and can put away childish things.

The same causes account for the innumerable anomalies of our polity. I own that I do not entirely sympathise with the horror of these anomalies which haunts some of our best critics. It is natural that those who by special and admirable culture have come to look at all things upon the artistic side, should start back from these queer peculiarities. But it is natural also that persons used to analyse political institutions should look at these anomalies with a little tenderness and a little interest. They *may* have something to teach us. Political philosophy is still most imperfect; it has been framed from observations taken upon regular specimens of politics and States; as to these its teaching is most valuable. But we must ever remember that its *data* are imperfect. The lessons are good where its primitive assumptions hold, but may be false where those assumptions fail. A philosophical politician regards a political anomaly as a scientific physician regards a rare disease—it is to him an 'interesting case.' There may still be instruction here, though we have worked out the lessons of common cases. I cannot, therefore, join in the full cry against anomalies; in my judgment it may quickly overrun the scent, and so miss what we should be glad to find.

Subject to this saving remark, however, I not only admit, but maintain, that our constitution is full of curious oddities, which are impeding and mischievous, and ought to be struck out. Our law very often reminds one of those outskirts of cities where you cannot for a long time tell how the streets come to wind about in so capricious and serpent-like a manner. At last it strikes you that they grew up, house by house, on the devious tracks of the old green lanes; and if you follow on to the existing fields, you may often find the change half complete. Just so the lines of our constitution were framed in old eras of sparse population, few wants, and simple habits; and we adhere in seeming to their shape, though civilisation has come with its dangers, complications, and enjoyments. These anomalies, in a hundred instances, mark the old boundaries of a constitutional struggle. The casual line was traced according to the strength of deceased combatants; succeeding generations fought elsewhere; and the hesitating line of a half-drawn battle was left to stand for a perpetual limit.

I do not count as an anomaly the existence of our double government, with all its infinite accidents, though half the superficial peculiarities that are often complained of arise out of it. The co-existence of a Queen's seeming prerogative and a Downing Street's real government is just suited to such a country as this, in such an age as ours.[1]

The effect of this history, and the consequent institutions, upon what our national character is, has been great; and its effect on the common idea of that character cannot be exaggerated. Half the world believes that the Englishman is born illogical, and that he has a sort of love of complexity in and for itself. They argue no nation with any logic in them could ever make such a constitution. And in fact no one did make it. It is a composite result of various efforts, very few of which had any reference to the look of the whole, and of which the infinite majority only had a very bounded reference to a proximate end. The French political work is just the same in like circumstances. Under the old régime, each province in France had most complex and traditional institutions, which have perished out of memory, very much because they were so involved that no one can describe them at once truly and graphically. They were so very bad that they have ceased to be remembered against the national character. Even under the present Government, whenever a large body of political relations is the gradual effect of changing arrangements,

---

[1] So well is our real Government concealed, that if you tell a cab-man to drive to 'Downing Street' he most likely will never have heard of it, and will not in the least know where to take you.

complexity comes out. Any one who will try to state at all accurately the relations between the French railways and the Emperor* will find that he has taken in hand a very difficult descriptive task, so complex is the present bargain, and so inexplicable, except by reference to previous bargains.

The evidence of language, the best single evidence of national character, goes to show that the English care more, even than the French, for simplicity, and are less patient of meaningless anomalies. If the facts were the other way, I am sure we should have many a pretty essay in Paris on the barbarous conservatism of the English in retaining genders. As *they* have kept and *we* abandoned them, we hear nothing about it; but a more meaningless anomaly, or one less explicable except by dim investigation into the far-off antiquity of language cannot be found. The plain English grammar is evidence all through of the fundamental simplicity of the English character. I believe it is admitted that the Americans are a logical people, and French and Germans, too,—so that the ingredients of the English people and the outcome of it are both logical, but that the nation itself is illogical. There is an obvious improbability in this theory which should keep people from asserting it.

But though I deny that the English Constitution is a result of an illogical intellect, and though I maintain that at bottom the English character is mentally and morally very consistent and straight-forward, yet I concede that the spectacle of this beneficial puzzle (for such our constitution is to most who live under it), is not a good teaching for symmetrical arrangements. Being in itself, as Englishmen think, so good and yet so illogical, it gives them a suspicion of logic. Seeing that the best practical things they know are produced by an inexplicable process, they are apt to doubt the efficiency of any explicable process. And as far as the constitution itself is concerned they are right in thinking it dangerous to apply to it quick and sweeping thoughts. You must take the trouble to understand the plan of an old house before you can make a scheme for mending it; simple diagrams are very well on an empty site, but not upstairs in a gothic mansion. Any good alteration of our constitution must be based on a precise description of the part affected, and that delineative premiss can scarcely ever be plain. So far the English suspicion of conspicuous logic is true and well-founded, but undeniably they have come to regard their constitution not only as a precedent but as a model, and so have sometimes a confidence in analogous compromises, rather than in contrasted simple measures. But the half measure must be one we understand. New complexity, as such, is detestable to the English mind; and let any one who denies it, try to advocate some plan of suffrage reform at all out of the way, and see how long it will be before he ceases to be able to count his disciples upon the fingers of a single hand.

And lastly, this history and its complex consequences have made the great political question of the day, the suffrage question, exceedingly difficult; have made it such that no perfect solution can be looked for, and that only a choice of difficulties, is possible.

There are two sorts of countries in which the suffrage question is easy. In a large community of peasant proprietors and no one else, where society is homogeneous, where comfort is universal, and where education is diffused, you cannot help having tolerable constituencies. You may draw parallelograms over the country of equal area, and call them constituencies, or you may make pens of equal numbers of persons, and call them constituencies, and either way the result will be about the same. A rough nation, where a common sort of education is plenty, and comfort sure, will yield a decent sort of parliament under any electoral system, though it cannot yield a refined one under any. We may frame likewise the image of a community, in which the less educated and less wealthy part of the nation yielded a conscious loyalty to superior knowledge. This would be a deference founded expressly on reason and justified by avowed argument. In that community it would be possible to give all some votes each, but to give the rich and wise each many votes. The fealty of the community being to certain specified classes and qualities, you might openly and plainly give to those qualities and those classes a superior power in the polity.

But England is not like either of these countries. We are (as I showed at, perhaps, tedious length in a former essay) a deferential nation, but we are deferential by imagination, not by reason. The homage of our ignorant classes is paid not to individual things but to general things, not to precise things but to vague things. They are impressed by the great spectacle of English society; they bow down willingly, but they do not reckon their idols, they do not rationalise their religion. A country village is very happy and contented now; it acquiesces in a government which it likes. But it would not be contented if any one put before it bare inquiries. If any one said, 'Will you be subject to persons who live in £20 houses, or £30 houses; or will you agree to take votes yourselves, on condition that those who live in big houses, or those who spell well, or those who add up well, shall have more votes?' If we wish to comprehend what England really is, we should fancy a set of Dorsetshire peasants assembled by the mud-pond of the village solemnly to answer these questions. The utmost stretch of wisdom the conclave could arrive at would be, 'Ah, sir, you gentlefolks do know; and the Queen, God bless her! will see us righted.'

Of course, as soon as we see that England is a disguised republic we must see too that the classes for whom the disguise is necessary must be tenderly dealt with. In fact, we do deal very tenderly with them, even the roughest of us. Our most bold demagogues steer clear of country villages, and small towns, and lone farmhouses, where those ideas are rife. They do not even descend into the 'lanes' of the city, and track the ignorant they there find. Probably if they did, they would not find the least wish for the suffrage, or the least real knowledge of what it means. These classes do often enough want much, and want it bitterly. But they would interrupt the best of Mr Bright's speeches, as the mob did in Paris, '*Pain, pain pas de longs discours.*'* Bonaparte, we know, hoped to gain the acquiescence of the Egyptians by promising them a constitution, which (as Mr Kinglake truly said*) was like a sportsman hoping to fill his game-bag by promising the partridges a House of Commons. Much the same would be the result of trying to make an explicit constitution for our ignorant classes. They now defer involuntarily, unconsciously, and happily, but they would not defer argumentatively.

The plain result is that on the whole England is not a bit like either a country where numbers rule, or a country where mind, as mind, rules. The masses are infinitely too ignorant to make much of governing themselves, and they do not know mind when they see it. Rank they comprehend, and money they comprehend, but, except in the vague phrase, 'He be a sharp hand,' their conception of the abstract intellect is feeble and inexpressible.

The existing system (as I have before shown) is a very curious one. The middle classes rule under the shadow of the higher classes. The immense majority of the borough constituencies at least belong to the lower middle class, and the majority of the county constituency is, I suppose, by no means of the highest middle class. These people are the last to whom any people would yield any sort of homage if they saw them. They are but the 'dry trustees' of a fealty given to others. The mass of the English lower classes defer to the English higher class, but the nominal electors are a sort of accidental intermediaries, who were not chosen for their own merits and do not choose out of their own number.

It is not pleasant to observe how artificial our system is, and to be convinced that no natural system would serve our turn. The result of our electoral system is the House of Commons, and that House is our sovereign. As that House is, so will our Cabinet be, so will our administration be, so will our policy be. We have vested, therefore, the trust of our supremest power in persons chosen upon no system, and who if they elected people like themselves would be unbearable. Yet a simple system would be fatal. Some eager persons, indeed, who are dissatisfied with what they call the imbecility of our present Parliament—meaning by that, not its want of sense or opinion, but its want of vigour in action—hope to get an increase of energy by a wholesale democratic reform. They give us metaphors about the Titan who touched earth, and I do not feel quite sure that this illustration does not, even with themselves, do duty as an argument. They think that as there are passions at the bottom of the social scale, so there is energy. But ideas are wanted as well as impulse, and there are no ideas among our ignorant poor. Let us examine the matter carefully.

Suppose household suffrage all over England with the present constituencies. The result would be that the counties would be still as much, even if not more than now, in the hands of the landowners. They would be able by means of the labourers—who never had a reasonable political opinion and who have no pretence of independence and intelligence—to control the entire constituency. The lower you go in the agricultural counties, under some limiting line, such as £20 or £15, the more you strengthen the present rulers; the tighter you bind the yoke of quarter sessions.

Then as to the small boroughs, the lower you go in them the more you aggravate the force of money. There are not in the enormous majority of country towns any working men who have much opinion about politics, or sufficient self-respect to abstain from selling their vote. Not twenty men in ten thousand in those classes can comprehend in the least why any one thinks votes should not be sold. They know, of course, that 'gentlefolks' say so, but they regard it as an error engendered by high living, and part of the nonsense the rich talk about the poor. Very good judges assure me that these feelings are not declining but growing. Not only is more and more wealth brought to bear on the constituencies year by year, but the class of questions which a poor person can understand is become exceedingly small. If Ritualism could be made a political question,* it might be different. I have no doubt a candidate who could say anywhere that he was for anti-Ritualism, and his opponent for Ritualism, would be elected by acclamation. He would be the genuine representative of the actual electors on, perhaps, the only question they care for. In many places it would be worth a man's life to take a bribe to 'vote for the Pope.' But if a person will try to explain administrative reform, or law reform, or even parliamentary reform, to a chance audience in a small borough, he will only find a dull languor. No common working man there really thinks of them by himself, or is able to enter into them when stated rapidly or orally by others. Persons, of course, interest the multitude more. A candidate new to the business not long since asked an old hand what he should speak about. The answer was 'Gladstone and Garibaldi.* Stick to them as long as possible, and get back to them as quick as you can.' There is so little to interest poor electors now-a-days, and so much money is all but thrown at them, that instead of wondering at their vice in being bribed, we should think them political anchorites if they were not so. The lower you go in the minor towns, the more sure and the more inflexible you make the dominion of wealth.

The larger towns are doubtless different,—at least, much more mixed. There are in them a considerable, though uncertain number of really intellectual artizans; and these are very well fit to form a political opinion, and far too well off to care much about a bribe. What the number of these thoughtful artizans is we cannot indeed tell. We can guess roughly at the number of the whole artizan class; but this includes many very different from those we speak of. There are many who never think of politics, who could not think of them, who care only for such pleasures as they can get. But what the proportion is between the good artizan and the inferior artizan—the artizan who is no better than other people—we have no means of even investigating. There are no 'mental and moral statistics' here to help us; and I do not claim to be able from personal knowledge to know the true ratio, while such estimates as I have been able to elicit from others differ immensely. We can only allege that as both classes largely exist, in a political estimate both must be carefully allowed for.

But the vote of the inferior working man is simply the vote of the 'wire-puller.' I am not competent to explain in detail how the inferior species of large constituencies are managed now, but in general everybody knows that money will buy them, and that certain persons will contract for them. They are mapped out, I believe, by the electioneering agents, and each contractor for a district, or a set of votes, has a subcontractor for bits of the district and parts of the set. This fate will happen to all but the most rigid and political artizans, as it happens to all except the most strict and most intellectual of the lower middle classes. Here again, is the rule of money, just as in the small boroughs.

The result of our investigations, therefore, is this. So far from an ultra-democratic suffrage giving us a more homogeneous and decided House of Commons, it would give us a less homogeneous and a more timid House. There would be first, a new element,—the representative of the intellectual artizan, but he would be in a vast minority, and only a new item in a motley crowd; next, there would be the rich member for the corrupt big borough; next, the rich member for the corrupt small borough; and, next, the county member, much as he is now, but perhaps intensified and more even still of a class member. Now wealth is the most timid of all things; and the kind of people most apt to purchase seats are the most politically ignorant of people. They are newly-made rich men, who by hard labour and great skill in business have made large fortunes; or again, they are new men, who wish to be thought rich, and are deeply engaged in traffic and companies. These people have never been much used to give much attention to politics; they have no leisure, and perhaps no inclination either, to begin to give real attention to them in middle age; they float with the opinion of the day; they are guided by what was in the newspapers last week, and change to what may be there next week. Such men are timid upon a double score: they fear as rich men, that their wealth may be endangered; and they fear as ignorant men, that they may be entrapped into something they do not comprehend. *They* will bring no vigour. The landlord will bring none either; and the House will be more heterogeneous and probably be more vacillating and timid than now.

This argument, I shall be told, assumes that the present constitution will be retained though the suffrage is lowered, and that the point of the demonstration depends upon that retention. But I answer by denial. I say that any readjustment of boundaries would leave the matter much the same. There are not enough pure and rigid citizens, under a very low suffrage, to elect above a fraction of the House, pick the electoral places where you like; but territorial and aristocratic influence has its indefeasible seats, and money its power everywhere. The nature of our constitution is not predominantly in fault, but the nature of our people.

As far as I can see, the theory of the augmented administrative power of a more democratic government rests not upon an accurate argument, but upon a kind of faith. Sanguine men assume that the English, somehow or other, ought to have the best possible government, and when they find that Parliament is not so decided as they like, they are angry, and clutch at the readiest means of altering Parliament. But it is of little use to alter the suffrage unless we alter ourselves. A free government cannot be wiser than a free nation; it is but their fruit and outcome, and it must be as they are. The real source of the weakness in our policy is in ourselves—in our ignorance. Let any one take to pieces the brains of any twenty persons he knows well, and think how little accurate knowledge, how little defined opinion, how little settled notion of State policy there is in any of them. Let him see, too, how each opinion flickers and changes with the patent facts of the day, and with what the last newspaper said; and note how various the opinions are. Perhaps no two heads will have any notion quite the same—some extrinsic notion—some cuckoo's egg, perchance, of stolid prejudice. Neither man nor nation can be vigorous except upon a defined and settled creed.

The advocates of the artizan's claims ought to take warning by France. The visible experiment there conclusively proves that universal suffrage will not necessarily help *ouvriers*. The intelligent workmen of Paris and Lyons, and elsewhere, are the most eager opponents of the Imperial Government. Their imagined socialism was the object—if not the real object, at least the alleged and believed object—struck at by the *coup d'état*; there is never an election of deputies at which they do not return as many opponents of the Emperor as they can. Yet the Emperor boasts, and truly boasts, that he rules by universal suffrage; firmly based on the fear and ignorance of innumerable rural proprietors, he despises the intelligent working men, as well as the literary classes of the great towns; he knows both hate him, and he lets both hate him. Because France, in comparison with England, is a homogeneous country, and because its rural population greatly outnumbers its town population, and because the nature of an elected empire abolishes the influence of minorities, the result of universal suffrage has no doubt there been the establishment of a strong government. But that government is established by the enslavement of the particular intelligent class whom here we wish to enfranchise; and as we are not a homogeneous country, and as we have a Parliamentary Government which preserves some influence for minorities, we should not get the good from universal suffrage that the French have, although we should get the evil, for the thinking artizan would be outnumbered here as much as there.

The very nature of our social system, therefore, forbids those rough and rude changes which the boldest political physicians prescribe. Those changes would not, indeed, as unthinking people fancy, cause massacre and confiscation. In spite of De Tocqueville,* in spite of a hundred similar teachers, the *instantia terrifica* of the original French Revolution still rules men's fancies. They think that democracy means the guillotine; that as Sydney Smith said,* 'it abolishes human life and human rents.' But here democracy would mean the rule of money, and mainly and increasingly of new money working upon ignorance for its own ends. It would not destroy our constitution by sudden revolution, but it would vitally impair it by spoiling our Parliament. What then must be done? Is our electoral system so refined, so delicate, that we cannot venture to touch it? Can we not meet the wants of this age as our fathers did that of other ages?

Something will have to be done. The numerous, the organised, the intellectual class of artizans who live close to our greatest wealth, and in the very *foci* of our most delicate credit, must not be teased with the continual proffer of the suffrage and the continued denial of it. Their physical strength we might indeed well cope with, if we had the rest of the nation to back us. They are a great and formidable number, but they could be coerced at once if they were the assailants of property or the enemies of order. If their cause was unjust, we could resist them; but we have neither physical nor moral force to use when their demand is judicious. They are a class fit to be entrusted with the franchise, and whom it is desirable to entrust with it.

The simplest expedient which has as yet been proposed for that purpose is to recur to the old English system of different suffrages in different boroughs, which existed down to the Act of 1832. Whether that system can or cannot be revived, I think there can be little doubt that its abolition was an error. It gave an element of variety to our constitution, exactly where it was wanted. Sir James Mackintosh and Lord Russell, and other Whig authorities, had written panegyrics on it.* In the hurry of a half revolution, and from the need of a simple bill, this valuable legacy of old times was unhappily discarded. But if it can be revived now, it affords the readiest and easiest help out of our palpable difficulty.

But I have not to deal now with this or that plan for representing artizans; I have to do here with the Reform question not as respects its solution, but as respects its difficulty. It affords the best illustration of the nature of our constitution, such as history and the nature of the people have made it. It shows the difficulty of maintaining and amplifying Parliamentary institutions in the midst of a various, and, at the bottom of the social scale, ignorant and poor nation; it brings out unmistakably the fact that our constitution is not based on equality, or on an avowed and graduated adjustment to intelligence and property; but upon certain ancient feelings of deference and a strange approximate mode of representing sense and mind, neither of which must be roughly handled, for if spoiled they can never be remade, and they are the only supports possible of a polity such as ours, in a people such as ours.

And thus I may fitly, perhaps, close these essays on the English Constitution. They will have served their purpose if they assist to break up obsolete traditions on an important subject; if they induce others to treat it according to the sight of their eyes, and not according to the hearing of their ears; if even by their errors they should stir some great thinker to embody the experience of England so as to be useful to mankind.

APPENDIX ON REFORM

IN a pamphlet published in 1859 I stated at greater length the mode in which the scheme of Reform, stated at the end of the last essay, might be effected. I had intended to have added here some quotations from that pamphlet, but I do not find them very suitable to my purpose. I prefer to cite the following article, stating the same plan, which appeared in the *Economist* for 24th December, 1864:–

'A SIMPLE PLAN OF REFORM

'We last week showed *why* the Reform question is so difficult. We showed that people must bend their mind to something new; must accept some anomaly; must admit something out of the way. If they do not, sooner or later democracy is inevitable. The great artizan class is augmenting in numbers, growing in intelligence, intensifying in political tastes. It *will* have before long some recognised place in the national system. The existing ideas, the common ideas, afford it no place but an exclusive place. Solely founded in all the constituencies on a uniform basis of mere number, it inevitably gives in all constituencies a uniform preponderance to the most numerous class. Throw open the door, admit the working class, and they will be everywhere the most numerous. Some new plan, some additional experiment, some uncommon conception is required, unless we wish to have a worse America, in which the lower orders are equally despotic, but are not equally intelligent. We must choose between *anomaly* and *democracy*. There is no third alternative.

'We have then to consider what is the *minimum* of anomaly which will be sufficient for our preservation. How can we best and easiest, in the most effectual way, the most comprehensible way, the most acceptable way, admit the working classes to some power without giving them the whole power? How can we concede to them a share in the Constitution without sacrificing the whole Constitution to them?

'We must look carefully at the real world before we try to solve this problem. It is no use upon this subject of all subjects to evade facts, amuse ourselves with theories, spin cobwebs. We are dealing with a plain rough matter of political business, and any misconception of our *data*, any misconception in our design, will be sure to lead us into grievous error. We must really face the question as it truly stands, or it is of no use facing it at all.

'But when we look at the Reform movement as it exists in the world, we immediately perceive that this question of the working men is in practice inseparably associated and confused with a very different question. There is another great interest in this country which conceives itself to be ill represented,—which believes that it does not occupy its true place,—which thinks that it is kept down, overshadowed, cast into the shade by other interests unequal to itself in value, feebler in intelligence, lower in vigour, and inferior in political capacity. We mean *new commercial wealth*. It cannot be denied that much of the wealth created in the last thirty years is dissatisfied with the settlement of the Constitution made thirty years since,— that it is restless and dissatisfied,—that it fancies older, more aristocratic, less energetic classes cast it into the shade. When the distribution of the English representation was originally made, the Southern part of England was not only the most gentle and agreeable, but the most rich and energetic. The ports of Devonshire were celebrated wherever the English navy was known. What are now old and mouldering seaport towns were then active victorious marts, eager with enterprise, and sparkling with the intelligence of the day. England north of the Trent was in old times a less cultivated, a harsher, and less populous region. Naturally, therefore, the duty (the *charge* was the phrase of those times) was entrusted to the towns which were the most eminent for industry and for wealth. Parliamentary boroughs were placed in the South because it was adapted for Parliamentary boroughs: they were not placed in the North, beacuse it was not adapted. Centuries of change and industry have altered all this. The North is now the industrial region, the vigorous member, the growing part of the Commonwealth, and we are only carrying out the original design of the English representation, if we take from the parts which were then living but are now dead, and add to the parts which had not been born but now live and thrive.

'No one who observes the Reform agitation closely can fail to see how closely this feeling—this *sensation* of the insufficient representation of commercial wealth and manufacturing industry—is associated with the cry for working-class representation. It is the master manufacturers who agitate for the enfranchisement of their own workmen. The classes whose immediate interests are most clearly opposed, who are constantly and of necessity driving unpleasant bargains with each other, who often are at bitter feud, are on this subject at one. The capitalist heads the movement of the citizen; he is sometime more clamorous for the rights of labour than the labourer himself. The explanation is simple. The capitalist and the labourer have a united interest—a common object—in this matter. They wish to push forward the present seats of their common industry into the places now occupied by the mouldering remains of past industry. When a great manufacturer says at a West Riding meeting, "I wish to alter the Constitution, so that the working classes around me should be represented," he means that undoubtedly very sincerely, but he means also, and more sincerely, because half consciously, "We—I, and such as I—ought to have more power. The stationary South must no longer govern the advancing North."

'Examined by the grave tests of sound philosophy, it cannot be denied that the whole new world of the North has its grievance as well as the artizan part of that world. Neither has such a place in the community as it ought to have. The effect of the Act of 1832 was to lessen the powers of the working classes in the country: the Act of 1832, though it did something to remedy the inequality between North and South—though it gave something to the new and took something from the old—did not adjust the balance even in the inequality it stood then; it did not transfer enough for a just rectification at that time, much less did it adjust matters as they should stand now that, after thirty busy years, the claimant has achieved such vast progress, and the possessor has plainly made so little. A good scheme of reform would *both* increase the power of what we must roughly but intelligibly call "the North," at the same time that it gave some power to the whole working classes, though denying them the whole power.

'We would propose to effect both these objects by the following means. Transfer a certain *considerable* number of members from insignificant boroughs,—from the well-known boroughs which have uniformly figured in every schedule of proposed disfranchisement,— to the great seats of industry, and in those seats of industry, and there *only*, lower the franchise, so as to admit artizan classes. This would give the necessary representation to the working classes, and it would give them only that necessary representation. Being only possessed of a certain number of seats, they could not rule the country, they could not impose on it their enthusiasms, their prejudices, or their fancied interests. Their members would be only one sort of members out of many sorts. They would contribute an element to a Parliament; they would not elect a Parliament. At the same time, this plan would cure the now faulty division between the more progressive part of England and the less progressive. The proposed transfer would give to those who ought to have, and take from those who ought not to have; and this is what is wanted.

'It may be justly objected that this plan would throw the representation of the great seats of industry, of the most intelligent part of the country, into the exclusive power of the least intelligent inhabitants in those places. But we would meet that objection. We would give to each of these great cities with low suffrage as many as three members, and allow all voters to give their three votes to any one candidate. This would give the rich and cultivated one member at least; for they would always be a large minority, and any minority greater than a fourth is by this plan sure of a vote.

'It may also be objected that this plan is an unjust plan. It gives, it may be said, a vote to an operative in borough A, and denies a vote to a precisely similar operative in borough B. But there is no injustice when we examine the matter. No one has a right to a political power which he will use to impair a *better* man's political power. The real injustice would be to give votes to all the working classes, for then, in substance, all the better classes, the more instructed classes, the more opulent classes, would have no votes at all. Supposing this selection of special constituencies to be the best mode of admitting the operative to a limited share of power, we need not fear the accusation of its injustice. It will be for the excluded operative to suggest some better plan for giving his class some power, and not giving them the whole power. Till he has given us a better scheme, we may rightfully act on what we think best. And, unquestionably, the operative in the *un*selected is not injured by the enfranchisement of the operative in the selected place. We take from him nothing; only we do not see our way to give him that which we see our way to give to another man.

'The common sense of this plan is the great recommendation of it. You have a great intelligent class to enfranchise, and by lowering the franchise in great cities you will enfranchise it. But in the mass of the boroughs there is no such class. Where, as the *Times* justly asked, is "there in *Thetford* the instructed, intelligent political class that our reformers speak of?" Why, then, touch Thetford? We wish to lower the franchise because we wish to give votes to a special class. In the mass of boroughs that class is not to be found; why, then, alter the franchise in the mass of boroughs? A great argument for this plan, too, is that which Mr Buxton put so happily in his letter to the *Times*,*—"a Parliament composed of human beings might vote for it." He found, he said, that the indiscriminate adoption of the minority principle, as it is called—of the permission, that is, to concentrate his votes on any candidate he likes—would change so many seats at the next election, that it could never be got through the House of Commons. So many people would feel they were voting for their own destruction. We rather fear that the same objection would apply to the plan which Mr Buxton proceeded to suggest, the giving a greater number of votes to the rich than to the poor. This, too, being a great diffused change affecting all constituencies, and affecting them much, would be very difficult to *pass*. Everybody would feel "that may hurt me in my borough. It is an unknown element. I am *in* now, but after this newfangled thing is introduced I may not come in." We fear the universal action of selfish fear upon every member for every seat.

'But, according to the plan we have put forward, the great mass of seats and boroughs would not be touched at all. Their members would say, "This is a good Bill; this does not 'touch us.'" Of course, the members for the places from which seats were to be taken would be sure to complain, and perhaps the places where the constituency was to be augmented might also complain. But the virtuous indignation of an uninjured majority would soon tread down the selfishness of these few. Mr Roebuck would rise* and ask "If the selfishness of a small minority was to be despotic in this country?" And the vast majority, happy to escape being hurt themselves, would feel a pleasant patriotism in the necessary immolation of the selected few.

'As we said, we propose this plan—saying that it includes an anomaly, and even because it includes an anomaly. Nothing, as we before proved at length, which does not include an extraordinary uncommon element will achieve the work which there is to do. We concede the exceptional nature of our scheme, but we believe that

M.P. for Sheffield

something exceptional is necessary and that this is the minimum of exception.'

I do not know whether such a scheme as this is now possible. Perhaps the passions of men have become too excited, and a more commonplace plan is all which can be hoped for. But I am sure it was possible when the above article was written, and that it would have saved us from many evils.

THE END

EXPLANATORY NOTES

3 *Lincoln's death*: Abraham Lincoln (1809–65) was assassinated on 14 April 1865 by John Booth, a Confederate sympathizer. His running mate (and therefore Vice-President) Andrew Johnson (1808–75) then succeeded him as US President. By 1867 (when this edition of Bagehot was published) Congress had opposed Johnson's policy of readmitting Southern representatives. Johnson vetoed Congress's measures and Congress overrode his veto. (He later narrowly survived an impeachment by one vote.)

5 *Mr Mill*: John Stuart Mill (1806–73), philosopher and MP for Westminster, 1865–8.

10 *ex vi termini*: by definition.

11 *Sir R. Walpole*: Sir Robert Walpole (1676–1745), First Lord of the Treasury and Chancellor of the Exchequer from 1721 to 1742, is usually regarded as the first Prime Minister.

The discriminating favour of William IV . . . rivals: in July 1834, on the resignation of Earl Grey, William IV surprisingly appointed the inexperienced Lord Melbourne (1779–1848) Prime Minister.

Lord Palmerston: Henry John Temple, Lord Palmerston (1784–1865) was Prime Minister in the years 1855–7 and 1859–65. Visibly weak when Bagehot commenced the *English Constitution* he died on October 18, 1865.

13 *Lord Melbourne put his back to the door and said . . .* : Melbourne is reported to have made this comment following a cabinet meeting in March 1841.

15 *Indian Chancellor . . . England*: following the Government of India Act of 1858 a Governor General of India (based mainly in Calcutta) had his own financial department, whilst back in Britain the Secretary of State for India had an advisory council, including a financial member. In theory all Indian expenditure was controlled by the Secretary of State.

an angry financial correspondence with Jefferson Davis: on 13 March 1865 Jefferson Davis (1808–89), President of the Confederate States, sent a message to the Confederate Congress at Richmond, accusing it of holding up the mobilization of troops. On 18 March the Congress assembled for what proved the last time and gave Davis's message a critical reception.

16 *I leave this passage to stand . . .* : Abraham Lincoln (1809–65) was assassinated on 14 April 1865 by John Booth, a Confederate sympathizer. Andrew Johnson (1808–75), the new President, declared that 'Treason must be made infamous, and traitors must be impoverished.'

19 *Confederate rebellion*: the American Civil War effectively began in

February 1861 with the secession of six southern states and the election of Jefferson Davis as President of the Confederacy.

19 *Mr Breckenridge*: John Cabell Breckenridge (1821–75), Vice–President, 1856–60 and unsuccessful pro-slavery Presidential candidate in 1860.

20 *Washington and Hamilton*: George Washington (1732–99) was the first President of the USA (1789–97) and Alexander Hamilton (1757–1804) was the first Secretary of the Treasury. Both men attended the convention in Philadelphia in 1787 which drew up the constitution.

22 *Lord Liverpool . . . Chatham . . . Louis Philippe . . . Napoleon*: Robert Banks Jenkinson, Lord Liverpool (1770–1828), was Prime Minister between 1812 and 1827 and was known for his pragmatic approach to government. By contrast, William Pitt, 1st Earl of Chatham (1708–78), Secretary of State and effectively Prime Minister between 1756 and 1761, was a strident Foreign Minister. Louis Philippe (1773–1850), was King of France between 1830 and 1848 and proved more of a constitutional monarch than any of his predecessors. Following his military successes Napoleon Bonaparte (1769–1821) became Emperor of France in 1804.

Cavour: Count Camillo Benso di Cavour (1810–61), Prime Minister of the Kingdom of Sardinia between 1852 and 1859 and the behind-the-scenes architect of Italian unification.

23 *at the Crimean difficulty*: in February 1855 the government headed by Lord Aberdeen, a coalition of Whigs, Peelites, and Radicals, resigned over accusations that it had mismanaged the war effort. Aberdeen, who had sought a negotiated peace with Russia from the outset of the difficulties, was replaced by Lord Palmerston, who favoured direct Franco-British action against Russia.

the Reform Act: the 1832 Reform Act, which not only overhauled the electoral system, but also contributed to the growth of parliamentary government.

the singular defect . . . President: Johnson, the military governor of Tennessee, was Lincoln's vice-presidential running mate in the 1864 Presidential campaign, and, not long after inauguration, was rushed into office as President after Lincoln's assassination.

24 *the first election of Mr Lincoln*: although well-known in Illinois, Lincoln was a relative newcomer in the presidential campaign of 1860 and won largely because the two Democrat party candidates, Breckenridge and Douglas, split the vote.

our great Satirist: Bagehot is probably alluding to the satirical journal, *Punch*.

29 *summum bonum*: highest good.

34 *the £10 borough renters, and the £50 county renters*: the 1832 Reform Act enfranchised occupiers of property worth £10 rental per annum in the boroughs and £50 in the counties.

38 *'The political condition,'* says Mr Grote: George Grote, *A History of Greece*, 12 vols. (1846–56), ii. 82–6.

41 *the marriage of the Prince of Wales*: the Prince of Wales and Princess Alexandra were married at Windsor on 10 March 1863.

Court Circular: then, as now, most newspapers included a column listing events involving the royal family. There was also a 'society' newspaper of the same name which commenced publication in 1856.

the Queen's letter to Mrs Lincoln: Queen Victoria sent a letter of condolence to Abraham Lincoln's widow soon after his assassination.

42 *After the Revolution*: the 'Glorious revolution' was the bloodless coup of 1688 whereby James II abdicated and William of Orange and Mary acceded to the throne. When Anne (1655–1714), Mary's sister, succeeded in 1702, her father, James II, had already died, but her brother James Stuart (1688–1766), the 'old Pretender', remained as a claimant to the crown.

43 *the Pretender*: see previous note.

44 *by virtue of 6 Anne, c. 7*: 6 Anne c. 7 is the 1707 Act of Succession.

45 *utilitarians*: the followers of the philosopher Jeremy Bentham (1748–1832), who, among other things, demanded cheap government.

They quote Napoleon's saying: Napoleon disapproved of the 1799 constitution, in which the Abbé Sièyes (1748–1836) had a hand and in which the 'grand elector' would rule alongside two nominated consuls. Formerly French Foreign Minister in 1836 and 1840, Louis Adolphe Thiers (1797–1877) was one of the foremost historians of his generation, the author of *L'Histoire de la révolution française* (1823–7) and *L'Histoire du consulat et de l'empire* (1845–62).

46 *Lord and Lady Derby*: Edward Stanley, 14th Earl of Derby (1799–1869), Prime Minister 1852, 1858–9, 1867–8, and Emma Caroline, Lady Derby.

47 *an 'upper ten thousand'*: contemporary slang for the social elite. The phrase originated in New York in the 1840s.

Socrates: Greek philosopher *c.*470–399 BC.

52 *it would have been impossible for Italy . . . than his*: as King of Sardinia, Victor Emmanuel (1820–78), helped unite Cavour's Piedmontese nationalists in the north with Garibaldi's redshirts in southern Italy.

the failure of Louis Philippe: in February 1848 at the first sign of unrest, Louis Philippe (1773–1850), the King of France, panicked and dismissed François Guizot (1787–1874), his Foreign Minister and de facto head of the administration.

53 *Lord North*: Frederick, 8th Lord North (1732–92), Prime Minister between 1770 and 1782.

54 *the Queen very wisely attempted to make life Peers*: in 1856, seeking to increase the number of Law Lords, Lord Palmerston recommended that the judge James Parke (1782–1868) be made Baron Wensleydale for his

lifetime. However, a House of Lords committee of privileges decided that the Crown's power to create life peers had fallen into disuse.

54 *Comyn's 'Digest'*: Sir John Comyn's *Digest of the Laws of England*, 5 vols. (1762–7).

55 *Mr Fox . . . 'of an infernal spirit'*: attributed to Fox, speaking in the House of Commons, 22 February 1782, by Horace Walpole, *Journal of the Reign of King George III, from the Year 1771 to 1783*, 2 vols. (1859), ii. 507.

Lord Thurlow: Edward, 1st Baron Thurlow (1731–1806), Lord Chancellor, 1778–83, 1788–92.

the Queen used to sign all military commissions: the Officers' Commissions Act of 1862 removed the necessity of obtaining the royal signature.

57 *There must be a meeting at 'Willis's Rooms'*: on 6 June 1859 the whole of the Liberal party in the House of Commons met at Willis's Rooms in central London in order that Lord Palmerston and Lord John Russell might patch up their differences.

58 *at the Schleswig-Holstein difficulty*: in July 1864, having been defeated on the issue in the House of Lords, Lord Palmerston's government survived an attack by Disraeli on its handling of the Prussian occupation of Holstein.

59 *Almost at the beginning of his career*: in 1762 George III ousted Chatham in favour of the Marquis of Bute. In 1805 he rejected William Pitt's suggestion that Charles James Fox be invited to join the ministry. (Chatham is William Pitt the elder; Bute is John Stuart, 3rd Marquis of Bute (1713–92); Pitt is William Pitt the younger.)

Addington: Henry Addington, 1st Viscount Sidmouth (1757–1844), former Speaker of the House of Commons, led an unremarkable ministry between 1801 and 1804.

60 *The events of 1858*: in February 1858, led by Thomas Milner Gibson (1806–84), many radical MPs joined with the Conservative opposition to defeat Lord Palmerston's government over the Conspiracy to Murder bill.

61 *Duke of Newcastle*: Thomas Pelham Holles, 2nd Duke of Newcastle (1693–1768), Prime Minister between 1754 and 1756, and nominally head of the ministry between 1757 and 1762 (although Pitt the elder was Prime Minister to all intents and purposes).

62 *Madame de Walmoden*: in 1738, a year after Queen Caroline's death, George II moved his mistress, Amalie Sophie Wallmoden (1704–65), into St James's Palace. She was created Countess of Yarmouth in 1740. NB: Wallmoden is the German spelling given in standard histories. Presumably Bagehot is using the Frenchified version.

the Marchioness of Conyngham: Elizabeth, Marchioness Conyngham (1770–1861) lived, along with her husband, in the royal household of George IV.

63 *In 1851 Louis Napoleon had his coup d'état*: in a remark made to the French ambassador, Lord Palmerston (1784–1865) expressed approval of Louis Napoleon's overthrow of the republican constitution. Under pressure from Queen Victoria, Lord John Russell (1792–1878) advised him to resign as Foreign Secretary.

66 *King Leopold has exercised immense power . . . I have described*: elected in 1831, Leopold I (1790–1865) was a constitutional monarch. He himself described his situation as one in which 'the state was in reality a republic with the shades of monarchical forms'.

a commanding influence over Lord Malmesbury: James Howard Harris, 3rd Earl Malmesbury (1807–89), Foreign Secretary in 1852 and again in 1858–9.

'The divinity which doth hedge a king': Shakespeare, *Hamlet*, IV. v.

The best instance is Lord Chatham: William Pitt the elder, 1st Earl Chatham (1708–78), enjoyed great popularity following British successes in the Seven Years' War (1756–63).

67 *Mr Burke*: Edmund Burke (1729–97), Whig MP and political writer. Letter to the Marquis of Rockingham, 5 January 1775, in Burke, *Correspondence between 1744 and 1797*, 4 vols. (1844), i. 503–8.

the 'doubtfulness things are involved in': Joseph Butler (1692–1752), Bishop of Durham and moral philosopher. Author of *Analogy of Religion Natural and Revealed* (1736).

69 *the reply of the Emperor Alexander to Madame de Stael*: a comment made in 1812 and cited in Maria Norris, *Life and Times of Madame de Stael* (1853), 354.

71 *says Swift*: Jonathan Swift (1667–1745), satirist and politician. Swift to Mrs Dingley, 7 April 1713; *Letters written by the late Jonathan Swift . . . 1703–40*, 4 vols. (1776–8), i. 373.

corruptio optimi pessima: corruption of the best is worst.

72 *Mr Pitt's wise plans*: after the Union with Ireland came into effect in 1801 Pitt proposed the emancipation of Catholics, against George III's wishes.

76 *As our great satirist has observed*: again, probably *Punch*.

The 'wicked Lord Lowther': James Lowther, Earl of Lonsdale (1736–1802).

77 *a Duke of Devonshire, . . . Duke of Bedford . . . Thurlow*: the Cavendish family (the Dukes of Devonshire) and the Russell family (the Dukes of Bedford) were amongst the wealthiest landowners in Britain. Edward Thurlow (1731–1806) was Lord Chancellor between 1778 and 1783.

county members . . . borough members: in the years before the 1832 Reform Act it was calculated that around 200 parliamentary seats were 'nomination boroughs', that is not available for open election but controlled by the Crown or aristocratic patrons.

78 *The Upper House of our Victorian Constitution*: in 1864 the Upper House

in the Australian colony of Victoria blocked the new government's Appropriation bill, as it contained tariff measures. The deadlock was not resolved until 1866.

79 *The Crown has the authority to create new peers ... to create them*: in January 1832, following the defeat of the Reform Bill in the House of Lords, William IV agreed to Earl Grey's request that he create at least twenty-one new peers in order to prevent further opposition.

the great Aylesbury case: a protracted legal wrangle in 1700 between the two Houses of Parliament over the right to vote of Matthew Ashby, an elector at Aylesbury. The Commons insisted it was the sole judge of election matters.

80 *he wrote a very curious letter to the present Lord Derby*: in February 1846 the Duke of Wellington (1769–1852) sent a memorandum to the then Lord Stanley (1799–1869), from which Bagehot quotes; G. R. Gleig, *The Life of Arthur, First Duke of Wellington* (1862), 569–72.

81 *Captain Elliott, in China*: in 1840 the Chinese, attempting to end the opium trade, blockaded the port of Canton. Charles Elliot (1801–75) led the British attempt to break the blockade.

83 *the 18th Brumaire*: returning from Egypt, Naploeon Bonaparte overthrew the French Directory government on 9–10 November 1799 (18th Brumaire in the revolutionary calendar), and established the Consulate.

84 *the present Lord Grey*: Henry, 3rd Earl Grey (1802–94), Colonial Secretary 1846–52, and author of *The Colonial Policy of Lord John Russell's Administration* (1853) and *Parliamentary Government considered with Reference to reform* (1858; 2nd edn. 1864). Both were works which influenced Bagehot.

85 *'members for railways'*: MPs who were railway directors. There were some 125 such MPs in 1868: Geoffrey Alderman, *The Railway Interest* (Leicester, 1973).

86 *the Private Bill Acts*: private bills, i.e. legislation such as local government, railways, as well as legislation such as divorce and naturalization relating to individuals, constituted the main workload of the mid-Victorian House of Commons, their volume doubling between 1852 and 1866.

87 *Swiss state-right patriot*: until 1874 Switzerland was based on a loose confederation of independent cantons, each with their own institutions.

88 *A severe ... critic of our institutions*: untraced.

a few years ago when Lyndhurst, Brougham and Campbell were in vigour: John Singleton Copley, Lord Lyndhurst (1772–1863), was Lord Chancellor in the years 1827–30, 1834–5, and 1841–6; Henry, Lord Brougham (1778–1868), in the years 1830–4; and John, Lord Campbell (1779–1861), in the years 1859–61.

89 *'the House of Commons has more sense than any one in it'*: source of quotation not traced.

Lord Chesterfield's axiom: Philip Stanhope, Earl of Chesterfield (1694–1773), author of a famous series of letters to his son.

92 *foster a new breed*: the recruitment, qualifications, and pay structure of the Indian Civil Service were overhauled by series of reforms beginning in the mid-1850s.

93 *Mr Bright will sometime use*: John Bright (1811–89), radical MP for Durham, 1843–7, Manchester, 1847–57, Birmingham, 1858–89.

95 *Lord Macaulay was to have been amongst the first*: Thomas Babington Macaulay (1800–59), the MP and historian. He was ennobled in 1857.

96 *the trial of O'Connell*: in September 1844 the House of Lords reversed the guilty verdict passed by a Dublin court on the Irish leader, Daniel O'Connell (1775–1847), 'the Liberator', who advocated repeal of the Union with Britain.

97 *Mr Lowe*: Robert Lowe (1811–92), Vice-President of the Education Board, 1859–64. Cf. Lowe in the House of Commons, *Hansard*, 177, 28 Feb. 1865, col. 875.

104 *Paley said many shrewd things*: William Paley (1743–1805), author of *Principles of Moral and Political Philosophy* (1785).

105 *combating its cattle plague*: in June 1865 reports of an outbreak of rinderpest in England and Wales began to appear. By the end of the year 8,000 cattle had died.

Lord Brougham and Lord Bolingbroke: Brougham (see also note to p. 88) was author of *The British Constitution: its History, Structure and Working* (1861). Henry St John, Viscount Bolingbroke (1678–1751), opponent of Walpole, and author of two famous attacks on government by party: *A Dissertation on Parties* (1733) and *Idea of a Patriot King* (1738).

An old secretary of the Treasury: Bagehot is probably referring to Charles Arbuthnot (1767–1850), one of the longest-lasting secretaries to the Treasury in the pre-reform era, who held the position of patronage secretary in the Tory party between 1809 and 1823.

106 *'finest brute votes in Europe'*: sometimes attributed to Benjamin Disraeli (1804–81).

Mr Cobden most justly said: Richard Cobden (1804–65), free trade advocate and MP for Stockport 1841–7, West Riding of Yorkshire 1847–57, Rochdale 1859–65.

107 *Father Newman complains*: John Henry Newman (1801–90), Catholic theologian.

'no stays in Peel's argument': stays were corsets stiffened by strips of whalebone, worn to shape and support the figure.

110 *the scheme of Mr Hare*: Thomas Hare (1806–91), author of two influential works on proportional representation, *The Machinery of Representation* (1857), and *A Treatise on the Election of Representatives, Parliamentary and Municipal* (1859).

119 *'D-mn me,' said Lord Eldon*: John Scott, Baron Eldon (1751–1838), Lord Chancellor (1801–6, 1807–27), an 'ultra-Tory' opponent of the Reform Bill in 1831–2.

120 *Bolingbroke and Disraeli*: for Bolingbroke see note to p. 105. Benjamin Disraeli (1804–81), Prime Minister in 1868 and between 1874 and 1880.

121 *Mr Bright . . . working man*: Bright, whose family owned carpet mills, was the parliamentary figurehead of the parliamentary reform campaign in 1866–7.

122 *'Jacobins to a man'*: a paraphrasing of the words used by Edmund Burke (1729–97) in his *Thoughts on French Affairs* (1797).

ceteris paribus: other things being equal.

127 *Gatton and Old Sarum . . . good members*: Gatton in Surrey and Old Sarum in Wiltshire were two of the smallest and most notoriously corrupt of the old nomination boroughs in the pre-1832 electoral system. They were disenfranchised.

Mr Carlyle: Thomas Carlyle (1795–1881), author of *The French Revolution* (1837), *Past and Present* (1843), *Latter Day Pamphlets* (1850), and other works.

128 *'Mr Gladstone and Lord Russell may have been wrong about reform'*: the Liberal government resigned in 1866 following the defeat of their reform bill.

What could be more absurd than what happened in 1858?: the popularity of Palmerston's government was fatally undermined in 1858 by a combination of factors, including his inclusion in his Cabinet of John de Burgh Ulick, 14th Earl of Clanricarde (1802–74), who had been named in a court case involving the estate of an Irish widow (in which he was accused of being her son and heir's real father), and Palmerston's own careless handling of diplomacy with Count Walewski, the French ambassador.

Lord Cranborne: Robert Cecil, 3rd Marquis of Salisbury (1830–1902), was known as Viscount Cranborne between 1865 and 1868, after the death of his elder brother. He was Secretary of State for India until he resigned over Disraeli's reform bill in 1867.

131 *'Darby Griffith destroyed Lord Palmerston's first Government'*: in the House of Commons on 16 February 1858 Christopher Darby Griffith (1804–85), MP for Devizes, 1857–68, asked the question about Lord Palmerston's reply to Count Walewski which precipitated the defeat of Palmerston's government.

132 *green coffee to the Crimea*: inefficiencies in the supply of military, medical, food and clothing resources to the British forces in the Crimea brought about the collapse of the Aberdeen coalition in February 1855.

133 *M. Guizot tells us*: Guizot's (see note to p. 52) *Memoirs* were published in English in four volumes between 1858 and 1861.

134 *quaestiunculae*: trifling questions.

136 *the three kings of Somerset House as they were called*: established by the Poor Law Amendment Act of 1834, the three-man Poor Law Commission was based in Somerset House and was responsible for the co-ordination of poor law relief in England and Wales. The first three commissioners were in fact Thomas Frankland Lewis (1780–1855) (George Cornewall Lewis's father), John Shaw-Lefevre (1797–1879), and George Nicholls (1781–1865).

Mr Chadwick: Edwin Chadwick (1801–90) was one of the authors of the 1833 Poor Law report, and was Secretary of the Poor Law Board from 1834 to 1846.

Sir George Lewis: George Cornewall Lewis (1806–93), Chancellor of the Exchequer 1855–8, Home Secretary 1859–61, Secretary for War 1861–3.

138 *the triumph of the Prussians*: in 1866 Prussia defeated Austria at the Battle of Sadowa, and also annexed much of the former German Confederation.

Mr Grant Duff . . . delineates them: Mountstuart E. Grant Duff, *Studies in European Politics* (1866), 228–9.

cap-à-pie: head to foot.

139 *as Burke put it*: Edmund Burke, *Speech on American Taxation* (1774).

'Frederic the Great lost the battle of Jena': Frederick the Great (1712–86) reformed the Prussian bureaucracy. However, twenty years after his death, the Prussian army was defeated by Napoleon at the Battle of Jena. Napoleon himself, it should be noted, thought the Prussians would not have been defeated had Frederick been in charge.

140 *'Every imaginable and real social interest,' says Mr Laing*: Samuel Laing, *Observations on the Social and Political State of the European People in 1848 and 1849* (1850), 184–5.

Voltaire says somewhere: 'Money', *Philosophical Dictionary* (1764).

141 *the great joint stock banks of London*: following the Bank Act of 1833, which extended the joint-stock principle to banks as long as they were not note-issuing, London-based joint-stock banks such as the London and Westminster, and the National Provincial Bank, began to surpass the traditional private banks.

143 *The late Sir George Lewis*: George Cornewall Lewis (1806–93).

The Duke of Newcastle was of this use at least in the Crimean war: Henry Pelham Clinton (1811–64), 5th Duke of Newcastle, became Secretary of War in 1854 when the Department of War was separated from the Colonial Office.

144 *The 'dyer's hand would be subdued to what it works in'*: Shakespeare, Sonnet 111.

147 *the Great Duke*: Arthur Wellesley, 1st Duke of Wellington (1769–1852).

150 *'pretentious, insufficient, and unsound'*: source not traced.

150 *Tocqueville and Lavergne have shown . . . the old régime*: Alexis de Tocqueville's *L'Ancien Régime et la Révolution* (1856) and Léonce de Lavergne's *Les Assemblées Provinciales sous Louis XVI* (1864) had both argued that centralization in France long preceded the imperial rule of Napoleon.

151 *Comptrollership of the Exchequer*: Thomas Spring Rice, Baron Monteagle (1790–1866), was the last person to hold this office which, under the Exchequer and Audit Departments Act of 1866, was replaced by the position of Comptroller and Auditor General.

the O'Connell case: in September 1844. See note to p. 96.

Lord Westbury . . . 'Essays and Reviews': Richard Bethell, Baron Westbury (1800–73), Lord Chancellor between 1861 and 1865, who sat on the committee of the Privy Council in 1864 that heard and upheld the appeals of the authors of a volume of biblical criticism entitled *Essays & Reviews*, a controversial book written by clergy which had been condemned by Convocation.

153 *A new India Office . . . had to be made*: the Government of India Act of 1858 transferred the administration of India to the Crown, in the shape of a new Secretary of State for India, advised by a council.

Mr James Wilson: James Wilson (1805–60), proprietor and editor of the *Economist* and member of the Council for India. Bagehot's father-in-law.

eo nomine: explicitly, under that name.

155 *Hobbes told us long ago*: Thomas Hobbes, *Leviathan* (1651).

156 *A fundamental article of the Federal constitution*: the four articles of the American Constitution to which Bagehot refers are Amendment 10 (1791), and Articles I 1:2a, II 1:2a, and II 2:2a of the original Constitution.

157 *Mr Johnson*: see notes to pp. 3 and 23.

163 *'an organised hypocrisy'*: House of Commons, 17 March 1845.

164 *particeps criminis*: a partner in the crime.

Dei ex machinâ: 'gods from the machine' (a device of ancient Greek theatre), i.e. a quick-fix solution.

166 *'That in 1802 every hereditary monarch was insane'*: source not traced.

168 *In 1835 William IV dismissed an administration*: in November 1834 [Bagehot got the date wrong], alarmed at the Whigs' policy towards the Church of Ireland, William IV failed in his attempt to use the accession of Viscount Althorp, the Whig leader in the Commons, to the Lords, as an excuse to dismiss Melbourne's ministry, although Lord John Russell had been chosen by the party to take over from Althorp in the Commons.

172 *One was in Queen Anne's time*: in 1712 twelve new peers were created to strengthen the ministry of Robert Harley, the Earl of Oxford (1661–1724), and increase parliamentary support for the Peace of Utrecht.

Swift bitterly and justly said: Swift, *Memoirs relating to that change which happened in Queen Anne's ministry in the year 1710*, in *Swift's Works*, ed. Thomas Roscoe, 2 vols. (1843), i. 273.

Mrs Masham: Abigail Masham (1670–1734), Queen Anne's dresser and court favourite.

Lord Grey promises the correspondence: published in two volumes in 1867 as *The Correspondence of the late Earl Grey with His Majesty the King William IV and with Sir Herbert Taylor*, edited by Henry, Earl Grey.

174 *like Count Moltke*: Helmuth, Count von Moltke (1800–91), Chief of Staff of the Prussian Army, since 1858. A learned man, who wrote widely on military strategy, he was known as 'the Silent'.

our very supporter of Divine Right . . . Count Bismarck: the unification of Germany entailed the end of power for the smaller German monarchies and duchies. At the same time Otto von Bismarck behaved autocratically towards the Prussian Parliament, suspending it temporarily in 1862.

175 *Mr Darwin begins*: Charles Darwin, *The Origin of the Species, By Means of Natural Selection, or the Preservation of Favoured Races in the Struggle for Life* (1859), 1.

'that most skilful breeder, Sir John Sebright': Sir John Sebright (1767–1846), MP and author of *The Art of Improving the Breeds of Domestic Animals* (1809). Darwin mentions him in *The Origin of the Species*, p. 31.

176 *réalisme impitoyable*: merciless realism.

178 *the masterly book of Hallam*: Henry Hallam (1777–1859), author of *The Constitutional History of England from Henry VII to George II* (1827).

182 *a modern Parliamentary agent*: by mid-century there were sixty or so solicitors' firms dealing with the draughtsmanship of parliamentary legislation, principally railway bills.

183 *Even in the 'Great Charter'*: the Magna Carta, agreed to by King John and the rebel nobility, was sealed at Runnymede on 15 June 1215.

'converted the right of taxation into the shield of liberty': James Mackintosh (1765–1832), Whig politician and historian. Author of *The History of England*, 10 vols. (1830–40), i. 221.

184 *Lord Macaulay is right in saying*: Macaulay, *The History of England*, 5 vols. (1848–61).

just as Hooper tells us his father was: John Hooper (d. 1555), Bishop of Gloucester and Worcester, executed by Mary I.

Charles II said that he would never go on his travels: Charles's forces were defeated by Cromwell's army at Worcester in August, 1651, forcing him to flee into exile.

186 *Mr Perceval's government*: Spencer Perceval (1762–1812), Prime Minister from 1809 until his assassination in 1812.

an indescribable life in St James's Street with Mr Fox: in the 1780s, much to his father's despair, the young Prince of Wales gambled and got into debt in the company of Charles James Fox and other Whigs, such as the playwright Sheridan.

186 *'he lived by being a royalist'*: cf. Chateaubriand's description of Louis XVI, that no one should be more royalist than the king': *De la monarchie selon la chartre* (Paris, 1816), 27.

187 *'un vrai peuple moderne'*: cf. De Tocqueville, *L'Ancien Régime et la Révolution* (1856), 27: 'une nation toute moderne'.

the census of 1851: the Census of 1851 was the most extensive to date, based as it was on the new administrative framework established by the Civil Registration Act of 1837. Two separate censuses on religious attendance and educational provision were also carried out.

188 *the Long Parliament*: the City of London provided financial support to Parliament during the 1640s, and the Corporation supported parliamentary control of the militia. On 5 January 1642, Parliament decided to meet in the Guildhall, where 'all members that came were to have voices': *The History of the Rebellion and Civil Wars in England, beginning in the year 1641* (1702), iv. 159.

Down to George III's time: the mayoral campaign of John Wilkes in 1774 was the last famous occasion when the Corporation showed its radicalism.

189 *De Tocqueville . . . founded what may be called the culte of corporations*: De Tocqueville's *Democracy in America* (1835) included an attack on French-style centralization and praise for the Puritan settlers who took old English habits of local autonomy with them.

191 *the relations between the French railways and the Emperor*: in the 1850s Napoleon III embarked on an ambitious scheme of railway building, revolutionizing the system of public credit in France to pay for it all.

193 *'Pain, pain pas de longs discours'*: 'Bread, bread, no long speeches.'

as Mr Kinglake truly said: in 'The French Lake', *Quarterly Review*, 75 (March 1845), 542. Alexander William Kinglake (1809–91), MP and author of *Eōthen* and a history of the Crimean war, was a neighbour of Bagehot's in Somerset.

195 *If Ritualism could be made a political question*: by the 1860s there was increasing concern over the lack of control of ceremonial practices in the Anglican church.

Gladstone and Garibaldi: in the 1865 election campaign Gladstone, as Chancellor of the Exchequer, personified the Liberal party's slogan of 'peace, retrenchment and reform'. Garibaldi, the popular hero of Italian unification, made a very successful visit to Britain in 1864.

198 *in spite of de Tocqueville*: De Tocqueville's *L'Ancien Régime et la Révolution* emphasized the continuities between Bourbon France and the Jacobins.

as Sydney Smith said: Sydney Smith (1771–1845), canon of St Paul's Cathedral and political essayist.

199 *Sir James Mackintosh and Lord John Russell . . . had written panegyrics on it*: Mackintosh, in the *Edinburgh Review* (1820), and Russell, in his *Essay on the History of the English Government* (1821), had both supported the *de facto* existence of mixed suffrages.

205 *Mr Buxton . . . in his letter to the Times*: *The Times*, 9 Dec. 1864, p. 5.

Mr Roebuck would rise: John Arthur Roebuck (1801–79), MP for Sheffield 1849–68 and 1874–9, a Benthamite radical in the 1830s and 1840s, who from 1859 onwards proved unpredictable on the parliamentary reform issue.

*The
Oxford
World's
Classics
Website*

www.worldsclassics.co.uk

- Information about new titles
- Explore the full range of Oxford World's Classics
- Links to other literary sites and the main OUP webpage
- Imaginative competitions, with bookish prizes
- Peruse *Compass*, the Oxford World's Classics magazine
- Articles by editors
- Extracts from Introductions
- A forum for discussion and feedback on the series
- Special information for teachers and lecturers

www.worldsclassics.co.uk

American Literature

British and Irish Literature

Children's Literature

Classics and Ancient Literature

Colonial Literature

Eastern Literature

European Literature

History

Medieval Literature

Oxford English Drama

Poetry

Philosophy

Politics

Religion

The Oxford Shakespeare

A complete list of Oxford Paperbacks, including Oxford World's Classics, OPUS, Past Masters, Oxford Authors, Oxford Shakespeare, Oxford Drama, and Oxford Paperback Reference, is available in the UK from the Academic Division Publicity Department, Oxford University Press, Great Clarendon Street, Oxford OX2 6DP.

In the USA, complete lists are available from the Paperbacks Marketing Manager, Oxford University Press, 198 Madison Avenue, New York, NY 10016.

Oxford Paperbacks are available from all good bookshops. In case of difficulty, customers in the UK can order direct from Oxford University Press Bookshop, Freepost, 116 High Street, Oxford OX1 4BR, enclosing full payment. Please add 10 per cent of published price for postage and packing.